In the Shadow of the Bomb

In the Shadow of the Bomb

The Legacy of the Cold War
in *Dr. Strangelove, End Zone,
Crash* and *The Wire*

NIALL HEFFERNAN

McFarland & Company, Inc., Publishers
Jefferson, North Carolina

LIBRARY OF CONGRESS CATALOGUING-IN-PUBLICATION DATA

Names: Heffernan, Niall, 1977– author.
Title: In the shadow of the bomb : the legacy of the Cold War in Dr. Strangelove, End Zone, Crash and The wire / Niall Heffernan.
Description: Jefferson, North Carolina : McFarland & Company, Inc., Publishers, 2018 | Includes bibliographical references and index.
Identifiers: LCCN 2018005666 | ISBN 9781476664668 (softcover : acid free paper) ∞
Subjects: LCSH: Neoliberalism in popular culture—United States. | Dr. Strangelove (Motion picture) | Wire (Television program) | Ballard, J. G., 1930–2009. Crash. | DeLillo, Don. End zone. | Cold War—Influence.
Classification: LCC E169.12 .H434 2018 | DDC 320.510973—dc23
LC record available at https://lccn.loc.gov/2018005666

BRITISH LIBRARY CATALOGUING DATA ARE AVAILABLE

ISBN (print) 978-1-4766-6466-8
ISBN (ebook) 978-1-4766-3041-0

© 2018 Niall Heffernan. All rights reserved

No part of this book may be reproduced or transmitted in any form or by any means, electronic or mechanical, including photocopying or recording, or by any information storage and retrieval system, without permission in writing from the publisher.

Front cover *insets*: photographs from a Civil Defense nuclear test in the Nevada Desert in 1953; background photograph of nuclear explosion © 2018 estt/iStock

Printed in the United States of America

McFarland & Company, Inc., Publishers
 Box 611, Jefferson, North Carolina 28640
  www.mcfarlandpub.com

To my parents, Kit and Sean,
for the long road travelled in grace.

Table of Contents

Preface   1

Introduction: The Cold War, a Forge for Capitalist Technocracy   5

  I. *Dr. Strangelove*: The Secular Apocalypse and Its Technical Imperative   35

  II. *End Zone* and *Crash*: Hollow Creeds and Monstrous Rituals   68

  III. *The Wire* and Game Theory: "All in the Game"   123

Conclusion: Imagination Is Irrationality   174

Chapter Notes   183

Bibliography   189

Index   197

Preface

In *The Wire's* season 5, Detective McNulty, an apparently well-intentioned miscreant, applies bite marks to the posterior of a homeless man's corpse with a set of dentures. Thus begins a story line in the show's final season that shows the mainstream media's complicity in fabrication. This adds to the powerful critique the show puts forward in its entirety of a system that is fueled by fabrication, from the top down. McNulty commits this foul deed in order to create a big enough political embarrassment—a homeless serial killer—that he may siphon off the money invested into it to his investigation of a real serial killer, a drug kingpin who has murdered dozens in West Baltimore. In so doing, McNulty gives in to the requirement of the politico-economic system for fabrication to do the job his institution nominally purports.

McNulty sets off a chain reaction that implicates virtually all the municipal bodies of Baltimore in its merry bullshit. *The Wire* is not just taking aim at the media and political apparatus's complicity in obfuscation. Most significantly, it accurately demonstrates the exact ways in which all of these institutions are held utterly captive by the ruling economic ideology. The market, which presides over all our lives, does not require a true picture of reality in order to generate growth and profit. Neoliberal capitalism, in fact, requires a *statistical illusion* of low crime rates, school pass rates, democratic participation, equal opportunity and other measures of a functioning society so that the minimum need be invested in the social realm in order to keep fed the system's insatiable requirement for growth. Cast aside in the neoliberal age are older, linguistically derived and qualified human judgments of how a society may function or how we may live well together. The notion of "fake news," then, is old news. Misinformation, fabrication, untruth, illusion, obfuscation, porky pies, rancid lies, call it what you will, is the fuel that drives neoliberalism. This situation is similarly dangerous and untenable as the wanton plundering of natural resources, as political disaffection among the masses means a turn towards "a virulent anti-politics in which facts and arguments are replaced with slogans, symbols and sensation" (Monbiot, "Neoliberalism: The Deep Story that Lies Behind Donald Trump's Triumph").

In *Dr. Strangelove*, the Russian doomsday machine has been set off to irrevocably destroy the earth by the entry into Soviet air space of Captain "King" Kong's errant bomber. The eponymous doctor tells the American President "Muffley" with gleeful admiration that the machine is utterly irrevocable and impervious to "human meddling" and so in its stupendous rationality cannot be shut off. When Strangelove realizes the doomsday machine's whole point as a deterrent has already been bypassed he asks the Russian ambassador why the Russian premier did not inform the United States of the existence of such an irrevocable weapon. De Sadesky sheepishly replies, "it was to be announced at the Party Congress on Monday. As you know, the Premier loves surprises." *Strangelove*'s technocrats, in thrall to the rationality of machines and quantified science, have failed to take into account the fact that human rationality is a conceptual state, not a factual one.

The character most in love with the idea of machine rationality is Doctor Strangelove himself, who speaks of a post–Holocaust breeding policy among survivors who would be selected by "computah" for their characteristics. While speaking, however, he wrestles with his right arm as it spontaneously gives Nazi salutes. Kubrick gives a clear hint that he believes jostling for control and sexual dominance play a much larger role in the psychology of those at the upper echelons of power than some magical form of rationality that somehow exists in a vacuum, free of messy human arbitration.

The system to which we are beholden defines human rationality simply by the motivation for self-advancement. Anything that lies outside of this is unquantifiable, including empathy and altruism, according to the market-derived models that underpin our institutions. Our current political scene is one that has a frightening lack of rationality or empathy. If systems or institutions try to corral human behavior according to very narrow and dangerous definitions, the result will most likely be unpredictable and destructive. Altruism and empathy are evolutionary drivers of the human animal, yet they are denied by the ideology and undermined by the mechanics of neoliberalism.

In the near future of Margaret Atwood's *Oryx and Crake*, the mechanically minded Crake has engineered a global pandemic to kill off the human race, leaving behind his own race of genetically altered humanoids to live in harmony with nature and each other. While having the corporeal ability to live sustainably, Crake has also designed them to mate in such a way as to remove romantic love, and thus the violence born of sexual jealousy. With it, too, goes the urge in them to create music, poetry and art. He has also made them immune to the urge to create symbols, hence the conditions for future religious wars. Crake has left only one person alive to be their custodian, his friend, Jimmy. He does so because he has detected an overabundance of empathy in Jimmy, knowing he will care for the "Crakers." Jimmy's overabundance of empathy, however, is linked by Atwood in the narrative to his love of language and storytelling (a useless and arcane skill in this science-dominated world of corporate compounds). Jimmy makes up all kinds of tales when questioned by the Crakers as to their origins and by the end of the novel, Atwood has the Crakers making effigies and chanting. Her point, when distilled, is a straightforward one: language and the need to narrate our own stories, not just individually, but collectively too, is innately human. The world before the global genocide in her novel was one in which the doctrine of a science utterly beholden to the marketplace had supplanted language as a way to navigate and understand the world. The dominance of quantified, or market-based means of understanding the world, over linguistically based consensual *human* judgments of how we might live well together, is a feature of neoliberalism, and Atwood's point is well made.

From language stemmed the human ability to think abstractly and to imagine that which did not exist in material form. Hence, the many gods of human history. We need collective stories that can incorporate the individual, that give purpose and meaning to our lives, in order to survive. Language and collective purpose are under attack by the current system; there is a void of meaning at the center of life in the post-industrial West and it needs to be filled with a narrative that facilitates our nature and who we are, and soon. Small-scale community cooperation and support, as Atwood's follow-up novels, *The Year of the Flood* and *Maddaddam*, suggest, may be the narrative we need. So, from art comes the storytelling, creativity and imagination that humans need as much as bodily requirements, lest we continue to make the environment more hostile to our lives and those of the animals with which we share it.

I have chosen these three anecdotes to highlight the relevance of the texts analyzed herein, and some others, to the world we occupy. The book demonstrates the importance of the texts analyzed within for what they reveal of the influence the Cold War has had on shaping the world we currently occupy. Fake news is simply part of the systemic logic. The attempt to contain, coerce or corral rationality is dangerous and what is defined as irrational according to the logic of the dominant system—namely altruism, empathy, imagination—are in fact, vital to us. These vital forces are transmitted in narrative form, in the novel, in a well-told story or dance or song, and from the bounties of the imagination spring new possibilities and new life.

It is with this in mind that this book's weakness is its strength. It is not exhaustive; its approach is varied, slanted and flawed and is perhaps not as rational as some may like, but that it may stoke, enlighten and interest its readers is its aim. The book's argument comes from a process involving years of research and thought. The analysis of each text, it is hoped, will work as stand-alone analyses of the texts within themselves. The varying approach to, and style of analysis of, each text is a required reaction and response to the methods and themes of each. The aim is to draw out their unique observations and critiques of the postnuclear world and incorporate them into a larger picture that has been hitherto obscured.

Introduction
The Cold War, a Forge for Capitalist Technocracy

There lies the true nuclear fallout: the meticulous operation of technology serves as a model for the meticulous operation of the social.
—Jean Baudrillard, *Simulacra and Simulation*, 34

The modern mind has become more and more a calculating one. The calculating exactness of practical life which has resulted from a money economy corresponds to the ideal of natural science, namely that of transforming the world into an arithmetical problem and of fixing every one of its parts in a mathematical formula. It has been the money economy which has thus filled the daily life of so many people with weighing, calculating, enumerating and the reduction of qualitative values to quantitative terms.
—Georg Simmel, *The Metropolis and Mental Life*, 177

Woe to those who, to the very end, insist on regulating the movement that exceeds them with the narrow mind of the mechanic who changes a tire.
—Georges Bataille, *The Accursed Share*, 26

The individual's self-preservation presupposes his adjustment to the requirements for the preservation of the system.
—Max Horkheimer, *Eclipse of Reason*, 143

Scientism in the Postindustrial Age

Science and technology are broadly accepted as the only rational basis for a *terra firma* upon which we can build our modern civilizations and societies. They are, after all, the sources of great tangible and material power, built upon human rationality and reason, not reliant on faith or guesswork and proven by their advances and marvels. Science and technology are not as secular and separated from human idiosyncrasy as we think, however. Permeating life in the technologically advanced Western world is an unthinking assumption that science contains the power to *save us*. Added to this is the vague belief that science and technology will make the lives of the future lives of leisure, entertainment and bliss, where our organic frailty too, will no longer cause us to suffer. Future technology will undoubtedly improve quality of life and save lives in ways that are not now possible. In truth, however, the presiding system that supports and shapes that technology is not geared towards the best outcome for the largest number of people, only towards profit in the largest possible accumulations, which as we see, benefits a rapidly shrinking minority.

Ideas of human perfectibility persist despite all the historical evidence to the contrary. It is a form of utopian thinking, which has undergone a transference from religion onto science.[1] This strain of utopianism, however, offers much less comfort than older forms as its narrative contains none of the shared purpose or redemption older religious narratives did. *Scientism*, the exaggerated belief in the power of science and its universal applicability, is not a coherent belief system in and of itself, of course. It survives from the Enlightenment period in which it was believed by many that the universe was mechanically rational.

Traditional religions still have a huge bearing and currency in the postmodern world, of course, but the ways we organize our societies in the West no longer rely as they did until very recently upon common good and other similar linguistically qualified judgments that are mainly rooted in Judeo-Christian morality. These judgments have been replaced with the quantified means of capitalist technocracy. This does not mean that the realm of social organization has been rationalized and secularized, however. Faith in God has simply been replaced with faith in the marketplace. This faith is a vestige of Christian teleology, only instead of being supported by narratives of shared purpose there is the opposite, a non-narrative of radical individualism and expression through consumption, a hollowness at the heart of postindustrial ideology that defines the age.

A cursory look at the history books will show innumerable instances in which governance pertaining to Judeo-Christian morality caused death, suffering or dysfunction. Their replacement, since the Cold War, with judgments based upon the numerical values of the marketplace, however, has had a dramatic dehumanizing effect that is mortally dangerous to the species in an era of unprecedented destructive technological power. This market-based social model seeks to excise linguistic, communicative and empathetically qualified judgments from our social structures and so quality of life, it seems, is far less important than growth and profit maximization in our postindustrial world.

The Enlightenment saw a push to replace superstition and assumption with science and rationalism, especially in the arena of social governance, which began, according to Philip Ball, with Hobbes's *Leviathan* (1651) and William Petty's *Political Arithmetick* (1690) (1–38). While the scientific discoveries of the Enlightenment appear to rationalize the world according to quantifiable and mechanistic means, what is less often revealed is the extent to which they are founded upon a Christian understanding of the world. Eugen Weber writes: "much of the progress in mathematics and in the natural and the physical sciences is related to the religious quest for wisdom, especially about God's intentions. Piety and learning went together and science followed" (84). The Enlightenment, as Weber convincingly demonstrates, did not constitute a clear break from religious and mythological understandings of the world but that the advances in scientific understanding remained as imbued as ever with the Christian worldview. This is most certainly the case regarding ideas of progress and overcoming perceived human shortcomings in the realm of social organization. And so, teleological ideas of progress—derived from older Christian ideas of a progress that leads to the eventual dawning of heaven on earth—were secularized and given over to science.

We are enamored by the instruments we have created, beholden to them, in fact, and the destructive power with which we have imbued in them. While we are in love with these instruments, that show us an image of ourselves through technology's parallax view, we are failing to invest in the true understanding of our own nature and a solution for how we may live well together and in the world.

Our scientific and instrumental creations are not objective and free-existing, independent of human foibles. Nor are nuclear weapons secular, they are unconsciously understood according to the mythology of the biblical apocalypse. This mythology speaks of the dawning of heaven on earth for God's chosen people but through a cataclysmic event of purging violence. The mythology is deeply rooted and plays out in a recurring effect, as Richard

Slotkin points out, in American wars that seek "regeneration through violence." It is also evident in the sense that neoliberal capitalism appears to contain the seeds of an apocalypse. At the behest of accelerated capitalism, we seem to be marching ourselves toward an environmental apocalypse and the system's logic is so completely internalized that we, as yet, appear to be incapable of imagining how to live differently, even as many are aware of the approaching precipice. It seems as though only a global collapse of resources will cease the gears of this rapacious machine of our own making, taking billions with it in its collapse. The surviving "righteous" in this scenario, according to the biblical myth of the apocalypse, presumably, are the billionaires who could afford to hoard the resources needed, and many of whom, ironically, would be those who invested in thwarting environmental education and the decimation of the natural world. They would much resemble the surviving group of fittest at the conclusion of *Strangelove*'s nuclear apocalypse, who have, in fact, survived by a combination of privilege and dumb luck as opposed to fitness.

Arguably the most pernicious form of scientism that abounds in the modern world comes in neoliberal capitalism's claim that the free market can bring about a natural order to the world. The position that the free market is a naturally occurring phenomenon ruled by recurring universal laws, hence must not suffer interference, from governments or any other source, indicates a secular *faith* that is a distillation of Enlightenment teleology. Like the ordained of older religions, free-market evangelists demonstrate total devotion by preaching the removal of *all* barriers to the market's natural state, interventions like welfare, health care and education. If the market fails to deliver on its promise, it is because it is encumbered. Because there are non-believers.

Secular Faith and the Neoliberal Apocalypse

This book, through its detailed analysis of the chosen texts, makes the case that the Cold War more than any other historical force has shaped neoliberalism. The godfather of neoliberalism, Friedrich Von Hayek, along with his disciples in the Chicago School undoubtedly paved the way for the supporting ideology of completely unencumbered free markets, but the Cold War really was neoliberalism's crucible. The Cold War shaped neoliberalism in two ways that work in tandem. Firstly, the clash of economic ideologies during the Cold War meant a doubling down on capitalist principles and conversely the absolute rejection of all notions of collective economic agency. Secondly, the nuclear standoff of the Cold War called for a mechanically rational and supposedly objective means of managing the potentially world-destroying weapons. Building upon the radically capitalist notions that had arisen during the conflict, then, scientists, mathematicians and theorists working in government-funded think tanks settled on the newly formulated Game Theory as a means of doing so.

In the aftermath of the Cold War, the fall of the Soviet Union was mythologized as a great victory for capitalist democracy, and models based closely on those victorious Game Theory strategies of nuclear management began to be implemented in public institutions across the United States. In this way, the radically capitalist values that underpinned these models were made institutionally, and thus socially, preeminent. Individual interaction within public and private institutions now falls under the ordinance of efficiency and profit maximization and people are determinately forced to internalize the logic of the free market.

According to David Harvey in the comprehensive and defining *A Brief History of Neoliberalism*, it is an ideology that "seeks to bring *all human action into the domain of the market*" (3, emphasis added). In adapting to life within the system, as Horkheimer observes in one of the epigraphs above, a person is adjusting his behavior and his frame of thought to the requirements of the system. Collectively, this is a stark and dangerous situation as is evident in our apparent inability to see beyond the system's insatiable demand for growth. The spread of these statistical models spans the neoliberal West. This fact will be apparent to anyone who has ever been held to a quantified target, in the institutions within which we all live and work, be that as a teacher, a student, a retail worker, a nurse, doctor, patient and so forth. These quantified targets insert the underlying rules of neoliberalism—radical, market-based competition between individuals, acquisition and atomization—almost undetected, into our daily lives, making them *defining* social principles.

Thus, a distilled and radicalized version of Adam Smith's economic man, or *homo economicus,* was inserted into the heart of our institutions when previously it had been, at best, a conceptual economic reference point. In a very real sense, then, the nuclear weapons of the United States, (what is referred to hereon in shorthand as "the Bomb,") is an avatar for the neoliberal form of capitalism that rules the world. The mathematical models that are used to organize institutions as mini-marketplaces across the neoliberal West

Introduction

are based upon the same capitalist notions of competition and human motivation that were used to determine the zero-sum game of the nuclear stand-off. These models also contain and establish as our social currency the same in-built paranoia and enmity as those original models, the same dim view of human rationality, and the same contempt for empathy, altruism, social cohesion and language.

The Bomb works as an avatar for neoliberal capitalism too in its intrinsic capacity to destroy narratives. The quantification that the ruling cybermarket requires speaks of an ancient human desire for certainty. The idea of a form of knowing the world that is objective and scientifically unequivocal is irresistibly seductive to us, yet the nature of life and the universe belies this. The universe is fundamentally in flux and life, despite all our knowledge and technology, remains mysterious, possibly unknowable to us as animal organisms with limited senses and abilities. This fact appears to terrorize us Westerners to the degree that we have created a technology that can end all uncertainty, and so the logic of the Bomb is terminal, toward the only thing that is certain. The Bomb is the science of certainty, the science of death, and this appears to be borne out in the trajectory of radical capitalism.

The destructive power of the Bomb, if not physically utilized, is sublimated through the seemingly inexorable process of environmental destruction. The ideology is internalized to the extent, it seems, that we cannot imagine the end of neoliberal capitalism without it meaning a global apocalypse of some kind. This brings to our attention the seemingly inextricable entwining of capitalism and apocalypse in the formation of the idea of America. The Cold War, the Bomb and the radicalized numerical management systems that sprang forth from it, work against the idea of cooperation and of binding narratives. Ironically, if ever there was a narrative that the human species needs to believe in and internalize, one that could unite all in a common purpose and reveal an intrinsic connectedness and meaning in our lives regardless of creed, color or nationality, it is one of environmental welfare. That we cannot work towards the maintenance of the environment that sustains us and all other life speaks of social atomization, denial and probably the death wish implied by both the Bomb and the biblical narrative of apocalypse that underpins American exceptionalism. Of course, we need not follow and succumb to the apocalyptic myth if we can *imagine* a different way of living, even if it is simple changes to the way we live and, imagination, as this book argues, is the key to our survival.

Introduction

The Power of Binding Narratives: Why Choose These Texts?

There are two very good reasons for choosing these specific texts despite the fact that they are in many ways very different from each other. Firstly, the texts are arranged chronologically in order to build a historical picture of the influence the Cold War has had on shaping neoliberal capitalism. The first three texts examine the historical and social context while the final text, *The Wire*, looks at neoliberalism in effect in a typical American city. *Dr. Strangelove*, which was made and set in the mid–1960s, accurately portrays the thinking at the height of the nuclear standoff while also debunking it intellectually and philosophically with brilliant satire. The novels, set in the 1970s, in turn, address the cultural diffusion of Cold War thinking and nuclear paranoia and what it means to be a person under the shadow of these conditions. Finally, *The Wire* brings the reader to the contemporary moment where the critiques of the philosophical and instrumental legacy of the Cold War that were exposed in the previous texts can be seen for their practical and immediate relevance. In *The Wire*'s wide ethnographic purview, we see a typical modern Western city in which the terror of nuclear war has subsided but the mechanisms of distrust and paranoia are now institutionally embedded. The structure of the book, therefore, is laid out with the hope that the analysis of *Dr. Strangelove*, *Crash* and *End Zone* will illuminate and critique the forging of these conditions that underpin our systems and our ideological assumptions, whereas the analysis of *The Wire* hopefully shows the legacy of Cold War thinking in a typical Western city, *The Wire* being a unique work in its comprehensive, perceptive and searing critique of neoliberal ideology in action.

The second reason for choosing these specific texts and this approach to the mammoth topic of the Cold War and its legacy is the very fact of their power as *stories*. A frequently recognized facet of postmodernity or late capitalism is the difficulty facing storytelling, when alienation is the bedrock of consumer culture and meaning is eternally refracted through simulation and digital white noise. The human striving for the sublime, or a higher purpose beyond the corporeal and material world has long been the sole preserve of organized religions. For many, in a world ruled by science, technology and quantified materiality, religions are either irrational fantasies or means of exploitation and control. The narrative that has replaced the religious quest for the sublime or higher purpose, however, is the promise of a technological

Introduction

advancement that is yoked to market requirement for profit and by definition offers little in the way of a shared purpose for human life. The sacrosanctity of individual freedom is one side of the same coin, whose other side is a constant and sustained message of radical atomization, competition and expression through consumption, what George Monbiot calls "the age of loneliness" (*The Guardian*, 14 October 2014). Fragmentation and isolation appear to preclude cohesive narratives. Describing the world and how we live in it, thereby poses a serious challenge to writers and commentators from all fields.

Keeping this in mind, it may be the novel more than any other form of communication that retains the most direct power to work against power structures, requiring as it does in the reader a recognition of our commonality and our struggles as fragile beings. A well-told story, in any medium, indeed, can reveal more to us the truth of the world we have constructed than any other form of information. This is perhaps because, although fictional, in order for stories to be good and to reach its readers' interior lives they must seek essential truths about human life, thus are less invested in maintaining the fictions that power structures propagate, specifically those that adhere to consumption and profit.

Not only are binding and cohesive narratives under threat from capitalist hegemony but the very fundament of the *word* itself is also under threat. The world we occupy is increasingly understood according to the mechanics of quantification over and above the nuance of linguistic qualification. The cyber-market, to which we have made ourselves beholden, requires numerals to describe only efficiency and profit, it does not recognize indeterminacy, ambivalence, nuance and the radical flux of the world of human heat. So, in a world ruled by the electronic pulse of cyber-capitalism the word itself is impugned as a means of understanding how we live, in favor of the supposedly incontrovertible number. At the heart of the effort to exchange human irrationality for Game Theoretical mechanical and quantitative logic is an implicit attack on language. The objective of Cold War Game Theoretical models and their derivatives is to replace the problematic aspect of linguistic interpolations with the certitude of mathematics.[2]

For all the disdain shown to language and its indeterminate emotional offshoots by the technocrats who came to power in the United States during and in the wake of the nuclear standoff, their mathematical models and their strategies are nevertheless founded upon language and linguistic concepts. Cold War strategies such as MAD (Mutually Assured Destruction), despite their purported numerical objectivity, were nevertheless founded upon the

Introduction

assumption that the Russians were rational and what was rational was what it was assumed was in the Russians' best interest. Specifically, in this instance, they were assumed to be rational in their desire not to be obliterated in a nuclear storm. Equally, the Game Theoretical models derived from the Cold War that now underpin so much of institutional life in the Western world make the same assumption of individual agency that neoclassical economics makes, that what is in the individual's self-interest is rational. This logic is so embedded in Western capitalism now that the logic has become reversible. Self-interested actions are rational, but also rationality has come to be defined thus, as self-interestedness, and all agency that falls outside this narrow spoke of human behavior is dismissed. To put it simply, according to the economic philosophy that underpins the institutions of the Western world, altruism is irrational. All of the numerical models are based, therefore, on a specific concept of a linguistic term. No objections, it seems, have been made by those who support these ideas towards the relativity of the concept of rationality, nor for that matter on the implications of its precariously narrow definition.

So, the power of storytelling is most pertinent in an age in which no facet of public life, it seems, from politics to media to science and technology, is not beholden to the vagaries of profit making or sustaining the insane fallacy of perpetual growth in a finite world. The stories told in the chosen texts speak variously of the world we have created and inherited in the wake of the Cold War. *Strangelove* speaks of the dangers of placing the requirements of institutions over human concerns and of assuming that science and mathematics are infallibly logical in the realm of human affairs. The novels tell of the essential human need for collective meaning above and beyond acquisition and of the role of language in imagining this and resisting the power structures that wish to atomize human life. *The Wire* tells of people's struggle to survive in a system that values them less each day, and yet how even in this system of radical competition everyone is connected and lives do have consequence and meaning.

Game Theory and God-the-Bomb: A Brief Background and History

Game Theory features directly in *Strangelove*, *The Wire*, and *End Zone*, thus an explanation and analysis of its genesis and rise to institutional primacy is necessary to an understanding of the radical critiques and insights of the

Introduction

chosen works. The term "Game Theory" is used in this book as an umbrella term for a cluster of related statistics-based models which began as economic theory. It is very much entwined with neoliberal economics and as such it assumes the same fundamental self-interested drives for the individual. Game theory deploys what is called a performance target in its management model for any given institution, such as a university, hospital or police force. This target is a pre-determined quantitative value for the successful enacting of an employee's job; taking the above examples, that may mean, number of students successfully passing an exam, number of patients seen or number of successful arrests. The nominal objective of the quantitative value of an employee's task is to strip away bureaucratic impediments and to liberate the individual to do his job in the most efficient way possible. Underpinning this objective is the core principle of Game Theory and the performance target method, which is a maximization of profit. In state-run institutions, this effectively means a minimization of costs in every possible way. In essence, it is the wish to apply the macroeconomic basis for the free market to the micro level of the institution, to which all people in the first world are part of or beholden to in one way or another. The primacy of a quantified value system for the work that is done in institutions has brought the radical competition and radical cost-cutting aspect of the corporation and applied it to the individual. The simple, single-minded, quantified value of maximum profit, the unfettered aggression of the global market has entered the realm of the social. Adam Smith believed that the interdependence engendered in capitalism would (through the guidance of God) allow man to flourish in peace. Contemporary Game Theorists, however, appear to believe that life in modern liberal democracies is a virtual, muted war, where individuals constantly strategize and battle with each other, each for their own personal advancement. As argued, Smith's economic concepts regarding the effect of the hidden hand in market forces were very much predicated on a Christian view of the world. In *Black Mass* Gray writes: "Smith had little in common with secular evangelists for the free market like Hayek and Friedman. He viewed the emergence of commercial society as the work of divine providence" (121).[3] The difference between Smith and Friedman is the Cold War's technological quasi-apocalypse, which led to neoliberal capitalism's supposed defeat of communism. The God that Smith placed his faith in has been replaced in the post–Cold War era by the Bomb, the avatar for neoliberalism and Western technology's total dominance. It retains the ancient myth of apocalyptic cleansing, yet the conditions of its birth shape its mute decree

Introduction

for a rational, scientific approach to the world. In an era of polarized ideologies, however, its decree is not rational, per se, but the radically selfish rationalism that capitalism requires to make its economic models work. It is only scientific in so far as it adheres to this presiding ideology and it cannot be said to be secular either, as it merely facilitated the transference of religious faith and awe from God to American Capitalism and its technical offshoots. Gray is not acknowledging the role of nuclear technology in this difference, as is the case here, but he is nevertheless correct in his assertion that "the body of thought is markedly more dogmatic than Smith's faith-based political economy. The free market became a religion only when its basis in religion was denied" (123). According to this modern technocracy, (or economic theocracy, as Gray would have it), we may be interdependent to an extent, as Smith believed, but we are also in competition with each other in almost every facet of life. Modern Game Theory is a mathematical means of mapping strategies in this incomprehensibly complex competition. Game theory purports mathematical objectivity, yet as can be seen, it still relies upon conceptual judgments of value for the various outcomes of the games' scenarios. It seeks to quantify the merits of its outcomes, yet in ascribing numbers to the various outcomes of different strategies, it is nevertheless making an initial qualitative judgment. This simple truth undermines the mathematical objectivity to which it ascribes. In the search for certitude, both in broader terms regarding life on earth and our place in the universe and in the more quotidian aspects of how we organize our societies, the role of qualified human judgment has been diminished. What judgments there are adhere to the presiding logic of maximized monetary profit.

As is seen in the analysis of *Strangelove* and *The Wire*, which deal with Game Theory in the most direct terms among the texts examined, the actions of men and women serve the instrument—the mechanical processes of nuclear technology and technocracy in the case of *Strangelove*, and the processes of the free market itself in *The Wire*—to largely disastrous consequences. It sees the immediate destruction of humanity in *Strangelove*, while the result of the abdication of morality to instrumental processes in *The Wire* also promises a bad outcome. Game theoretical instruments served only a very small elite of technocrats during the Cold War, albeit in a very limited way, while the same applies now to those at the higher echelons of the capitalist hierarchy. To understand Game Theory's genesis as an instrument of power devised by very flawed people with radical beliefs is vital to understanding its true nature and that of neoliberal capitalism: not as an objective

Introduction

mathematical science but as a highly loaded instrument of a radical ideology.

Game Theory became a coherent formulation in 1944 with the publication of *Theory of Games and Economic Behavior* by the Hungarian-American mathematician John Von Neumann. It revolved around the assumption that human behavior and, by extension, economics were predictable given the right models. Although it began essentially as economic theory, the strategy-based aspect of its focus meant that human behavior was factored into its equations. For example, poker is a strategy game in which human actions are all-important. Like poker, Game Theory's emphasis is on formulating a strategy that factors opponents' actions into its theorems in the attempt to predict their moves. In effect, therefore, it seeks to quantify human agency. Von Neumann and his co-author Oskar Morgenstern began with what he called the "minimax theorem" (*Essays On Game Theory* x). Simply put, this is a strategy of minimizing one's maximum loss in a two-player game with fixed parameters, which, as discussed below, had huge implications for the Cold War nuclear standoff between the two superpowers.

John Nash, who was made famous in the 2001 Hollywood movie *A Beautiful Mind*, won the Nobel Prize for Economic Sciences in 1994 (along with John Harsanyi and Reinhard Selten) for his various improvements on Von Neumann's theories. His big breakthrough, according to Ken Binmore in his introduction to a collection of essays by Nash titled *Essays on Game Theory*, was his division of games into cooperative and noncooperative categories (ix–xx). Nash expanded the formulae along the complex and difficult calibration of strategies in a non-cooperative situation. His "Nash Equilibrium" seemed to prove in an ingenious set of theorems that a society of players all seeking their own advancement did not necessarily lead to chaos. Instead there was a point at which equilibrium was reached, with stability the proposed outcome. Nash's equilibrium, therefore, appears to mathematically prove Smith's hidden hand, Friedrich Von Hayek's self-directing automatic system, and generally justify neoliberalism's call for deregulated and unfettered institutional capitalism.

Both Von Neumann and Nash worked for a government think-tank in Santa Monica, California, called the RAND (Research and Development) Corporation. The strategic element of Game Theory meant it was deemed the perfect model for the Cold War standoff. Its complex formulae, it was thought, could potentially predict the actions of the Soviets in the strategy "game" the superpowers were playing with nuclear weapons. The equilibrium,

Introduction

after the fashion of Nash's Nobel Prize-winning theory, was MAD. According to the assumptions of the game, MAD ensured that it was in the Soviets' best interest, being rational, not to fire upon the United States, as this would bring about their own destruction. It was seen as the ultimate deterrent to nuclear war. The inherent contradictions in this situation are readily apparent and captured with all the implied irony in the acronym. Von Neumann, in particular, known as a zealous militarist, was an advocate of nuclear weapons and it was in fact his "Von Neumann Committee for Missiles" that proposed the strategy (Nasar 81).

The Prisoners' Dilemma is a simple hypothetical model upon which the Game Theoretical logic of the nuclear standoff can be tested. Ever since it was proposed in 1950 by Merill Flood and Melvin Drescher, the thought experiment has been reformulated in countless varieties, and in many of these forms seeks to demonstrate that the purely logical strategy is to distrust your partner. Balance could develop between the opposing super-powers if both sides armed themselves to the hilt.[4] According to the logic of Game Theory when applied to the Cold War standoff, a strategy of maximizing U.S. nuclear capabilities was the only rational solution. A situation where no mutual or global destruction could occur was, of course, the most desirable scenario, but in order for that to happen the United States would have to trust the Soviets to only arm moderately or disarm their arsenal before they, in turn, could disarm theirs. Trust, as a basis for disarming, with so much at stake was not viable as it left to chance the possibility that the Soviets would hide some of their missiles and destroy the United States as soon as they could. Disarmament, therefore, according to Game Theorists, was a logical impossibility. The equilibrium of Mutual Assured Destruction, then—the stability of the situation—derived from the assumption that the Soviet elite, being rational, with the prospect of a devastating American retaliation, would not act to bring about their own certain destruction. Equally, the Americans did not wish to initiate a nuclear holocaust, and thus the stalemate of the late 1960s Cold War, or in Nashian terms, the equilibrium arose.

In the eyes of the RAND employees, the Game Theorists and social scientists, notions such as trust, benevolence and decency, while nice, perhaps antiquated, abstractions of everyday life, had absolutely no place in the formulation of potential strategies in this incredibly dangerous situation. What was needed was a strategy of cold logic and clear rationality. Essentially, however, the Cold War strategy adopted by the United States is a mathematical formulation that expresses the paranoia of the time. It did not simply occur

Introduction

to von Neumann or Nash as objective and fully logical and complete sets of theorems that proved one thing or another; it was instead an *a posteriori* mathematical manifestation of multifarious subjective strands of thinking in a specific cultural and political environment.

The strategy's theorems were formulated according to the baseline assumption of a participant's rationality, and according to the presiding ideology the rational choice in any given situation is the move that advances the participant's gain the most. The idea that humans acted out of some form of common good was seen as naive at best and communistic at worst. Game Theory, being essentially an extension of the logic of unfettered free marketeering, was ideologically opposed to the centralized control of communism. It embraced competition, took account of human fallibility and distrustfulness, and rationalized them into a seemingly objective system that benefited from human selfishness. The theories amount to a concentrated form of capitalism that disregards any of the mediatory insight set out by Adam Smith.

In ascribing numerical values to various outcomes of a strategy, Game Theory must find a basis for the values. This is done according to what is rational for the agent to do based upon utility maximization. Game Theory does not go into the labyrinthine philosophical conundrum that such an abstract word as rational opens up, but Hargreaves-Heap and Varoufakis trace the thinking back to David Hume's *Treatise on Human Nature*. Hume's thesis on instrumental rationality is defined by the authors simply as "the capacity to choose actions which best satisfy a person's objectives" (7). In *Treatise*, Hume argued that the passions are what motivate a person to act and reason is their servant. Hargreaves-Heap and Varoufakis draw the argument in this way:

> Reason on this account merely guides action by selecting the best way to satisfy our "passions." This hypothesis has been extremely prevalent in the social sciences. For instance, the mainstream, neoclassical school of economics has accepted this Humean view with some modification. They have substituted preferences for passions and they have required that these preferences should be consistent. This, in turn, yields a very precise interpretation for how instrumental reason goes to work. It is as if we had various desires or passions which when satisfied yield something in common; call it "utility." Thus the fact that different actions are liable to satisfy our different desires in varying degrees (for instance, eating some beans will assuage our desire for nourishment while listening to music will satisfy a desire for entertainment) presents no special problem for instrumental reasoning. Each action yields the same currency of pleasure ("utils") and so we can decide which action best satisfies our desires by seeing which generates the most "utility" [7–8].

Introduction

Hargreaves-Heap and Varoufakis go on to criticize this simplification of human motivation in terms of Habermas's theory of communicative action. Communicative action argues that human beings reach understanding through language and that this is the essence of our rationality. In attempting to dismiss language as too abstract a basis for institutional frameworks, and in replacing it with the claimed objectivity of mathematical means, technocrats and politicians are subscribing to an essentially impossible goal, given that collective human life is fundamentally governed by the flow of linguistic meaning.

The assumptions that underpin Game Theory maintain that notions such as common good or benevolence are obsolete in the arena of politics and management, but it does not consider the rather abstract notion of human rationality as the subjective concept that it is. What is rational to one individual, group or nationality, even if we take Game Theory's narrow and simplistic criterion of self-advancement, in no way necessarily corresponds to the rationality of another group or nation. This rather obvious assertion has been proven and reproved repeatedly in international affairs: quantitative values will not bring about greater understanding between people. In the desire to modulate human life in this way, much of what makes us human is missed. The infinitesimal momentary occurrences that motivate us in every new second in which we find ourselves, the values we embrace, the pressures we endure and the meanings we invest in our own individual and shared existence are lost to techno-economic rationality. In their *Dialectic of Enlightenment*, Adorno and Horkheimer extensively argue a closely related point, in their setting out of the representational fallacies of instrumentalism, as they see them. "What human beings seek to learn from nature," they write of this concept of rationality, "is how to use it to dominate wholly both it and human beings. Nothing else *counts*" (2, emphasis added). In *Communication and the Evolution of Society*, Habermas sets out his argument that a different kind of rationality emerges from the understanding of shared communicative action and this book, similarly, is arguing for the primacy of language and the importance of shared narratives as a binding and cohesive force in society. The postnuclear techno-economic models that dominate the Western world today appear to act very much as a countervailing force to these social elements.

The Nash Equilibrium had much wider implications beyond the United States' Cold War strategy. Its assertion that large numbers of individuals in pursuit of their own self-interested goals does not necessarily result in chaos has had enormous political implications. The political right that came to power in the United States (and Britain) in the 1980s assumed the distrustful and pessimistic view of humanity that had germinated in the aftermath of World War I and on up to the early Cold War period, yet they still sought to implement the doctrines of liberal democracy. Game Theory had a perfect answer to this conundrum, and the eternal problem for the governing elites of liberal democracies, of the promise of freedom versus the (perceived) need for control of the masses. According to Berlin's two concepts of liberty, negative liberty could be formulated around the freedom that can be purchased in what was now mathematically proved to be a self-regulating market.

Self-fulfilling Corruption

Notions such as the common good, patriotism, and loyalty, upon which many bureaucracies and institutions had relied up to the 1980s, began to be seen as, at best, meaningless antiquated abstractions and, at worst, malignant sources of inefficiency and corruption. If such a thing as common good existed, the argument states, it was only an individual's or an elite group's *idea* of what the common good should be. The public choice/competition advocates from Reagan and Thatcher's administrations rejected this common good emphasis on the basis that it was paternalistic, interfering and inefficient. Individuals, it was understood, were simply seeking their own gain, while hiding behind the pretense of public service. In his interview in *The Trap*, Buchanan explains his rationale:

> There is certainly no measurable concept, that's meaningful, that could be called the public interest, because how do you weigh different interests of different groups, and what they can get out of it? The public interest as the politician thinks it, does not exist, it's what *he* thinks is good for the country, and if we come out and say that, that's one thing, but behind this is a hypocrisy of calling something *the* public interest as if it exists. That's what I was trying to tear down" ["F**k You Buddy," *The Trap*, Ep. 1].[5]

The Reagan and Thatcher administrations began to dismantle old bureaucratic institutions designed to serve the notion of common good and replace them with Game Theoretical models. These meritocratic models supposedly stripped away the pretense of public service in these institutions to make them transparent. It was seen as more honest and more efficient for a person within the new system to pursue selfish goals. The old National Health Service in Britain, for example, was dismantled under Margaret Thatcher's

Introduction

government (on the advice of James Buchanan) and reformed on a meritocratic basis, with performance targets providing the motivation to efficient work. The new performance target-run health service was designed by the former RAND technocrat Alain Enthoven, who also developed the body count method implemented by the United States military during the Vietnam War under then Secretary of Defense, Robert McNamara. The use of this infamous body count performance target undoubtedly added to the mismanagement of an already confusing and tragic period of interminable aggression. The denigration of unquantifiable concepts such as communication and empathy in favor of a balance sheet method of conducting the war engendered the dehumanization of the enemy, and in turn America's own troops, and certainly too, fostered the misunderstanding and entrenchment of enmity between the two sides. The realistic depiction of performance targets in *The Wire* manages to convey in subtle detail how they erode the possibility for communication between the *de facto* institutional enemies and preclude empathy and understanding. There are significant corollaries between the American running of the Vietnam War and the War on Drugs, as depicted in *The Wire*. The body count performance target led to the murder of civilians and an unmanageable war with no apparent end in Vietnam, while the wars on drugs and terror can be painted in much the same light, leading us to draw the conclusion that without true human values underlying our actions we are lost.

McNamara, as a past proponent of Game Theoretical strategic systems and a key figure in two of America's major twentieth century conflicts, and his story reveals two astonishing insights into the reality of these systems. The first, that the use of the body count performance target in the Vietnam War betrayed a brutal failure in this logical system to do the very things it was intended to do. It did not create a more efficient war; it had precisely the opposite effect. The second insight comes from McNamara himself. The Errol Morris documentary on McNamara's involvement in these episodes, *The Fog of War*, is divided into a sequence of lessons that McNamara had gleaned from his experiences. The second lesson is a direct quotation from McNamara, titled "rationality will not save you." McNamara oversaw the implementation of the systems-analytical attempt to rationalize the war as Secretary of Defense for eight of the fifteen years of large-scale American military involvement. Alain Enthoven, who was a mathematician and former RAND Corporation economist, served as his deputy assistant secretary of defense from 1961 to 1965 and from then until 1969 held an office called assistant sec-

Introduction

retary of defense for systems analysis. In the episode of the BBC documentary series *The Trap* called "F**k You Buddy," filmmaker Adam Curtis describes the circumstances in which the body count, at the hands of Enthoven and McNamara, came to be used by the United States military in Vietnam:

> Enthoven began by getting rid of the idea that patriotism should be the guiding force in America's defense, and replacing it with a rational system, based on numbers. What replaced patriotism and notions of public duty, were mathematically measurable outcomes, but McNamara's experiment had ended in disaster when he had tried to run the Vietnam War in a rational, mathematical way, through performance targets and incentives. The most infamous example had been the "body count." It had been designed as a rational measure of whether America was winning the war, but in fact, troops simply made it up, or even shot civilians, to fulfill their performance targets, and in 1967 McNamara had resigned.

The cheating of statistics that occurred in the Vietnam conflict, undertaken by American troops looking to fulfill the body count performance target foreshadows the juking of the stats that is so comprehensively detailed in *The Wire*'s depiction of American institutions. In its detailed analysis of *The Wire*, the final chapter of this book draws this comparison to explore the consequences of basing the (institutional) functionality of a society around the assumed tenets of self-interest and asks to what extent it may be a self-fulfilling imperative. In other words, human beings are inherently adaptable creatures, the adaptation to a distrustful and selfish presiding system creates distrust, paranoia, selfishness, factionalism and, it appears ultimately, a breakdown in society. Furthermore, the quantified system that alienated the Vietnamese from America and precluded understanding and dialogue between the sides is now creating precisely the same effect, according to *The Wire*'s depiction, in the War on Drugs and the War on Terror. The gaps between the institutional factions, namely the police and those in the street drugs trade, become ever wider and more entrenched in the statistics-driven Game paradigm, and, in turn, where face-to-face communication has been all but nullified as a police strategy, surveillance technology is used to bridge the gap. In *Strangelove* too, the means of communicative action, understanding and empathy are eliminated by technical rationality. The true irrationality of this situation is underscored by the almost genial telephone conversation held between American President Muffley and the Soviet Premier Kissoff, where both men seem to be locked into the intractable logic of their respective ideologies and are powerless to prevent the terminal conclusion of their machine-driven totalitarianism.

Introduction

Game Theory and all its derivatives and variations have nevertheless become the underlying institutional framework in the developed world, despite John Nash's suffering as he did from the effects of paranoid schizophrenia, despite von Neumann's extreme political views and despite its disastrous use in the Vietnam War. In placing the individual's self-interest at the heart of institutional life, these modes encourage the internalization of free-market values from the top of its hierarchy on down. The adherence of institutions to the bottom line above all else—even, as is demonstrated so convincingly in *The Wire* above their nominal functions—indicates an abdication to the totalitarianism of profit and efficiency. Likewise, just as the institutions are beholden to the vagaries of the free market, so too are the individuals working within these institutions beholden to the institutions' preserving need for efficiency. In other words, in order to preserve oneself, as stated above, an individual must do what has to be done to preserve the institution and its profitability even if this requires bending the rules or undertaking immoral actions. This abdication of moral human judgment to mechanical processes, as is currently seen in the abdication of so much human energy and agency to the requirements of the all-pervasive free market, is precisely what is satirized in *Strangelove*, and what leads to the annihilation of the species at the end. As is demonstrated in *The Wire*, the individual preserves his position, and the institution to which he belongs, by acting in ways that are detrimental to the institution's nominal function. The inefficiency engendered in the system is summed up by the everyday occurrence of juking the stats, the act of preserving the institution according to the free market dictates by creating the *illusion* of its efficiency. The juking of the stats that first occurred in the Vietnam conflict is now, albeit in less immediately brutal terms, institutionally endemic according to *The Wire*'s depiction.

Critiques of Apocalyptic Rationality

The Cold War victory over the Soviet Union has slotted into the formative American narrative of an apocalyptic battle between civilization and savagery, in which the chosen elect endowed by God with superior ideas and technology overcome the primitive forces that stand in the way of progress. The Cold War was a civilizing mission too, whereby those that followed unnatural and ungodly communism would be forced to give way to capitalism's anointed, natural and democratic way of life. Yet, for the first time, in this modern recapitulation of the formative myth it was science and not God that contained the power of apocalyptic awe. The millenarian belief in a cleansing apocalypse still loomed large, but in this instance the power had been transferred from God to man, via technology. The Bomb, as a simulacrum for God, decreed a specifically capitalist technocratic rationalism, one based not upon faith in God but upon the supposedly incorruptible certainty of numbers. The nature of the conflict too, steeped in the narrative of the battle of good versus evil, has inevitably led to a radicalization of the ideology. In this instance, Smith's *homo economicus* has become inculcated with the paranoia of the Cold War and the terror and awe of the apocalypse. To put it simply, neoliberal capitalism was conceived as a quasi-religion with the advent of the Bomb and the victory of the United States in the conflict. The many mathematical models that sprang forth from the attempt to control the nuclear standoff were variations of Game Theory and proposed a universalism of application. It was purported—by those who gained power through the Bomb—to be irrefutably true that individuals are fundamentally self-interested, and so the widespread application of the Game Theory models to civilian management systems and politics began. The Bomb decreed a radicalized economic quantification of human agency with faith placed not in God but in the objectivity of numbers and the American economic way. Its scripture is a belief in capitalist technocracy, the numerals of efficiency and profit that the market requires.

It is perhaps ironic but not surprising, therefore, that the apocalypse is a dominant metanarrative of the postmodern world. As is demonstrated in the analysis of *End Zone*, however, it lacks the redemptive aspect of God's apocalypse, and as a consequence leaves the technical certitude of postmodern life bereft of sublimity or narrative. In *Crash*, following his near-fatal car accident, the narrator Ballard is reborn into the hands of a paternal technology that tends only to his corporeal being. In this hyper-real world, devoid of binding narratives and pervaded by the specter of technology's destructive power, the narrator Ballard and the crash cult with which he becomes embroiled create their own technological communion via staged car crashes. Postmodernity in *Crash* is ruled by the motifs of violence and pornography. Under the shadow of the Bomb—using technology's most powerful conduits of desire, the car and camera—the crash cult create their own binding narrative. The orgasmic collective expenditure of energy promised by the Bomb is miniaturized (diffused subconsciously throughout society) in each crash, what Ballard calls "autogeddon." In this way, the energies of the crash fatalities can be released and co-mingled into the universe, while the crash will be filmed. Thereby, the filmed crash, in its infinite reproducibility adheres to the simulational logic of postmodern consumption.

In this book's final chapter, analysis of *The Wire* explicates its depiction of Cold War models in the institutional life of a representative American city. The reorganization of bureaucratic institutions around the tenets of Enthoven's performance target model began in the United States and Britain around the late 1980s. Now they are the foundational basis for institutions across the developed world. The creation of a work of art that recognizes this institutional framework and its consequences, and that explores its effects from micro to macro levels with pathos and balance, is remarkable. In its analysis of *The Wire*, this book reveals how the tenets of the self-interested institutional framework have a self-fulfilling effect on society, and examines the ways in which the paranoia inherent in its original genesis resonates throughout the Game-paradigm in modern society.

McNamara's first lesson—empathize with your enemy—remains unlearned or ignored by American political elites. The degree to which the United States military and political elites misunderstood the Vietnamese in that techno-economic civilizing mission precipitates the misunderstanding of the enemies in the War on Drugs and on terror on precisely the same basis. The statistics of performance target models, as is depicted in *The Wire*, enumerate mostly meaningless arrests for minor drug offences in order to create the illusion of effective policing. The consequence of this and its placing within the framework of war is to entrench opposition and enmity between two institutions within American society, instead of bridging the gap through empathy, communication and medical treatment. The attempt to fight and destroy what is, in actuality, a social problem is reminiscent of the American propensity to view apocalypse and violence as a means of purgation and a sort of reset-to-zero.

Just as the savages made way to technical and commercial progress, so too were the Russian savages subdued by the superior capitalist technique of the United States. In the technocratic and scientific models that emerged victorious from the Cold War were the means to organize society according to the ordained ideology, thus the War on Drugs and other problematic social issues could be managed rationally in a way that is, naturally, simpatico with the needs of profit-making in the natural free market system. As discussed in the next chapter, however, *Strangelove*'s satire reveals that the insanity of the Cold War standoff precipitated the rise not of rationality, but the insane situation in which moral human decisions were abdicated to mechanical and technocratic means.

What Do We Mean When We Say Neoliberalism?

This age of hyper-accelerated capitalism so far lasting approximately forty years, in which capitalist market values appear to trump all other considerations, can be named, neoliberalism. The book addresses the postnuclear world here in the introduction via the use of the term neoliberalism but the main body focuses closely on parsing the texts and so the term itself does not arise much, although very often the analyses of the texts reveals powerful critiques of the political, mythological, quasi-scientific and quasi-religious aspects of its formation and rise to hegemonic dominance.

The term itself garners reactions varying from belligerent denial, to confusion, to apathy and is only slowly entering the public discourse as a term of recognition for the radical and hyper-accelerated form of cyber-capitalism to which we are all beholden. This is strange, as Monbiot points out in his powerful article, "Neoliberalism—The Ideology at the Root of All Our Problems," when he asks the reader to imagine those living under communism had no word to name or define it. The point is that neoliberal capitalism is derived from a set of ideological propositions that are so deeply implanted in our culture that we seem to unthinkingly accept it as natural, despite the terrible social and environmental consequences it generates. This set of ideological assumptions has existed for a long time, born of the Enlightenment, yet only truly implemented in the last forty years. The paranoia, exaggerated capitalism and other peculiarities of the American Cold War, however, make up the mechanics, the politics, the mythology and the pathology behind neoliberalism. Although deeply ingrained, the tenets of neoliberalism are far from natural. As stated, neoliberalism is underpinned with assumptions about human motivation that are actively hostile to the notion of altruism, whereas it is intuitively understandable, without the help of science, that altruism is a function of human cooperation and thus evolutionary success. The active institutional models of neoliberal capitalism were designed in the crucible of the Cold War's madness. They married with existing ideas—coming from free-market evangelists like Friedrich Von Hayek and his followers regarding the destiny of a market that is truly unfettered and unencumbered by the needs of the social realm—and are now forcibly supplanted onto our social

Introduction

organization. The choice for so many ordinary people in the age of financial cyber-capital and rapidly increasing automation is to either attempt to adapt to institutional competition and its intrinsic alienation, or to opt out of legitimate capitalism and find different ways to eke out a living. Opting out or making a living illicitly means joining the growing underclass, disenfranchised, alienated and of ever-diminishing value to the ruling mechanism.

A life lived by a creed of acquisition and self-advancement is almost by definition a lonely one. It flies in the face of our intuition, it leaves us hollow, our lives appear to lack purpose and sublimity. The hollowness of this lack of shared purpose creates a disconnection from the natural world and each other that is exploited by commercial propaganda. There is a collective psychic or psychological rupture at the root of our rabid consumption that in turn facilitates our disregard for the environment that sustains us. The radical form of capitalism that emerged from the Cold War was naturally hostile to notions of collectivism but neoliberalism is hostile too to any binding or collective narrative as these social forces are antithetical to the creation of profit and an efficient system that serves profit creation.

While hostile to binding narratives and altruism, neoliberalism is based upon vast statistical fallacies that paint a false picture of a functioning society. Neoliberalism is an ideology that harnesses Enlightenment ideas of rationality, as well as older mythologies with Christian bases, such as those of progress and of utopia itself. This admixture constituting modern scientism is a narrative that is patently false, structurally, visibly false. It has presided over the greatest transfer of wealth from a majority to a tiny minority in the history of human life, yet it is a narrative that remains the most powerful non-story of the developed Western world.

In the epigraph Baudrillard makes a succinct and semi-cryptic but nevertheless monumental observation about the Cold War. It was, for Baudrillard, a strictly technical exercise. The point of the Cold War, per se, was to apply the scientific and mathematical techniques to the management of the social realm. Baudrillard's insight is a good starting point for this book, which analyses the chosen texts for what they reveal of the postnuclear moment and its aftermath. The Cold War was the eye of a needle through which American mythology, economic ideology, scientific thinking, religiosity, paranoia and tendency towards genocidal violence were squeezed and fused together in the nuclear heat.

Clearly it was never the desired outcome for either side in the Cold War to use the world-destroying nuclear weapons. The American goal, then, was to manage them as symbolic threats and proof of its scientific superiority. The war was one of technique, resources and ideology and this virtual conflict was won by the United States, thereby proving, according to its own mythology, its global preeminence. The United States' clear superiority and eventual Cold War victory reaffirmed its formative exceptionalist mythology, that it is the world's light for liberty and democracy. What is more, it did so in terms that were in symbolic accordance with those of a biblical apocalypse in which good would triumph over evil.

The victory in this final battle of ideologies proved once and for all that America's economic system and science were apodictically incontestable. The United States' Cold War created and facilitated the application of social science models based upon the unfettered free market. The Cold War embodied all the facets of America's formative mythology, most clearly that of its status as the torchbearer of civilization in its battle against savagery. This took ideological form in the construct of a democracy-versus-communism ideological framework, in which capitalism, the preordained economics of democracy, was set in polar opposition to collective economics and was thus pushed right and radicalized. The rule and control of the social realm by mini-market models is the true legacy of the Cold War, as Baudrillard so astutely and presciently observed.

Neoliberalism is a much more dogmatic and quasi-religious form of capitalism than Adam Smith envisaged when setting out the tenets of his economic system, which he believed was designed by divine providence and not a religion in and of itself. Neoliberalism can be most readily identified in its zealous pursuit of privatization, usually of formerly public services, a process which began in the 1980s in Britain and the United States under the patronage of Margaret Thatcher and Ronald Reagan. Privatization is coupled with the de-regulation of checks and balances on market forces and the prioritizing of financial capital over production. These developments, whereby industry, production and profit are highly mobile, and now facilitated by digital, robotics and emerging artificial intelligence technology have seen the triumph of capital over labor.

Neoliberalism as a political project and economic model is not long for this world, however, having been the dominant system for under forty years. Capital may have triumphed over labor but the fight may be moving to a new battleground, away from its traditional site at the place of production. This is because the system is ingrained with all the destruction implied in the conflict that forged it. The destruction is not apocalyptic and cleansing as the founding ideology would have it. Instead it is a destruction of social justice or equality and of the narratives that bind people and give them a common purpose and a meaning. In order to avoid the implied destruction humans must cohere around a narrative of shared interest, and against the tide of atomization and consumptive acquisitiveness that undermines it.

Postnuclear Culture and the Chosen Texts: A Closer Look

We see the non-sequitur austerity mantra of doing more with less dismantled as an abiding fiction of neoliberal ideology in the analysis of *The Wire*, and there is much more in each text that is revealing and directly relevant to the world we now occupy. There is a definitive connection between the rise of Game Theory with the ludic and virtual aspects of postmodernity, about which, many theorists and novelists have written.[6] It is immediately notable, of course, that the nuclear standoff itself was framed in game terms by the theoretical models, thus immediately drawing attention to fiction and hyperreality as conditions of postmodern life. The Game theoretical mathematical models, as is revealed in the analysis of *The Wire*'s critique, create a fabricated *numerical* description of society as fully functioning. The market requires this fabrication of its adjoining political apparatus. In this sense their *virtualness* and *gameness* fits perfectly with the presiding logic of late capitalism. The models are conceptually removed from quality of life criteria and human judgment, their sole rationale instead is efficiency, even as is depicted in *The Wire*, above the nominal functions of the institutions they underpin. For state and municipal institutions such as universities, police forces, schools and so on, the (desired) outcome is an absolute minimum of investment in their maintenance. Austerity, which is the broad scale implementation of this economic ideology, is therein presented as a devastating attack on the social realm by the accelerated forces of unfettered marketeering. Capital and investment are drained away from public resources, on the one hand, yet they pool in huge accumulations at the hierarchical apexes in *The Wire*, a trend that is borne out in reality by the monstrously unequal distribution of wealth that distinguishes this period in history.

The game, referred to repeatedly by characters from all strands of society in *The Wire*, usually in the tautology, "it's all in the game," is the great game of capitalism, for many a zero-sum game of do or die. Where once there was unionized labor there is now an illicit drugs trade. The enormous profits generated by narcotics sales, as *The Wire* demonstrates, end up at the higher echelons of the game's hierarchy regardless of who generates it. Money is an ephemeral form of information that is now utterly detached from the process of its gathering, be that through the street drugs trade or otherwise.

Analysis of *The Wire* in the final chapter unpacks its critiques of abiding fictions in how the modern world is organized. The market requires the *illusion* of a functioning society for the maintenance of its administrative political system and the sustaining (American) myths of democratic agency. This fiction is provided by the Game theoretical models by which Baltimore's institutions are run, (the city of Baltimore as an "everycity" of the post-industrial West, where these models are all-pervasive) a virtual reality of quantified proof that the institutions are functioning to effect.

We also see in the analysis of *The Wire* an interrogation of the denigration and militarization of the job of policing. This process has picked up speed in the United States in the intervening years since *The Wire* has ended, and has surely played a part in the spate of recent police shootings. In the analysis of *The Wire* this book examines its critique of the so-called War on Drugs and how at the time the War on Drugs was in the process of transitioning into another unwinnable but much more encompassing and global war, the War on Terror. Addressing the social problem of drug use in war terms creates the framework whereby, on the one hand the police are militarized, while on the other, those partaking in the capitalist system on its nominally illegal side are the enemy, and most often the enemy are disenfranchised and ghettoized African American youths.

The Cold War, along with every other American war, virtual or real, adopts the formative biblical framework of an apocalyptic battle of the forces of civilization versus the forces of darkness in which the latter, the *other* must be removed by any force necessary from the path of progress in order that the United States become the heaven on earth it is destined to be. It began with the savage natives who were found to be occupying the God-given utopia and the pattern repeats to the present, in which those who take or sell drugs are the other, the disenfranchised African American is the other, the Mexican or Latino who migrates north is the other and the Muslim is the terrorist other. (The latter a reconfiguration of the commie that so stirred up the fear and loathing of many before, during and after the Cold War.) Nowadays the removal of this barrier to progress does not necessarily entail a root-and-branch destruction or slow genocide but instead, particularly in the instance

Introduction

of the drug using or selling other, a highly profitable mass incarceration. The majority of the enormous profits generated by a privatized prison-industrial complex, again, feeds directly into the upper echelons of the game. The War on Terror too has facilitated immense profits for weapons manufacturers, defense contractors and their investors generated by weapons sales and security, internally and across the globe.

We see explorations of our destructive myths in all four texts examined. For example, we see how the technology and use of nuclear weapons, specifically in the United States, is a manifestation of apocalyptic modes of thinking that came across the Atlantic on the Mayflower and with those millenarians who followed to battle with the heathens for their utopia. Similarly, we see in *Strangelove* and *Crash* explorations of the posthuman and what it may mean to merge with technology or surrender our agency to machines completely, as we currently appear to be surrendering to dehumanized thinking and the prioritizing of the system's sole requirement for growth over human considerations. In all four texts is the embodied wisdom that imaginative engagement with these problems, and the agency of imagination itself is vital to our continued survival and that narratives that convey our connectedness and imagine how we can live well together can provide the means for our existence outside of destructive modes and frameworks.

The American tendency towards apocalyptic cleansing, as discussed, goes back to its formative period in which the savages made way for the commercial and technological progress of those ordained by God to hew Utopia from the wilderness. While under God's decree, the project has nevertheless always been a commercial and technological one, and thus the pattern remains in the Game Theoretical strategy models of the Cold War. The communists had backward, savage and unnatural collectivist notions that were an affront to the American project. Thus Game Theoretical strategic models automatically assumed the deepest principles of Smithian economics, fundamental self-interest harnessed for the natural benefit of society, while conversely ruling out any notions whatsoever of collective agency. It is not surprising, with this in mind, that a strategy based on a radically polarized economic theory was used to deploy America's God-given and God-like superior technological arsenal in the fight against communism.[7]

Thus, there is what may appear at first glance an unlikely connection between *Strangelove* and *The Wire*. It has been noted by ex-analysts and journalists in more recent years that *Strangelove*, despite its comedy, is supremely accurate in all its detailing of American Cold War protocols and logic, as well as its characterization of top military brass, politicians and the technocratic elite. The film's satire exposes a problem with the American faith in technology and technocracy that *The Wire*, by way of its urban realism, criticizes as par for the course of American dysfunction. The philosophical essence of much of Kubrick's life's work was an exploration of the effects on the evolution and behavior of human beings of ideology, institutions and technology. It is no surprise, then, that *The Wire*'s co-creator David Simon cites Kubrick, and in particular *Paths of Glory*, as an inspiration. Simon obviously took heed of Kubrick's insightful treatment of institutional orthodoxy and the effects on those within these institutions when writing *The Wire*. Far from the self-interested rationality that modern institutionalism assumes, individuals in both Kubrick's films and *The Wire* often rail against the constraints of the institutions in which they find themselves, in ways that are irrational and self-destructive. The totalitarianism of instrumental and mechanized thinking that is satirized in *Strangelove*, the selection of the survivors of the nuclear holocaust by "computah," for example, is echoed in *The Wire*'s depiction of a system that dictates the requirements of its maintenance to the individuals who populate it. Ironically, of course, while Dr. Strangelove gives this speech, extolling the virtues of a post-apocalyptic breeding policy selected by computer, the world and virtually everyone in it are about to be destroyed by the technology of the doomsday machine, which could not be stopped by mere "human meddling." The technology of the doomsday device in *Strangelove* and those of remote spying in *The Wire*'s War on Drugs and terror facilitate the gap between the nominal enemies, where communication clearly could have prevented the impending Armageddon in the first place or avoid the conditions for a permanent state of warfare in the latter.

In *The Wire*, the War on Drugs is a systemic construct, as argued above, that is facilitated, not prevented by remote spying technology. This reflects an ingrained belief, with both internal and external wars, in the possibility of solving conflict through superior scientific reasoning. Undoubtedly this is the case with the use of unmanned drones, for example in recent wars. The thinking, again, can be traced back to the Enlightenment notion that all human problems can be solved by science in a mechanically rational universe. Where communication, understanding and empathy may go some way towards bridging gaps and avoiding wars, the problem is instead treated as both a barrier to progress and a mechanically soluble problem. The result depicted in *The Wire*, however, is an entrenchment of enmity between two factions who are locked into an interminable autotelic system. The logic of American wars is techno-economic, towards growth, progress and the promised utopia, against the uncivilized, by way of the apocalyptic cleansing that the Puritans and Pilgrims imagined when they set about purging the savage from the wilderness.[8]

Chapter I

Dr. Strangelove
The Secular Apocalypse and Its Technical Imperative

> The drives of both Eros and Thanatos can be rechanneled both to abet and reflect the technocratic super-state's trend towards systematic dehumanization of both its warriors and its opponents. No other object has become a more effective medium for achieving these objectives than the atomic bomb, both in terms of the psychological force it exerts and in its significance as an icon that simultaneously embodies the yin and yang of both global destruction and sexual climax.
> —Charles Gannon, *American Science Fiction and the Cold* War, 111

Introduction: *Strangelove* and Techno-ideology

Given America's formative mythology and what Sacvan Bercovitch calls the "Puritan errand," technological and commercial means have clearly been at the center of American ideology since the beginning (*The Rites of Ascent* 30).[1] Not until the nuclear arms race of the Cold War, however, did technology become both (political) methodology and ideology.[2] The nuclear strategies with which America fought the Cold War were loaded with radical capitalist rationality, and the civilizing mission against the Soviets was pursued with the same zeal as the mission to tame the wilderness.[3] The perceived American victory has seen an acceptance of this form of technocratic management as a scientific and objective way to organize society. The tenets of free-market individualism have been implemented on a widespread institutional level because it is assumed that they are rational and scientific, thus objective and correct. The Enlightenment project to bring science to bear on social organization has finally come to fruition with the secularization of the apocalypse.

Where once the threat of God's apocalypse could be used to justify the removal of the savages in order to allow progress, the power the United States has to bring about a secular apocalypse is seen as testament that neoliberal capitalism is apodictic.

This chapter analyses what Stanley Kubrick's *Dr. Strangelove* may reveal of this crucial nuclear moment, when, as Baudrillard puts it in the epigraph above, technology became the model for "the meticulous operation of the social" (34).

Strangelove encapsulates the nuclear moment with great acuity. At the heart of its satire is the abdication of moral, and sane, decision-making to the rationality of machines and the means of quantified judgment. This aspect of its satirical focus remains as potent as ever, as its lesson addresses the neoliberal tendency to abide by the dictates and requirements of economic growth above all other considerations, human or global. In the destruction of the world at the end of the film, caused by the moral abdication to mechanical processes, can be seen the potential destruction of the world in our deferral to the market requirement for growth despite the obvious destruction this causes the environment that sustains us. While the political and technocratic elites in the film defer to mechanization and quantification they are nevertheless prone to all kinds of frailties and foibles that lie behind their motivations. This is particularly evident in the overt bawdiness of *Strangelove*'s satire. The film's unsubtle suggestion that subconscious sexual drives lie behind human motivations, not least the urge to kill and destroy, is also a central feature of Ballard's apocalyptic tale, *Crash*.[4]

Both Kubrick and Ballard employ Freudian elements in their rendering of technological domination under the aegis of the Bomb, however, Kubrick's employment of the sex allegory is more denotative.[5] It may have seemed a farcical comedy upon its release, but the film captures the paradigm-changing nuclear moment, in the protocols and mindset that arose and now shape the world we live in, with great detail and philosophical perspective. Therein resides one source of the film's power and its continued relevance. The film's satirical deconstruction of Cold War protocols reveals the same flaws that remain at the heart of postnuclear institutional frameworks today, as we shall see.[6]

In this analysis of *Strangelove*, the ideas of machine rationality in the ideal of an American Cold Warrior—a masculinity in which judgment remains unimpaired by sentimentality or fears of impregnation with weak communistic ideas—ties in with formative American fears of miscegenation.

I. Dr. Strangelove

Strangelove's allegory of distorted male sexuality is, therefore, not a trite joke, funny as it is in the film. For the early settlers fears of miscegenation and the pollution of the blood of God's chosen bearers of progress and civilization were expressed in representations of the dark and naked sexualities of the heathen savages.[7] The enemy during the Cold War was distant and unseen, and the fear of this inscrutable otherness manifested as an amorphous phobia of the red menace—the pollution and miscegenation of its own citizens with weak and sentimental communist ideas—an episode of paranoia that culminated in McCarthy's witch hunts. The prophylactic measure was the prescription of a machine-like rationality dictated, of course, by the apodictically correct economics of the free and just ideology, God's chosen way. Only by being ruthless in this way, as a machine would be, could American Cold warriors use the Bomb to defeat communism. *Strangelove* satirizes the fear of communist miscegenation and the inherent misogyny and homophobia attached to that, most pointedly in the scenes between General Jack D. Ripper (Sterling Hayden) and Group Captain Lionel Mandrake (Peter Sellers). The film also satirizes the abdication of moral judgments to machines and the concept of a machine-man rationality, most notably in the characterization of the eponymous doctor. Dr. Strangelove (Sellers) appears towards the end of the film to explain the flawless logic of the Russian doomsday machine, which is a perfect representation of the strategy of Mutual Assured Destruction pursued by the Americans in the late 1960s. Dr. Strangelove, although clearly in admiration of the unequivocal nature of mechanical logic, is shown to be motivated deep down by a tribal-sexual breeding urge. The connection of a desire for (genetic) cleanliness and perfection is thereby linked with the odious thinking of the Nazis, specifically, and with fascism in general. The framework of nuclear strategy and mechanical thinking, as revealed in *Strangelove*, therefore, is not a foundation for rationality, it is a supplanted system of mechanical processes that becomes the sublimated violence of a distorted tribal-sexual conflict. While the binary provided an us-versus-them narrative framework for American patriotism during the Cold War, there is no solidarity or binding effect in this narrative for those whose Americanness was to be defined, to a large degree, simply, by its non-communism.[8] The narratives of America's oft-recapitulated mythology, such as equal opportunity and social meritocracy are radically debunked, as only those already powerful enough would survive the nuclear war in Dr. Strangelove's mineshafts. What is also evident in the film is that abdication of moral judgment to technocratic processes means a denigration of communication and empathy in the realm of politics and general human interaction. This is seen most pointedly in the War Room, whereby President Muffley (Sellers) and Premier Kissoff clearly bear no animosity towards each other, and they are both obviously sane, yet their attempts to prevent a nuclear war are powerless against the irrevocable logic of the doomsday machine.[9] Here, the film's satire of the precedence of mechanical and quantified processes over communication, empathy and moral human judgment can be related to the later attempt to fight the civilizing mission of the Vietnam War by quantified means. In *The Fog of War* Robert McNamara cites the denigration of communication and empathy as one of the main reasons the Vietnam War became entrenched. In the final chapter's analysis of *The Wire*, also, we see in America's internal civilizing mission—the attempt to correct the drugs problem of the uncivilized other using the regenerative (sublimated) violence decreed by capitalist instrumentation—a factional entrenchment between two institutions in American society, predicated on a lack of communication, empathy and operational inflexibility. Powerful as surveillance technology is, it is nevertheless ineffective in the overall scheme of the War on Drugs. Binding and cohesive narratives seem to be unraveling and losing their power in postnuclear America, a side effect of the technical imperative and its adherence to free market values only.[10]

The Cold War may have been subconsciously perceived as a tribal-sexual conflict, but one, from the American point of view, which was largely defined by ideological opposition to collectivist ideas. Thus definition of one's own tribe was predicated on the assumed purity of their ideas, a dedication to individualism, the tacit acceptance that only the fittest survive through the will of their self-determination. *Strangelove*'s ending, in which most of the population of America, and the rest of the earth are killed, except the political elite and those selected by computer, suggests that this ideology, taken to its extreme via technical concepts of society, leads to fascism re-drawn.

Strangelove's sardonic ending of a carousel of nuclear explosions rolling to Vera Lynn's "We'll Meet Again" brings to mind the contradiction in the non-regenerative nature of a man-made apocalypse. The secular apocalyptic has no promise of regeneration; the only narrative it contains is one of the technical certitude of a science by which total destruction is eminently more feasible than redemption or transcendence. The common trope, therefore, that connects these four examined works is the unraveling of binding narratives caused by the all-pervasive technical imperative. With the transference of the religious power of apocalypse from God to man, and scientific certitude, cleanliness and airless modulation came the loss of sublimity. The secular apocalypse has no redemptive promise, as all previous pre–Christian and Christian apocalypses have had. In the pursuit of certitude, the postnuclear techno-ideology has created an atomized society, all in competition with all, in which narratives of solidarity belong to pre-scientific superstitions and defeated ideologies, and the myths of utopian progress are now carried by scientific and technological advancement. In *Strangelove* the subjection of moral judgment and the often essentially irrational affairs of human society to the means of quantification and technology, sees the literal death of meaning when the doomsday machine goes off. Similarly, devoid of a binding narrative the crash cult in Ballard's novel commune in the only way they see possible in a fully technological realm, and create their own binding narrative. DeLillo's novel sees the protagonist poring over nuclear technical tomes seeking the certitude that scientific means promise but finding only the certitude of death that the Bomb's secular scripture decrees. In *The Wire*'s ethnographic depiction of a typical American city there are the destructive effects of the loss of binding narratives of solidarity on a growing population of people who find themselves surplus to the requirements of the market. *Strangelove* marks the beginning of the new paradigm where humans came to wield the power of God, with the ability to unleash a violence more powerful than anything in nature, yet knew less than ever, seemingly, about our own nature. Fear and ignorance of human nature in possession of this force led to the rise of the protocols of quantification and mechanization to which we now defer, protocols that were derived from the dominant economic ideology.

Kubrick and Technology

Strangelove focuses its considerable critical force on the nuclear moment, and is clearly still relevant, but Kubrick expanded upon some of the themes he introduced in *Strangelove* in his later films. A major trope in his work during the 1960s and early 1970s, in particular, is an interrogation of the tendency of those in the Western world to defer to the prevailing scientific rationalism and institutional logic when it comes to making a moral choice. While Kubrick appears to have been pessimistic about the human ability to be moral, he was nonetheless a humanist. Not naïvely but in the sense that his films call for a stripping away of the falsehoods that underpin our institutions. His insight into the falsity of much of the logic of America's Cold War strategy is summed up beautifully by his assertion in an interview about *A Clockwork Orange* given to the *New York Times*, that "Any attempt to create social institutions on a false view of the nature of man is probably doomed to failure" (McGregor, Web. par. 3). Kubrick's films of the 1960s and '70s interrogate the assumed construct of human rationality underpinning Western capitalism and its institutional framework. In the same interview, Kubrick says, "Man isn't a noble savage. He is irrational, brutal, weak, silly, unable to be objective about anything where his own interests are involved—that about sums it up." Kubrick here is pessimistic, however, there is a subtle but crucial difference from the cynical and reductive doctrine that radical capitalism assumes. Kubrick did not assume that self-interested agency is the only rational agency, but that we are incapable of being objective about our own interests. Which is a pretty compelling argument for not placing the assumption at the core of our economic and social systems. Unlike the Cold War radical capitalist institutions that assume self-interested rationality, therefore, Kubrick's films question the notion of rationality itself. Furthermore, if a uniform and overarching rationality emerges and becomes *the* prescribed institutional rationality that humans must adhere to, it will invariably become a template for a new from of totalitarianism, as is so vividly depicted in *A Clockwork Orange*'s (1971) dystopian nightmare. In this regard, *Strangelove* and Kubrick's other films from this era form a prescient critique of neoliberal free-marketeering, as we in the developed world are all beholden to the statistics of the bottom line and the vagaries of the market, often to the detriment of our own well being, which is a prevalent element of the era of austerity. Of course, in *Strangelove* the substitution of moral human judgment with the requirements and logic of the system leads to the annihilation of life on earth, which is the same fate humans and many other species face, it seems, with the current rate of environmental destruction that a system based on infinite growth requires.

Kubrick's three films after *Strangelove* contain subversive anti-heroes: HAL 9000 in *2001: A Space Odyssey* (1968), Alex in *A Clockwork Orange*, Barry Lyndon in the film of the same name (1975), and each of whom embody in different ways an idful (human) primacy.[11] The ironic conceit of the humanity of each is that HAL is a computer, Barry Lyndon is a lying, cheating scoundrel and Alex is a violent and cruel brute. *2001* may be Kubrick's philosophical counterpoint to *Strangelove*'s giddy nihilism. The world as we know it, is, of course, destroyed at the end of *Strangelove*, and while *2001* is a paean to the "impending extinction of the civilization whose technology put him there," there is hope for a rebirth, a cosmic mystery awaiting mankind, in the birth of the star child at the end (Feldman 14). *Strangelove*'s pithy satire of the direction man had taken technology and, by extension, the increasingly mechanized concepts by which our societies are organized and humans are defined, is treated more philosophically in *2001*. Kubrick, Feldman writes, "perceives that man, separated from his primal self, has become a mere mechanical force and is now little more than the instrument of the abstractions that he once conceptualized to serve him" (14). This is personified in the juxtaposition of the flawless and emotionless astronauts with HAL, who displays human fallibility when he makes a mistake that jeopardizes the mission, and ends up committing murder and then begging for his life.

A Clockwork Orange's Alex, of course, obeys only his own brutal, primal instincts, but he is forcibly altered by the state to ensure the preservation of the society's prescribed conventions. Alex's choice is removed, and his brutality is subsumed by society's totalitarianism. Kubrick's muse in these three films is the inhibitive, narrow and destructive elements of technological and mechanical manifestations of mankind. This philosophy corresponds to *Strangelove*'s satire, and signals the beginning of a major trope in Kubrick's work. Kubrick's view of the narrowness of technocratic institutionalism, or any institutionalism that does not acknowledge the irrational, is one that resonates throughout his career and throughout this book.

Dr. Strangelove as Kahn and von Neumann: Through the Lens of Power, Paranoia and Psychosis

Kubrick's fastidious attention to detail in the making of all his films is well known. According to biographer John Baxter, even before the project that was eventually to become *Strangelove* was conceived, Kubrick had begun to research the peculiarities of the Cold War with a mixture of legitimate nuclear paranoia and an obsessive need to understand the details. Kubrick "found the mechanics of destruction intellectually fascinating. He read intensively on modern warfare. By 1963 he'd collected seventy or eighty books on nuclear strategy, like *On Thermonuclear War* by Rand Corporation strategist Herman Kahn" (Baxter 166). Along with Kubrick's obsessive need for accuracy and detail, other notable factors contribute to the film's accuracy. Peter George, upon whose novel *Two Hours to Doom* (1958) *Strangelove* was primarily based, was an ex–RAF flight lieutenant who had inside knowledge of nuclear war protocols.[12]

Kubrick's set designer, Ken Adam was able to glean acutely realistic details regarding the visual aspects of the war's settings. Kubrick's co-script writer, Terry Southern also contributed a powerful insightfulness to the film. It is, however, the film's almost preternatural accuracy in depicting the nuclear protocols, as well as the rationale and mindset of the political, military and technocratic elites of the time that is key to the continued relevance of its satire. The subtext to *Strangelove*'s bawdy allegory and Kubrick's views of human motivation is that the rise to influence of one theory, of one man, or one clique of technocratic elitists, has more to do with the complex interplay between the people who develop and campaign for a political instrument, their psychological proclivities, their pre-existing beliefs and how all this fits with the dominant paradigm of their society, than it has to do with the instrument or theory's supposedly objective and incontestable logic. Game Theory was conceived by a person with strong and specific beliefs that were in dialogue with the political situation of the time, and in which he and an elite group of technocrats at the RAND Corporation gained enormous political power from their claims to a scientific orthodoxy attached to the Bomb. The theory (along with all its offshoots and derivatives) cannot possess the objectivity it claims, as it takes its assumptions from a highly ideological concept of motivation. Neither, for that matter, can those who formulated it be said to be objective, or, in some cases, sane. All of which, Kubrick was aware, as the film dismantles this flawed logic with a furious glee. In episode two of Adam Curtis's *Pandora's Box* series, "To the Brink of Eternity," Sam Cohen, a former employee at RAND offers a revealing perspective on the technocratic elite of the time[13]:

> These analysts were human beings but they were no ordinary human beings. They had more than a smattering of megalomaniacs—Herman Kahn was one of them, Albert Wohlstetter was another megalomaniac—there was this feeling that they could gain control and a huge degree of power by doing these studies, and so these analysts indeed achieved their grandiose dream, they were in full control ["To the Brink of Eternity" *Pandora's Box*, Ep. 2].

Strangelove's acute satire of the psychological proclivities and the prevailing mindset of this powerful elite ensures the film's continuing relevance. *Strangelove*'s satirical deconstruction of the abdication of morality and the denigration of communication and empathy to mechanized concepts remains as valid as ever, and most pertinently when looking at *The Wire*'s depiction

I. Dr. Strangelove

of game-paradigmatic neoliberalism. The steep slope of this neoliberalism benefits the few, in *The Wire*, as did the currency of power generated by learning the technical scripture of the Bomb for the elite of nuclear technocrats at the height of the Cold War. Capitalism became radicalized by the conflict, while the preachings of certitude and total control—by those who adopted its most radical forms as offerings of prayer to the Bomb and the American civilizing mission it facilitated—have remained at the heart of American institutional life, unopposed. Cohen's observations are very pertinent in this regard:

> When we started all this systems analysis business all these many, many years ago, we stepped through the looking glass, where people did the weirdest things and the most perverse kind of logic imaginable, and yet claimed to have the most precise understanding of everything and would give these perversely superbly rational and logical explanations as to why they were doing all these perverse and irrational things. That is a world which has always existed; it's always been a perverse and irrational world. That was the world that these systems analysts stepped into—that's in the mirror—they should have stayed on the right side ["To the Brink of Eternity" *Pandora's Box*, Ep. 2].

America and much of the developed world, it seems, has inherited the constructs of the currency of power, by a small elite of men, in love with their own mathematical models, in a very short, but highly dangerous, paranoid and ideologically polarized period of history.

Strangelove's satirical characterizations are achieved through the lens of its sex allegory. The film's juxtaposition of male sexuality with the processes of war strongly suggests that the subconscious forces at work in human behavior are psychosexual, in the vein of Freud's theories on the primacy of the libido in human agency. In Kubrick's films, Feldman argues, "Political activity is ... no more than the sublimated urge to overpower all that is outside the id" (16). Feldman focuses on Kubrick's later films in his analysis, but this argument can certainly be made as strongly for *Strangelove* as Kubrick's subsequent work, in that all the farcical events that culminate in Major "King" Kong (Slim Pickens) riding the nuclear bomb to oblivion appear to be driven by sexual urges, as is evident in the constant ribald references and the oversexed jigging of George C. Scott's Buck Turgidson and Sterling Hayden's General Ripper. In *Strangelove*, then, the urge toward virtual annihilation is an amplified expression of distorted male sexuality; the technology and technocracy of Cold War jousting are sublimated political manifestations of the death instinct.

The American President Merkin Muffley, played by Peter Sellers, was "modeled in style and appearance on Adlai Stevenson" (Seed, *American Science Fiction* 153). "George C. Scott's Buck Turgidson was a caricature of the cigar-chomping, war-loving head of the Strategic Air Command in the fifties, General Curtis LeMay," according to Baxter (181). There has been much critical debate about who exactly the eponymous doctor was modeled on, with Henry Kissinger, Edward Teller, Werner Von Braun and John von Neumann being mentioned, but the reality is that elements of all these people can be seen in Dr. Strangelove's characterization.[14] Teller and Von Braun connect the doctor to destructive technologies and the use of Nazi scientists by both the United States and Soviet Union during the Cold War. The visible aspects of von Neumann and Herman Kahn in Dr. Strangelove's characterization are most interesting and pertinent to the thrust of its satire. In particular, those aspects between them would be anti-communism, hyperactive sexuality, deferral to mechanical rationality and absolute faith in the redemptive power of the free market. When the eponymous doctor first appears in the film he refers to a study he has commissioned by the "Bland Corporation." Dr. Strangelove is wheelchair-bound, like the later-life von Neumann, has a nondescript mid-European accent, and espouses the "prodigious breeding" that will have to be done in the post-apocalypse mineshaft life, where there will be a ratio of ten women to every man. At the beginning of the atomic age, when the RAND Corporation went on its speedy trajectory from conception and nascent development to the seat of authoritative scientific knowledge, von Neumann was the most influential mathematician and scientist in America. His new theory was accepted in the halls of RAND since it "showed not only how to banish for ever economic uncertainty, but also how to rule the world by nuclear force" (Strathern 2). The virulent anti-communism of the time, however, undoubtedly had a profound bearing on how Game Theory was conceived:

> Von Neumann grew up in Hungary, coming to the United States in the 1930s, retaining a bitter hatred of Communism, an uncharacteristically fervid emotion about the subject which lasted the rest of his days and which also allowed him—in contrast with J. Robert Oppenheimer and many other leading scientists of the day—to work enthusiastically on the H-bomb project with no moral qualm. "I think," Von Neumann wrote to Lewis Strauss in November 1951, "that the USA-USSR conflict will very probably lead to an armed 'total' collision, and that a maximum rate of armament is therefore imperative" [Kaplan, *Wizards* 63].

The claim of von Neumann's theory to objectivity, however, may be brought into doubt, not only by his views on communism but also by his own psychological make-up. *Strangelove* is determined to show its viewers that the Cold War standoff and the arms race has less to do with scientific reasoning and more to do with oversexed masculinity. Strathern spells out what Kubrick certainly knew long before he began writing the script: "Von Neumann's continuing obsession with game theory may well have been linked to his compulsive sex drive" (3). Strathern cites von Neumann's penchant for trying to look up the skirts of secretaries who might happen to be in the room he was occupying, and notes the frequent extra-marital affairs von Neumann conducted, seemingly as par-for-the-course of the game he was playing, as evidence of the links. Given Kubrick's obsessive attention to detail and his access to political insiders and their knowledge, it's fair to say it is most unlikely he didn't know of von Neumann's proclivities. The possibility that Von Neumann's violent anti-communist feelings, his hyperactive (hetero) sexuality, and his extra-marital strategizing might have been evident in the theory he had produced is one that certainly fits with *Strangelove*'s satire. Buck Turgidson and General Jack D. Ripper, as their names suggest, match their over-sexed antics with their enthusiasm for a strike-first strategy, while Dr. Strangelove's advocacy of mechanistic rationality is equated with his post-apocalyptic fascist breeding policy. To what extent sexual aggression, distrust and paranoia influenced von Neumann's formulation of Game Theory can never be known, but for all his undoubted mathematical genius, his theory is nevertheless based upon ideologically loaded, aggressive and reductive assumptions.[15]

Kubrick's libidinal satire is an astute critique of the theories of those elite technocrats. *Strangelove*, from the opening sequence of the mating planes refueling in the sky, to the bomber proceeding through stages of sexual readiness; from foreplay, to primed, to dropping its payload and on to Dr. Strangelove's mineshaft breeding policy, leaves the viewer in little doubt as to what the real subconscious driving force behind the weapons and deterrence protocols might be. Charles Maland's assertion that Kubrick is "suggesting that man's warlike tendencies and his sexual urges stem from similar aggressive instincts" is well observed (704). Claims for Game Theory's objectivity and scientific rationality are thereby disrupted by its creator's psychosexual proclivities and his pre-existing beliefs, as well as those of the technocratic elite of the RAND Corporation, and the overall dominant political paradigm of the United States.[16]

In her essay "Dr. Strangelove," Sharon Ghamari-Tabrizi reveals the links between Kubrick and Kahn in the period of Kubrick's researching of the film, referring to the latter as "the period's most felicitous grotesque," while James Naremore compares quotations from Khan (and Henry Kissinger to a lesser extent) to lines spoken in the film by Turgidson and Dr. Strangelove. Fred Kaplan chose "Dr. Strangelove" for the title of his chapter of *Wizards of Armageddon* about Kahn, and Grant Stillman also, notes that Kubrick was "in fairly frequent contact with Thomas Schelling (another notable RAND Game Theorist) and Herman Kahn, who could feed him the latest scary strategies, such as Mutual Assured Destruction (MAD), or limited nuclear war on the battlefields of Europe" (492). Kahn's concept of survivable and winnable nuclear war, based upon his escalation ladder concept, often made distinctions between the preferable scenario of two million deaths as opposed to fifty million, for example, and the instrumentalism of his thinking is satirized in *Strangelove* as monstrously callous, particularly in Dr. Strangelove's mineshaft speech at the end of the film.

The first evidence of the film's satirical exposition of the callousness of Kahn's thinking can be seen in Turgidson's inhuman hawking of a strike-first strategy against the Soviets. Turgidson leaves Miss Scott (Tracey Reed) in their bedroom and we next see him in the War Room, whereupon, after learning of the errant bomber's irretrievable misadventure, he espouses the virtues of following up the bomber's strike with an all-out attack.[17] In keeping with the film's ribald allegory, Turgidson explains that in doing so, "we've got a good chance of catching them with their pants down." In what is almost a direct quotation from Kahn, Turgidson explains that the choice is between "two admittedly regrettable, but nevertheless, distinguishable post-war environments: one where you've got twenty million people killed, and the other where you've got one hundred and fifty million people killed." On the desk in front of Turgidson can be seen a folder called "World Targets in Megadeaths," a phrase coined by Kahn and used in *On Thermonuclear War*.

Interestingly, however, while the connection between distorted male sexuality and an overzealous desire for a strike-first against the tribal enemy is played up in Turgidson's characterization, Kahn himself was not an advocate of an all-out strike. Kahn believed in a rational nuclear war, as is apparent in his escalation ladder concept, which revolved around an unofficially agreed-upon set of rules, and which would make nuclear war survivable in his eyes. Kahn referred to an all-out strike as a "wargasm," indicating his awareness of the element of distorted sexuality in strategies of nuclear aggression, yet his own notions that nuclear war could be fought according to an agreed upon set of rules was apparently not ridiculous in his view ("To the

I. Dr. Strangelove

Brink of Eternity," *Pandora's Box*, Episode 2). This naïve faith in the rationality of humans to *play* by the rules in a terminal war indicates a fatal blind spot in Kahn's viewpoint, linked to his own deeply rooted faith in the power of the free market. According to the film, then, he is guilty of the conceptual flaw of moral abdication to the means of the market, which persists in the postnuclear world.

After Major Kong succeeds in bombing his target and thereby triggering the Russian doomsday machine and initiating a global nuclear holocaust, Dr. Strangelove and Muffley discuss the possibility for survival of the human race, which Strangelove proposes can be done underground. After Dr. Strangelove describes, with a lascivious grin, the "prodigious breeding" that will be required of their new mineshaft-life, he explains to President Muffley, that while survivors will be selected by "computah" for their favorable genetic attributes, the political and military elite will, of course, have to be preserved to carry their leadership qualities into the future mineshaft society. Dr. Strangelove stands from his wheelchair, still clutching the slide rule he had been previously been wrestling his black gloved hand for possession of, and bellows, "Mein Fuhrer, I can walk!" The film ends with footage of various nuclear mushroom clouds rolling to Lynn's soothing tones. Dr. Strangelove walks when he finds full expression of the fascist fantasy his Nazi allusions entail. The various factors of distorted male sexuality, technical prowess, faith in logical cleanliness and elitism are shown to be the ingredients of fascism redrawn in Sellers' ingenious clowning at the end of the film.

The subtext to this discussion is that those in the War Room are privileged enough by their power to survive the holocaust, at least initially, and likewise the currency of Kahn's power also allowed him the facility to survive nuclear war. This factor underpins the apparent callousness of Kahn's instrumental thinking, a radical disconnection from the enormity of suffering and death that would occur in the event of a nuclear war. Perhaps the power Kahn gained through his nuclear scripture, and the fact that he and his loved ones would be able to survive a nuclear war, insulated him from considering the reality of the horror upon which his power was predicated. The callousness and irrationality of Kahn's thinking is closely satirized in this scene when President Muffley asks Strangelove if the survivors would lead such a poor quality life that they would envy the dead. Dr. Strangelove's response is a rambling nonsense that is closely related to text from a chapter of Kahn's *On Thermonuclear War* called "Will the Survivors Envy the Dead?" As Kaplan points out, "The chapter began with an air of scientific rigor and mathematical precision. It ended with rambling, uplifting rhetoric: 'We may not be able to recuperate even with preparations, but we cannot today put our finger on why this should be so and I, for one, believe that with sufficient preparation we actually will be able to survive and recuperate if deterrence fails'" (Kaplan, *Wizards* 230). In the film, Dr. Strangelove rants about a "bold curiosity for the future," before springing out of his wheelchair and giving the seig heil salute. *Strangelove* thus makes a clear statement that the callous and disconnected instrumental thinking of Kahn and other likeminded elite nuclear technocrats is fascism redrawn.

Whatever the merits or otherwise of Kahn's nuclear rationality, there is no doubting that he, like von Neumann, became very powerful in the late 1960s on the basis of his ability to speak the esoteric language of the Bomb. In the RAND Corporation and his own think tank, The Hudson Institute, Kahn retained the status of what Kaplan calls a "thermonuclear Jesuit," and as such, the scripture was one of capitalist logical orthodoxy (*Wizards* 11). Kaplan writes here of Kahn's hypothesis about post-war life, which the last scene of *Strangelove*, as mentioned, so incisively and mercilessly mocks:

> The rest of Kahn's book crucially depended on the feasibility and success of a nationwide civil-defense program. Yet, in the final analysis, proof of this feasibility rested not on the rigorous thinking that Kahn elsewhere celebrated, but on faith in the basic goodness of the free market even under the most catastrophic circumstances, faith in the ability of quantitative analysis to solve problems even when faced with unpredictable, largely unquantifiable variables [*Wizards* 231].

It is clear that both Kahn and von Neumann approached the Cold War stand-off not from an objective point of view, but from deep within their ideological paradigm. Von Neumann's hatred of the Russians and his hyperactive sexuality are apparently conflated in his theory's rationalization of a strike-first strategy. The theory absorbed the distrustful paranoia of the time too, taking a radically solipsistic view of humanity, an effect that is very much in tandem with the theories of his contemporaries, Friedrich Von Hayek and Milton Friedman, who are the fathers of neoliberalism. That von Neumann's hatred of the Russians is rooted in a tribal-sexual aggression, and that Game Theory absorbed these elements of his being, is clearly evident in *Strangelove*'s close parodying of the mathematician. Dr. Strangelove's megalomaniacal urges actually come to fruition with the global destruction at the end of the film, as this will allow the "prodigious breeding" that lies at the root of all the political and theoretical machinations, the sublimated aggression of the theories. The theory's continued claim to mathematical and scientific objectivity, however, as well as its concomitance with neoliberalist ideology, has apparently ensured its survival thus far.

Dr. Strangelove's rambling rhetoric also contains the film's most enduring critique of Cold War instrumentalism. Moral abdication in favor of mechanical processes, over and above communication and empathy, sees the destruction of the species at the end of the film. The rigorous thinking and scientific objectivity that Kahn (and the rest of the elite analysts of the time) claimed, was ultimately predicated on the forces of the market to solve the problems of post-war life. Kahn's callousness about the suffering and death of millions that his escalation ladder model predicted is matched by the ludicrous naivety of his blithe assumption that the enemies would play by the rational rules set out in capitalist ideology in a real war situation. The anomalous situation that facilitated the rise to power of these priests of scientific objectivity, according to *Strangelove*'s vaudevillian comedy, was ludicrous and insane. There is an enduring lesson imparted by *Strangelove*, which is that deferring morality, communication, empathy and flexibility in human judgment, flawed or not, to the processes of our equally flawed technological or technocratic instruments and institutions, will undoubtedly lead to catastrophe. This is a Kubrickian assertion that is evident especially in his films from this period, that man is undoubtedly irrational and silly, but attempts to modulate or circumvent these animal traits that have come to be accepted as flaws in our nature are much more dangerous than our actual nature, and that prudent social governance lies in an honest understanding of human beings. Dogma, power, ideology and institutionalism often obscure clear understanding of human beings, as is so dramatically evident in the Cold War's rise to dominance of the mechanized concepts of a few delusional men in an insane situation. Here the text will turn to an examination of how these mechanized concepts, in particular the idea of the ruthlessly efficient modern man, are predicated on a particular idea of masculinity that arose in the Cold War stand-off, and this is also, as ever, in dialogue with formative American mythology.

The "De-libidinized" Machine-Men of the SAC Movies

Dr. Strangelove's grotesque technocratic fantasies are an insightful critique of the cultural paradigm that emerged in RAND and the other power elites at the time of the nuclear standoff. The culture was one that required the deferral of moral and human considerations in the *calculation* of agency, thus the grotesqueness of von Neumann, Kahn and Nash's theories. "Indeed, the association between nuclear responsibility and diminished human effect," Gannon writes astutely, "began to become one of the most common tropes in nuclear war fiction. From the characters in the film version of *Fail-Safe* to the partially mechanical Dr. Strangelove, nuclear war narratives (particularly films) have brooded not only upon the physical mutation caused by the bomb, but upon the psychological degeneration of those who live in proximity to it" (113). It is noteworthy in this regard, that ruthlessness in decision-making is a highly venerated trait in modern capitalist ideology. The Bomb played a role in this socializing effect, as its techno-economic requirement for an ultimate male rationality required a more machine-like decision making process that was to be devoid of emotion or sentimentality.

The Bomb's destructive power required a ruthless efficiency; to think as a machine thinks is to remove all sentimentality and irrationality, thereby ruling out any catastrophic miscalculations. As seen in Ripper's anti-fluoridation rant (discussed in detail below), American Cold War paranoia revolved around a fear of impregnation with weak and feminine communist ideas. Irrationality and sentimentality, in the inherently misogynistic and homophobic right-wing thinking of the time, were assumed to be female or homosexual traits and intensely dangerous. A Cold War outline of masculinity was thus conceived, whereby feminine weaknesses were to be excised in favor of ruthless efficiency. *Strangelove*'s sex-allegory revolves around a distorted male sexuality, in which the drollest joke is one of missile jousting. Von Neumann and his over-sexed philandering is the obvious target for this kind of joke, yet Kubrick and his co-script writer Terry Southern had undoubtedly watched the Hollywood Cold War movies of the late 1950s/early 1960s in which the concept of masculinity was recapitulated in very bald terms. *Strangelove* was not the only American text to satirize the Cold War, but it was the first popular film to do so. Southern's own novels, *Candy* (1958) and *The Magic Christian* (1959) were, like *Strangelove*, bawdy and anarchic satires that had a cult following at the time. "His additions to the script," Baxter writes of Southern, "recalled *Evergreen Review*, Paul Krassner's acerbic *Realist* and Harvey Kurtzman's magazines *Mad* and *Help*, with some of their comic-book parodies of Hollywood clichés" (178).

Those Hollywood films that did deal with the Bomb and with the Strategic Air Command (SAC) help to illuminate *Strangelove*'s satire of machine-

I. Dr. Strangelove

masculinity and provide an important context to this reading of the film. While the films are important cultural artifacts, they differ from *Strangelove* in that they accept the prescribed paradigm that nuclear policy is rational, that the military and political elites are rational and doing their best in an intractable situation. Although Lumet's *Fail-Safe*, unlike the others, is critical of mechanized thinking, it falls short of the removed critical perspective that *Strangelove* achieves, portraying the nuclear standoff as tragic but inevitable. *Above and Beyond* (1952), *Strategic Air Command* (1955), *A Gathering of Eagles* (1963) and *Fail-Safe* (1964) all concern themselves with the nuclear subject, and all were more or less officially sanctioned: "General Curtis LeMay, commander of the SAC, took a personal concern in *A Gathering of Eagles*: he stressed the need to explain how many safeguards had been created to prevent accidental war" (Maland 715). Sidney Lumet's *Fail-Safe* can be set apart from Melvin Frank's *Above and Beyond*, LeMay's *A Gathering of Eagles* and *Strategic Air Command*, which together complete a trio of Cold War movies that are part domestic drama and part paean to military technology. The story, theme and message of these three films are remarkably similar.

A credit at the opening of *Above and Beyond* cites the "wholehearted cooperation of the Department of Defense and the Air Force."[18] The film tells the story of the real-life pilot of the *Enola Gay*, Paul Tibbets (Robert Taylor), who is drafted to pilot the plane that will drop the first atomic bomb. The mission is, of course, top secret and nobody, not even close family members including spouses, can know anything about it. Tibbets' wife, Lucy (Eleanor Parker), quickly begins to resent his secretiveness, believing he has delusions about his work and is simply shutting her out of his life. It is only after Lucy hears the broadcast on the radio announcing the dropping of the atomic bomb on Hiroshima that she realizes the error of her ways. She picks up a framed picture of Tibbets and weeps on it while assuming a contrite, prayerful pose. The message of the film is clear: to be a good Air Force wife, and a good American patriot, she must learn to make sacrifices and not question her husband's work. Tibbets, on the other hand, has learned not to let (female) sentimentality and emotion get in the way of his primary function.

In *Strategic Air Command*, directed by Anthony Mann, and starring James Stewart and June Allyson, "Dutch" Holland (Stewart) is a major league baseball player doing quite well for himself and his new wife Sally (Allyson), when he is re-drafted to the Air Force bomber division. Dutch is reluctant, but comes around to his patriotic duty, while his wife also dutifully gives up her domestic dream. Dutch comes into conflict with the LeMay-like General

Hawkes (Frank Lovejoy), but his diligence and dedication win the day in the end. His job is to help iron out flaws in the new bomber, the B-47, which is depicted through a long series of montages of flying bombers, including, like all of the films mentioned, a mid-air refueling scene. Interestingly, in this particular version of the scene, the non-diegetic music is incongruously romantic and an electronically transmitted voice intones, "your slipway doors are open, receptacle clear, ready for contact." Again, given Kubrick's extensive research on all his films and Southern's penchant for Hollywood mockery and ribald punning, these films may have had an influence on *Strangelove*'s outcome as a satire and not a straight Cold War film, not only in the sense that these films gaze at military technology with an awe that approaches (unintentional) sexual arousal but also, of course, in the consistently recapitulated call for unsentimental, ruthless masculinity.

A Gathering of Eagles, staring Rock Hudson, completes the trio of domestic drama Air Force movies. Colonel Jim Caldwell (Hudson) is given the job of heading up a wing command, which is overseen by a notoriously perfectionist Major. Caldwell's friend, Colonel Hollis Farr (Rod Taylor) doubts that nice guy Caldwell is ruthless enough to bring the wing up to speed. Caldwell proves him wrong by being utterly ruthless, so much so, that he fires Farr for a mistake. Caldwell's wife, Victoria (Mary Peach), believes he has changed for the worse, that this ruthlessness is not in his nature. At the end of the film however, Caldwell's ruthlessness is justified. His wing command's takeoff procedure, which is charged with the vital job of a counter-strike against the Russians in the event of an attack, is now flawless and Victoria learns the error of her doubting. She has the last line of the film, as she dutifully picks up the emergency Air Force phone and places it beside him in their small Air Force base apartment and cheerfully says, "You'll have to live with these things in SAC." In these three films, the male identity and role is constructed around a need for a machine-like perfectionism, as a function of Cold War patriotism. Feelings must not get in the way of duty; a man must be as ruthless in his judgments as the computers that provide the technological precision to bomb the enemy. The wives in these three movies represent overwrought emotion. The male heroes in all three, by way of instruction as to how men should be in Cold War America, overcome weak, feminine emotions in order to do their duty and reap the rewards of their ruthless efficiency.[19]

The novel *Fail-Safe*, co-written by political scientist Harvey Wheeler and Eugene Burdick (who wrote the bestseller *The Ugly American*), concerns itself with an errant bomber that exposes a flaw in the fail safe system, and

I. Dr. Strangelove

the film follows suit. In this particular story, the bomber manages to bomb Moscow, but reasonableness and communication between the American President (Henry Fonda) and the Russian Premier prevail, and the crisis is solved when America agrees to bomb New York in order to redress the imbalance.[20] The news that Lumet was making a film concerning the same subject matter as *Strangelove*, and which would be released at around the same time, may ultimately have been the most compelling, among other factors, in Kubrick's decision to switch from a straight adaptation of George's novel to a satirical-farcical approach. The decision to switch was in retrospect very wise. Although Lumet's film is quite insightful in its critique of mechanized thinking, it, unlike *Strangelove*, has all but drifted into obscurity. Having said this, it is worthy of separation from the other nuclear films mentioned above. In it Walter Matthau plays Professor Groeteschele, a Kahn-esque mouthpiece for the strategies of deterrence. Once the President and the rest of the military and political elite realize that the bomber cannot be recalled, Groeteschele adopts the same stance Turgidson does in *Strangelove*. He demonstrates Game theoretical logic by extolling the need for America to take advantage of the situation and strike a decisive blow against the Russians. The pivotal scene of the film sees Groeteschele argue his point while General Black (Dan O'Herlihy) calls for restraint. The exchange reveals the philosophical heart of the film. In response to Groeteschele's call to annihilate the Russians, Black asks "In the name of what? To preserve what? Even if we do survive, what are we, better than what they say we are?" Those that survive, Groeteschele retorts, are the only ones who deserve to survive. In this proclamation, Groeteschele is restating the essence of Dr. Strangelove's faux–Darwinian, fascist survivor breeding fantasy, and by extension, the fascist undertones of Kahn's elitist theories. The RAND technocratic elite controlled the language of the Bomb, the vastly complex argot that spoke to its essence; their rationality deemed them fit enough to survive its devastation, along with the military and political elite. They were, as Kaplan so astutely observes, its "thermonuclear Jesuits."

Fail-Safe's Groeteschele is the embodiment of machine-man rationality, and as in *Strangelove*, it is equated with a form of fascist thinking. The sum and substance of this, however, are imparted more memorably in Sellers' antics than the dry and somber treatment it is given in *Fail-Safe*. *Strangelove*'s satire of machine-man is much more allusive and much more biting than the critique offered in *Fail-Safe*, particularly in Dr. Strangelove's mutual fondness for logical cleanliness and his obvious fascist tendencies. Allusions to Nazism and totalitarianism in *Strangelove*'s satire are not only based on real figures of the Cold War, but there are also notable intertextual references. Contemporary Hollywood Cold War films are fodder for *Strangelove*'s satire but there are also more reverential allusions. For example, Kubrick, it seems, is giving a nod to Rotwang, the "maimed technocratic genius" from Fritz Lang's *Metropolis* in Dr. Strangelove's errant black-gloved hand (Baxter 187). *Metropolis*'s depiction of technocratic dystopianism undoubtedly did not escape Kubrick's attention. In Lang's film, the scientist's arm is mechanical; in *Strangelove* it is unclear whether the arm is mechanical or Strangelove's own. In either case, Dr. Strangelove's increasing loss of control over the arm in the final scenes of the film, in which the hand refuses to relinquish a slide rule to his other hand, gives impromptu Nazi salutes and attacks its owner's throat as Dr. Strangelove explains the merits of the computer-selected breeding program, is ingenious satire of the rationale. If Dr. Strangelove's arm is mechanical, it reflects man's loss of control over technology. Strangelove and his errant arm in this context signal an irrevocable rupture between the Bomb (as an avatar for the systems and machines of late modernity) and the practical needs of man's survival. If the arm is Strangelove's own, however, it is a case of agonistic apraxia, or alien hand syndrome, a kind of physical Tourette's, signaling the human inability to control irrational impulses. Despite Dr. Strangelove's total faith in technology and its logic, human beings will always be irrational, as his inability to control his own arm signals. Worthy of note too, in this context is the definition of agonism, which is a political theory that emphasizes the inevitability, and positive aspects of conflict, the favorable breeding opportunities for the survivors being the positive aspects of the conflict from Dr. Strangelove's point of view.[21] Dr. Strangelove, an amalgamation of Cold War technocrats, demonstrates the psychological degeneration that proximity to the Bomb engendered in an insightful and unforgettable way. Far from being "de-libidinized," *Strangelove*'s "Bland Corporation" elite expressed their sexual aggression through the sublimated violence of their bomb-derived social engineering models.

In contrast, as Maland correctly points out, *Fail-Safe* "does nothing to suggest, as *Strangelove* does, that national policy is ridiculous" (715). Instead, Lumet's film and the other Hollywood nuclear movies of the time portray a military that is doing its best in a tragic situation. The viewpoint that military and government leaders are doing their best to protect the nation's civilians is one that emerges very much from within the prescribed understanding of the Cold War. In addition, Charles Gannon argues convincingly that the

I. Dr. Strangelove

Bomb was viewed in America in a much more utilitarian way than it was by the British. He contrasts the explicit rendering of thermonuclear blast in American post-war films, such as *The Day After* (1983) or the memorably fetishized detailing of the explosion in *Terminator 2: Judgment Day* (1991), with the more circumspect treatment of the matter in British films such as *Threads* (1984) or *The War Game* (1965). Nuclear war was seen as survivable, partly due to the sheer size of the United States and partly because apocalypticism is in tune with American frontier mythology. On the other hand, however, Britain's bombing during World War II and its relatively small size meant there was a much different attitude to nuclear war.[22] Thus can be seen the British movie's tendency to look away from the holocaust and the American movies' tendency to look as closely as possible, in an attempt to engender a "psychological prophylaxis" (Gannon 106). By rendering a nuclear war in images, Gannon suggests, people could be in some sense prepared for its occurrence and perhaps also contain or manage what is untamable. Gannon doesn't engage with the centrality of apocalypticism in the American psyche, however, his argument does shed light on von Neumann, Kahn and the general RAND attitude to nuclear weapons as utilitarian. A weapon that for the British meant total annihilation of all life became for the Americans an elite tool with which to wield and control global American political dominance. It is in this sense also that the Bomb is treated in *Fail-Safe*. "The bomb serves as a means of redistributing international justice and balance," Gannon writes. "This cultural perspective also helps us grasp the logic underlying the use of the bomb at Hiroshima itself—the use of a nuclear tool, justified by claims that it would ultimately save lives by making Operation Olympic (the planned American invasion of Japan) unnecessary" (110). The Bomb's power, of course, is not just effective as a weapon against outside enemies; its effects have permeated the core of American life in the capitalist technical imperative that has become central to the running of institutions and the internal wars, on drugs and on terrorism.

The American view of the Bomb as a tool is inherently bound up with the transcendence implied in apocalyptic regeneration. America's large geographic space precipitated the construct of the frontier mythology in the American psyche, and the transcendence implied in the myth is an expression of Christian utopianism. While the secular apocalypse that the Bomb signifies has no promise of transcendence, beyond that of the transcendence of life itself, its use as a tool of global dominance betrays an anachronistic frontier attitude to its utility. In other words, the frontier myth implies limitlessness, eternal expansion, eternal growth but all of this is contradicted by the existence of world-destroying technology. *Strangelove* satirizes this erroneous frontier attitude to the Bomb in the cowboy Kong's rodeo-riding "Hi There" to oblivion.

This is seen in the distorted sex-allegory that happens on the bomber on its way to bomb Laputa.[23] When the bomber receives the go code, Kong dons his ten-gallon hat and declares with gusto "we gotta get humpin," a pun that is soon to be given the visual impetus of Kong riding the phallus all the way down to the earth. Kong's enthusiasm for this outcome belies the totality of what he has initiated. In this anachronistic frontier act, the Bomb is just another tool in the civilizing mission to conquer the Indians, and, as such, reflects how nuclear war was seen by military and civilian hawks at the time of the nuclear standoff. On a more immediate level, Pickens' goofy cowboy character could be Kubrick and Southern's swipe at the ubiquitous Hollywood western of the time. Slotkin points out in *Gunfighter Nation* that American culture consistently recapitulated the myth of the frontier and the conquest of the red man in so many westerns of the middle twentieth century, and the conceiving of the Cold War was no different, as seen in *Devil's Doorway* and *Broken Arrow* (both 1950).[24] American exceptionalism is very much wrapped up in its frontier mythology, the notion that American greatness was forged in the taming of the wilderness, its civilizing mission in which savagery and godlessness was overcome eventually by the implementation of equality, justice, liberty and most importantly, commerce. The great irony in Kong's case, however, is that he rodeo-rides the bomb to the destruction and end of all frontiers.

The advent of the Bomb, along with its attendant cultural and psychic effect on America, was integral to America's evolution into the world's dominant superpower. Of course, this is one concern of *Strangelove* and Kubrick's later films including *2001*, and what Baudrillard means when he argues that the Cold War was a technical exercise, a model for the mechanical operation of society. In a strictly utilitarian sense, the Bomb's destructive power rendered its use as a weapon unthinkable, thus the actions of man had to become machine-like, to become subjugated to its discipline. Precisely what *Strangelove* satirizes, what *Fail-Safe* merely laments as inevitable, and what the SAC movies call for, is a more mechanically rational man to manage the reality of a world with the bomb:

> America's technocratic solution to this vulnerability was not merely the creation of machines that could do the work of men, but of men that could work like machines.

I. Dr. Strangelove

> The stoic, inflexible demeanor of totemic warlords such as General Curtis LeMay (the architect of American nuclear Strategy) and Admiral Rickover (the driving force behind the nuclear submarine) set a standard that not only "trickled down" into their own branches of the armed service, but into the narrative characterizations of the de-libidinized machine-men who were charged with controlling and unleashing the arsenals of Armageddon [Gannon 114].

The "de-libidinized" men of the SAC movies, in which masculinity is restructured around ruthlessness and unsentimental rationalism in the workplace, are parodied mercilessly in *Strangelove*. If politics is the sublimation of subconscious libidinal urges, as *Strangelove* is suggesting, the Bomb, and the protocols that surrounded it became the vehicle for these displaced libidinal urges. Contrary to the machine-men of the SAC movies that live in domestic bliss with faithful and obedient wives, *Strangelove*'s machine-men espouse their uber-rational theories of destruction and holocaust in what is clearly an insane distortion of primitive male sexuality. The view of the Bomb as a symbol of sexual potency in the American psyche goes back, according to David Seed, to the first official accounts of the atomic bombs, by the *New York Times* journalist William L. Laurence. Laurence, who witnessed the bombing of Nagasaki, recounts not the destruction of the city, but "concentrates instead entirely on the implicitly sexual process of orgasm and birthing of a titanic monster" (*Imagining Apocalypse* 91). The SAC movies stand as evidence as to how much the idea of mechanized, unsentimental rationality had permeated the culture but *Strangelove*'s outlandish sex-allegory shows that this rationality in action is far from being de-libidinized. It is tribal-sexual, as much politics seems to be, and if not overtly violent all the time, the violence is sublimated through dehumanizing systems and brutal logic.

The Bomb and American Millenarianism

The American attitude to the Cold War conflict, its technology and its systems reflects, in particular, the millenarian aspect of America's mythological inception, whereby the dawning of heaven on earth is precipitated by a cleansing apocalypse. It is the myth of destruction and rebirth that Laurence subconsciously fell back upon when describing the bombing of Nagasaki.

The means of science, going back to Newton and far beyond, according to Eugen Weber, were utilized to reveal the mechanics of God's divine plan. Weber argues that we tend to read the history of science forward, for what it predicted, instead of backwards to show its connection to the ideas and mythologies that preceded it. "If we do that we discover the intimate connection between science and theology" (*Apocalypses* 84). The application of science and technology was certainly integral to the spiritual mission of the Pilgrims and Puritans in the New World. The powerful auspices of technology, commerce and Christianity strengthened the mission to hue and carve the new land into the promised utopia, while also cementing the apodictic view that the natives were savages, in direct opposition to their Godly civilizing mission: "They envisioned a continual increase of moral, spiritual, and material goods in this world—an age of sacred-secular wonders within history. They inherited the hope of supernatural things to come, and they altered this to mean an indefinite course of human progress" (Bercovich, *The Puritan Origins* 37). Technology, then, has been integral to American mythology in tandem with the religious promise of utopia.[25] For pre-millennialist Puritans and Pilgrims, the apocalypse preceded the dawning of heaven on earth. The H-bomb can be understood in millenarian terms, therefore, as the way to utopia and the transcendence at the core of the American Dream. Subservience to mechanical processes, as is personified by those in *Strangelove*'s War Room, is religious faith which has been transferred to the new source of apocalyptic power, technology. Faith in technology, technocracy, and rationalism imbues a religious faith in a higher power, but there are no guiding moral principles to base the faith upon, this system only requires efficiency and clean logical thinking.

The Cold War was mythologically conceived as a civilizing mission, a battle between the Godly force of liberty and light against the inscrutable heathen other, who sought to corrupt America and the rest of the world with unnatural collectivist ideas. The old Puritan fears of the dark and heathen other resurfaced in the fears of the red menace, in similar sexual and breeding terms—fears of miscegenation and the corrupting influence of Godlessness on their own population. This manifested during the Cold War in fears of a pollution or infection of their own citizens with communism; citizens, who may have been predisposed to queerness in some way, thus open to corruption. The Bomb, as the source of a religious power of certitude provided a scripture for straight, modular and masculine thinking, a protection against queering othernesses. *Strangelove* addresses these conflated fears of miscegenation, femininity, homosexuality and predisposition to communist ideas in the interaction between General Ripper and Group Captain Lionel Mandrake, and to a lesser extent between President Muffley and the military hawks of the War Room, as is discussed below.

I. Dr. Strangelove

Ripper and Muffley: Miscegenation, Misogyny and Homophobia

In the Cold War's civilizing mission, the battle between capitalism's civilization and communism's savagery, the original fears of miscegenation and the othering of the enemy's sexuality are present, yet because of the distant and non-combatant nature of the Cold War, these fears were diffused and dispersed in a different way throughout the culture. The fears of miscegenation revolved around a rampant paranoia that communism was spreading and infecting the population in unseen ways, like a viral disease, but one in which females and homosexuals, the internal others, were susceptible to communism's weak collectivist ideas. Masculinity in the ideal Cold warrior, as presented in the SAC movies, was to revolve around the ability to be ruthlessly rational in one's judgment, primarily by excising and denying the influence of feminine sentimentality. What were perceived to be softer attributes, such as empathy and care, as well as the quotidian attendances of domesticity were the preserves of the woman, to be separated and prevented from infiltrating the calculations of the machine-man warrior.

In the paranoid atmosphere of McCarthy's trials, fears of impregnation with weak collectivist ideas were rampant, taking shape most pointedly in the fears that water fluoridation was a communist plot to impregnate the population with communism. The Cold War was framed in the United States as the great battle of ideologies—that of a God-given freedom of self-determination, versus a heathen and unnatural centralized-rule totalitarianism—carried out under the specter of the apocalypse that millenarian settlers expected would bring a conclusion to their battle. The miscegenation that was feared by the Americans in the tribal-sexual aspect of the Cold War was one in which femininity or homosexuality opened the door to communism. These aspects of the era's paranoia are satirized in *Strangelove*'s distorted sex-allegory, in the interactions between Ripper and Mandrake, Ripper and Colonel Bat Guano (Keenan Wynn) and between President Muffley and Turgidson.

Ripper's office is the scene of the General's initiation of "Wing Plan R," whereby the directive to bomb is sent via code to the "CRM-114" communications devices aboard a squadron of bombers flying fail-safe missions. Group Captain Lionel Mandrake, a British officer on exchange at Burpelson, quickly discovers the General's insane plot and tries to foil it. The following exchange between Mandrake and Ripper satirizes the conflations, in right-wing thinking at the time, of communist infiltration with male sexual impotency, homosexuality and impregnation. Ripper takes Mandrake hostage in his office after the latter has discovered his plot, and then begins to explain the thinking behind his actions:

RIPPER: Mandrake, do you realize that in addition to fluoridating water, why, there are studies under way to fluoridate salt, flour, fruit juices, soup, sugar, milk ... ice cream. Ice cream, Mandrake, children's ice cream.
MANDRAKE: Lord, Jack.
RIPPER: You know when fluoridation first began?
MANDRAKE: I ... no, no. I don't, Jack.
RIPPER: Nineteen hundred and forty-six. 1946, Mandrake. How does that coincide with your post-war Commie conspiracy, huh? It's incredibly obvious, isn't it? A foreign substance is introduced into our precious bodily fluids without the knowledge of the individual. Certainly without any choice. That's the way your hard-core Commie works.
MANDRAKE: Uh, Jack, Jack, listen ... tell me, tell me, Jack. When did you first ... become ... well, develop this theory?
RIPPER: Well, I, uh.... I ... I ... first became aware of it, Mandrake, during the physical act of love.
MANDRAKE: Hmm.
RIPPER: Yes, a uh, a profound sense of fatigue ... a feeling of emptiness followed. Luckily I ... I was able to interpret these feelings correctly. Loss of essence.
MANDRAKE: Hmm.
RIPPER: I can assure you it has not recurred, Mandrake. Women uh ... women sense my power and they seek the life essence. I, uh.... I do not avoid women, Mandrake.
MANDRAKE: No.
RIPPER: But I ... I do deny them my essence.

Ripper's theories parody what Baxter calls a "fashionable right-wing obsession of the period, fluoridation of the public water supply, which some of the more volatile elements of the idiot fringe regarded as a Communist plot to poison America" (181). That the communists infiltrate through "the precious bodily fluids," suggests not only impregnation of America with weak communist ideas, but also an emasculation, and denial of male sexual release.[26]

Ripper's fluoridation rant also speaks to the framing of the Cold War, in the minds of many, as the apocalyptic battle redrawn. The civilizing mis-

I. Dr. Strangelove

sion for the Puritans and Pilgrims in early colonial times was threatened by the heathen natives whom they believed lived in sinful carnality and bestial savagery. The rhetoric of sexual otherness that informed the early colonial justifications for enmity and destruction of the natives resurfaces in the fears of Communist infiltration during the Cold War, but now conceptualized not in terms of the female body but of the body politic, which is assumed to be male. Thus the fluoridation conspiracy, the notion that the Soviet enemy could impregnate the American body politic with their unnatural, weak and feminine ideas, is the Puritan fear of miscegenation redrawn to fit a new holy mission against a new savage.

The scene presents Ripper as a macho military action man, the epitome of a commie hatin' Cold Warrior, albeit in the film's characterization it quickly becomes more than apparent that he is insane. Mandrake, on the other hand, who does not share Ripper's communist paranoia and tries to foil his efforts, is portrayed as camp and effete. The unfolding scenario between Ripper and Mandrake, in which Ripper explains his theories to Mandrake, (while producing his obviously phallic machine gun to shoot out the window at the forces ordered to retrieve the recall code) is oddly flirtatious. Mandrake lies belly down on the couch and almost whispers to Ripper that he can't help him because of his "gammy leg." Ripper finally realizes he cannot fight off the troops and takes his own life (with a pistol). In this scene, with Mandrake lying on the couch, dappled in light from the venetian blinds and being almost coy with Ripper, there is the ostensible suggestion, firmly tongue-in-cheek, that Mandrake's unwillingness to side with Ripper in his crusade marks him out as homosexual. Similarly, in the War Room, President Muffley's reasonableness, and his attempt to prevent the nuclear war is equated, via his ribald name, with femininity, and thus weakness, from a certain reactionary point of view. If we recall Von Neumann's philandering, his hatred of the communists and his willingness to strike first we see a certain right-wing ideal of patriotic masculinity exemplified. Conversely, traits such as reason, restraint and communication, *Strangelove* suggests, are implicated in the minds of the hawks, strike-first technocrats and paranoids as weak and feminine.[27] Mandrake and Muffley's suggestive names are part of the sport the film makes of this odious attitude, whereby their reason and their sanity makes them queers and pussies in the eyes of the hawks.[28]

Strangelove also makes fun of an unenlightened attitude that some Americans may have held towards the English during the post-war and Cold war era, specifically their revulsion of, and unwillingness to engage in a nuclear war. Mandrake's interaction with the commanding officer of the strike force, Colonel "Bat" Guano, who finally breaks into the office after Ripper's suicide, certainly bears this out. Guano is immediately suspicious of Mandrake's gentrified English accent and strange uniform and assumes that he is some kind of "prevert." Mandrake's Englishness/reasonableness/homosexuality strikes at the basest fears of Bat Guano, that he may be impregnated with Communism and "perversion"[29]:

MANDRAKE: Colonel! Colonel, I must know what you think has been going on here!
BAT GUANO: You wanna know what I think?
MANDRAKE: Yes!
BAT GUANO: I think you're some kind of deviated "prevert." I think General Ripper found out about your "preversion," and that you were organizing some kind of mutiny of "preverts." Now move!

Once he has convinced Guano of what is occurring, Mandrake is forced to use a telephone box to call the president with the codes. Running out of coins, he pleads with the operator to allow a trunk call, which the operator refuses. Mandrake, after much pleading, convinces Guano to shoot a nearby Coca-Cola machine for change to make the call. The scene ends with the machine spitting cola in Guano's face, a visual pun on the imagery of a golden shower, but the act of "perversion" here belongs to a machine and not a man. The image of a machine pissing on Guano's face, of course, is also in keeping with the film's general theme of human subservience to machines and systems. In contrast to *Fail-Safe*, for example, where the President manages the red alert situation by way of telephone communication with the Russian Premier, thus averting a global holocaust, in *Strangelove* the technology of communication consistently breaks down, while on the other hand, the technology of destruction is all too efficient. In both the technology and the Game Theoretical technocracy of the Cold War, communication, empathy and reason were denigrated in favor of the implied threat and aggression of nuclear arms. The abdication to the modular certitude and clean logic of machines leads to nuclear annihilation in *Strangelove*, despite Muffley and Kissoff's attempts to divert disaster by means of communication, reason and empathy. The doomsday machine is emblematic of the lunacy of replacing judgment with machine logic. Muffley's attempts to divert disaster by way of reason and empathy—or his feminine weakness as per the views of both fictional and real warmongers—are trumped by the inexorable logic of the doomsday machine.

I. Dr. Strangelove

The viewer only gets Muffley's side of the conversation with Kissoff, and it is clearly fraught with irrationality and pandering, which is in direct contrast to the prescribed enmity between the superpowers and the brutal logic of the machines of destruction with which they threaten each other. Muffley's attempt to explain the American mistake, the nuclear attack on Russia, is delivered in an amusingly simpering tone: "Dmitri, you know we've always talked about the possibility of something going wrong with the bomb ... the bomb Dmitri. The hydrogen bomb! Well now, what happened is, ahm, one of our base commanders, he had a sort of.. he went a little funny in the head.. you know ... just a little funny. And, ah ... he went and did a silly thing." Muffley's reasonableness in the War Room is offset by the MADness of Turgidson and Dr. Strangelove, both of whom espouse the irrefutable mathematical logic of a strike-first policy and, of course, display the concomitant infatuation with (heterosexual) sex and breeding. Muffley's reason, calmness and unwillingness to proceed with a strike-first policy, marks him out, like Mandrake, as effeminate, and thus weak. In this context, it is noteworthy that relations between military brass and the Kennedy Administration at the time were notoriously poor, due in part to Kennedy's reluctance to accept a strike first stance.[30] Muffley's retort to Turgidson's urging the launch of an all-out assault: "I will not go down in history as the greatest mass-murderer since Adolf Hitler" probably sums up Kennedy's attitude quite well, and marked him out, undoubtedly, as weak among those who subscribed to the logic of the Cold War as the civilizing mission redrawn. While Muffley and Kissoff's interaction is reasonable, deferential and sane, it is nevertheless, replete with human silliness and irrationality. This is best encapsulated in Muffley's strained attempts to convince the Russian Premier that the two are, indeed, friends. The silliness and childishness of the conversation seems a reassurance that the situation is not serious and the problem can be solved with communication. It is the indeterminate mix of human irrationality and mechanized processes, however, which ensures the outcome, and specifically the placing of machine processes above irrational communication in the realm of decision making.

The Doomsday Machine and the MADness of Moral Abdication

After his conversation with Muffley, Premier Dmitri Kissoff asks to speak to De Sadesky at which point the Russian doomsday machine is introduced to the film. The doomsday machine is a giant bank of nuclear bombs, which will be triggered automatically by computers once the American weapon falls. Any attempt to disarm it will cause it to explode immediately and the Earth will be enshrouded in a cloud of material that has a radioactive half-life of 93 years. The so-called doomsday machine, as Kubrick presents it in the film emulates perfectly the logic of deterrence as conceived by Cold War Game Theory. The incentives not to attack are obvious.[31] The device is controlled by immutable mechanical processes, not fickle and unreliable humans, thus its potency as a deterrent is rationally maximized, according to the strategic logic. The theory's founding principle of self-interest ensures that no one would risk an attack on a doomsday machine because its mechanical logic ensures that no irrational human factors such as empathy or mercy can interfere with its programmed retaliation. This apparently perfect logic, however, is undermined by Premier Kissoff's failure to inform the Americans of the doomsday machine's existence, thus completely negating its power as a deterrent. Characters in the film are often presented as sexually obsessed or repressed, or just silly and frail, but as Stillman points out, their irrationality is "vastly to be preferred to the rationality of the Doomsday Machine" (10). Humans, of course, do not think like machines and it is a silly human foible that ultimately brings about nuclear apocalypse in *Strangelove*. Kissoff's doomsday machine mistake, and indeed the film's entire premise, whereby nuclear war is initiated by a lone lunatic general, critically deconstructs both the deterrence strategy of Mutual Assured Destruction, and the belief in the infallibility of mechanical processes that abided among the power elite at the time.

Dr. Strangelove appears out of the shadows for the first time in the film when asked by President Muffley if the Americans had considered such a thing as a doomsday machine. In this scene Dr. Strangelove describes the essence of the Game Theoretical strategy of Mutual Assured Destruction, as derived from the Bland Corporation study he had commissioned: "Deterrence is the art of producing in the mind of the enemy, the fear to attack, and so because of the automated and irrevocable decision-making process, which rules out *human meddling*, the doomsday machine is terrifying and simple to understand, and completely credible and convincing." This pristine logic is undermined in the end, of course, by the Kubrickian observation that humans are not motivated by clean, quantifiable rationality. Dr. Strangelove snaps out of his fond ruminations on the incorruptible logic of the doomsday machine to ask, "But the whole point of having a doomsday machine is lost

I. Dr. Strangelove

if you keep it a secret. Why didn't you tell the world, eh?" De Sadesky dryly informs him, "It was to be announced at the party congress on Monday. As you know, the Premier loves surprises." Kubrick's films bear out the consistent viewpoint that humans are not rational, at least not according to the simplistic techno-capitalist rationality that Mutual Assured Destruction and other Game Theoretical models ascribe, and here an innocuous human triviality leads to nuclear apocalypse.[32]

The faith in rationality and mechanical logic among the analysts and mathematicians of the RAND Corporation, and the political elites who couldn't resist the lure of the certainty that they purported, revolved around the quasi-religious belief that science can correct human failings. This exchange in *Strangelove* collapses that logic. Rationality, if such a thing exists in human society, does not adhere to the perfect rationality of machine logic, and if it is nevertheless imposed in the form of the Bomb's enormous power, its incongruity with the complex realities of human motivations, according to *Strangelove*, will result in annihilation for mankind. President Muffley and Premier Kissoff's attempt to prevent the impending attack on Russia and thus the retaliation of the doomsday machine, for all their communication and reasonableness and empathy, nevertheless succumbs to the inexorable logic of the machine. The same criticism that is leveled at the technical imperative of Cold War ideology in *Strangelove* holds true to the technical imperative as it operates today in its free market-derived ubiquity. The primacy of technical or quantitative logic in our social interactions negates the means of communication, empathy and negotiation that are necessary at every node of human interaction. This was exemplified with horrific consequences in the Vietnam War, whereby the United States conducted their side of the war in the mode of an exercise in mathematical technique. The intractably rational mode of the United States' war prevented and eliminated the possibility of communication between the enemies, which McNamara claims, may likely have alleviated the conflict. Quantitative and technical logic is modular and inflexible, thus redundant as a framework for human decision-making.

Postmodernity's Grand Narrative of Apocalypse

Technique and paranoia, as characterized by American Cold War strategy and the scientific management models that arose from it, are part and parcel of the continuing dynamics of postmodernity. Distrust of man's nature and judgment in the wake of World War II, and the entrenchment of opposition between the superpowers, meant a concentration of effort in the areas of technology and technique and a deepening mutual fear and paranoia. *Strangelove* marks the beginning of the epoch of postmodernity in the Lyotardian and Baudrillardian sense, with the twin elements of technique and paranoia in America's Cold War underpinning the period. The Christian narratives that informed the Puritans and pilgrims—whereby faith was placed in a benign God—were replaced with the ameliorative certainty that the means of science promised. In other words, man's imperfections could be overcome with science and technology. Thus, a tangibly strong current of Christian thinking is evident in the American faith in science, technology and rationality to bring about progress.

It can be inferred from Baudrillard's essay "The Precession of Simulacra" (1981) that the predominance of Cold War-derived technocracy in Western institutional life is an underpinning factor in dehumanization and alienation in postmodernity. *Strangelove* is no more postmodern than it is modern, in that its distrust of prescribed Judeo-Christian morality or its distrust of technology can be equally attributed to tenets of modernism, yet it is the first film or text to deal with the postmodern elements of technique and paranoia in a way that was both insightful and widely influential. *Strangelove*'s insight into the religious and sexual aspects of America's relationship with technology reveals not a simple dissipation of religious narratives but a transference of the power of their mythologies into new narratives that claim, not mere faith, but scientific objectivity as their basis. The ostensibly secular arenas of science and technology have been imbued with the biblical mythology of progress and utopia.[33] The Bomb is the symbolic vestige of both the glorious apocalypse prophesized in *Revelations*, and the distorted and displaced sexuality implicit in America's formative rhetoric. The paranoia of miscegenation becomes a paranoia of infiltration or impregnation with weak, uncivilized, un–American ideology, becomes a vague all-pervasive paranoia of nuclear annihilation, of viral pandemic, of natural disaster, of environmental disaster, technological collapse and so on. Marina Benjamin, taking up Frank Kermode's central point in his *The Sense of an Ending*, argues that apocalypse is a grand narrative that has survived since the year 1200 B.C.:

> Apocalypse is a grand narrative unlike any other. It may be antiquated, arcane and crypted, having every appearance of redundancy, but it is able to account for the way things are in a manner that our other grand narratives cannot. It provides locations, a cast of players, a coherent script for the human story and it has an agenda. In all

I. Dr. Strangelove

these regards it shares the specificity of, say, history or science, but—and this is the source of apocalypse's strength—its symbols are so rich, or else so vacant, that they lend themselves to endless interpretations and uses. Effectively, in apocalypse, we possess a grand narrative that refuses to die [Benjamin 25].

Strangelove is not a postmodern film in its form or narrative methods, instead it marks historically the political and social effects that shaped the postmodern period to come, specifically, the Cold War's legacy of free-market technical primacy and the prevailing cultural tropes of paranoia and apocalypticism. In this regard, it precedes a number of important texts and films that deal with this complex knot at the heart of American mythology and postmodernity in general. Among these, *End Zone* and *Crash* are natural successors of *Strangelove*, marking as they do, a transmutation of cultural paranoia from that of Communist and nuclear war paranoia, into a more insidious and pervasive postmodern paranoia.

Chapter II

End Zone and *Crash*
Hollow Creeds and Monstrous Rituals

> In a novel about conflict on many levels, this was the primal clash—the tendency of language to work in opposition to the enormous technology of war that dominated the era and shaped the book's themes."
> —Don DeLillo, "The Power of History"
> (*New York Times*, September 7, 1997)

> Thermo-nuclear weapons systems and soft-drinks commercials coexist in an overlit realm ruled by advertising and pseudo-events, science and pornography. Over our lives preside the great twin leitmotifs of the 20th century—sex and paranoia.
> —J.G. Ballard, Introduction to *Crash*, 1995[1]

Introduction

These two novels—*End Zone* from 1972 and *Crash* from 1973—to greater and lesser extents respectively, assume and elaborate upon certain religious and sexual distortions in our postnuclear relationship with technology and technique, which *Strangelove* had already brought to light.[2] The novels engage with the formative period in postmodernity and offer enlightening insights into the role nuclear thinking and technology has played in shaping our cultural epoch. Both novels address a culture where the virtual and the spectacular—along with the machinery that produce them—have assumed prime currency.[3] At their core, they are concerned with the individual and collective struggle to find meaning in an ever-more confusing hyperreal world. This hyperreal world, as set out in *End Zone*, is one in which rationalism is prescribed from the dictates of deterrence logic and in *Crash*, in which the realm of the social and sexual has been sublimated through technology, specifically its destructive potential.

II. End Zone *and* Crash

The two novels upon which this chapter focuses are very different in terms of style and approach, but both are as perceptive as *Strangelove* in the manner in which they engage with life under the sign of the Bomb. The novels respond in their very different ways to the technology of global destruction and the peculiar rationality that arose from the American effort to manage the Bomb's existence and the Soviets' apparent ideological opposition. *Strangelove* reveals much about the Cold War from the American perspective: the kind of men in power at its height and the thinking at the root of America's approach. The novels, however, are set in the aftermath of the Cuban Missile Crisis, when the visceral fear of annihilation cooled and sublimated into a paranoia that diffused throughout the culture. In the novel's expansive forms is a response to the cultural *zeitgeist* that is more personal and philosophically complex than *Strangelove*. The following chapter therefore, will begin by discussing the thread of apocalypticism that connects *Strangelove*, *End Zone* and *Crash*.

It is noteworthy, for those who may be interested, that Baudrillard wrote extensively on the effect of technology on society and very perceptively on the implementation of Cold War-derived economic models on social institutions. There is much in Baudrillard's theory that corresponds with the themes engaged by the novels, particularly in his 1981 text, *Simulacra and Simulation*. The novels and Baudrillard's theories diverge, however, in their respective beliefs in the possibility for a radical interrogation of capitalism from within its seemingly totalizing logic. As DeLillo states, language contains the possibility to work against the "enormous technology of war" and hopefully the following analysis reveals the ways in which the novels successfully critique the totalitarianism of apocalyptic neoliberal instrumentalism.

The analysis of *End Zone* in this chapter—in its examination of the fate of narratives and its engagements with formative apocalyptic American myths—acts as a conceptual bridge between *Strangelove*'s revelation of the advent of scientific management and mechanical rationality, and the following chapter's discussion of *The Wire*. These texts are ostensibly very different yet are thematically linked. The dehumanizing mechanistic rationality with which Harkness struggles so profoundly in *End Zone* is an elaboration and personification of that which is first revealed in *Strangelove*'s comedy and can be seen in effect in *The Wire*'s more contemporary examination of neoliberal America. This chapter also investigates the novel's expansion upon the religious aspects of nuclear annihilation that are revealed in *Strangelove*, and the powerful current of apocalyptic thinking that is so embedded in the American way. The chapter will move on to discuss *Crash* and its examination of the

American technological apocalyptic in terms of subconscious sexual desires and how technology has and will change human subjectivity now and into the future.

The Apocalypse Still Looms: Sex and Religion in *End Zone* and *Crash*

End Zone, more directly than *Crash*, engages the religious aspect of the American relationship with technology in its narrative of Gary Harkness's ascetic journey to "Logos" College in the West Texan desert to play American football. Harkness seeks refuge from all the complexities of contemporary life in the carefully systematized violence of American football, and ironically, in the terminal logic of nuclear war. *Crash*, on the other hand, focuses more on the sexual element of our relationship with technology. James Ballard finds a new sexuality developing through technology's pseudo-womb—the car. In Ballard's novel the car is emblematic of all technology, and technology has become a conduit for our refracted and destructive libidinal urges. Each car crash, each sex act, opens the door a little more to death—the apocalypse in miniature, each fatal car crash an infinitesimal part of the greater "autogeddon." The novels express the apocalyptic in different ways, yet in both it is evoked as a nebulous and fractious entity that has disseminated throughout the culture. The apocalypse has been personalized and individuated in both novels, expanding and complicating the thematic can-of-worms that *Strangelove*'s nightmare comedy pried open.

Both novels present the idea that technology has taken the place of the Christian paternal God figure. Technology's destructive potential affords it the power to channel the apocalyptic mythologies that until then were conveyed in biblical narratives. The American relationship with technology is inextricably bound up with apocalyptic mythology and as a global leader in culture-making (primarily via entertainment and media technology), the United States has exported its peculiar apocalyptic sense of postmodernity to the rest of the media-industrialized world. Our attitudes to technology are complex and often ambivalent. We have charged it with our need for spiritual sustenance, yet simultaneously fear its destructive and dehumanizing effects. It would be unwise, herein, to insist that our collective relationship with technology in the postindustrial world is simplistically bound to the destruction/utopia mode of the apocalyptic; however, there is the simple truth that our

II. End Zone *and* Crash

destructive power far outstrips our life-giving powers. The morbid spectre of nuclear destruction still falls across all the amazing scientific and technological advances that save, ease or prolong human life. Thus, it is evident that the apocalyptic (American) mythology with which both of these novels engage is a powerful structural undercurrent in postmodern culture.[4]

Both *Crash* and *End Zone* reveal ways in which our ancient and sometimes unconscious needs—for meaning, for communion, nurturing and sexuality—now reside with scientism and the seemingly inexorable machinery of the capitalist instrument. The novels warn that the loss of binding narratives that is caused by subservience to this machinery is not only the source of our great loneliness in the world but also poses a grave danger to our survival if we cannot imagine a unified purpose. We have, in a sense, finally elevated ourselves to the status of God, but in solipsistically worshipping our own technique we find ourselves in a lonely universe. Our new secular mythologies lack the paternal comfort of either a disciplinarian or a loving father figure. John Gray argues in *Black Mass* that the rise in fundamentalism, particularly in the United States, is not a sign of a religious resurgence, but a desperate reaction to the instrumental secularization of the West. The attempt to revert back to pre-scientific myths and the denial of evolution, for example, is evidence of a doomed attempt to reinstate a purposive narrative for mankind, according to Gray. Technology's utopian narrative is humanist, thus secular, and thereby there is no divinity in its conception of humanity. The desperation with which fundamentalist Christianity is pursued by its proponents is evidence of the impossibility of reinstating pre-scientific belief systems in a techno-secular world. Gray does not denigrate the role of spiritual beliefs in the contemporary world, instead he seems to suggest an evolution or emergence of a new kind of spirituality that is adapted to life in a fully technologically immersed world. This is precisely what *Crash* proposes, albeit the new spirituality it presents is one that is deemed psychopathological by our current mores.

The myth of apocalyptic destruction and rebirth has existed, of course, in a rich variety of cultures since history has been narrated. Frank Kermode argues in *The Sense of an Ending* that the fear of an apocalyptic cataclysm was no more real and visceral for those living in the era of the Cuban Missile Crisis than it was for millenarian Puritans who awaited Armageddon. "We think of our own crisis as pre-eminent, more worrying, more interesting than other crises.... But it would be childish to argue, in a discussion of how people behave under eschatological threat, that nuclear bombs are more real and make one experience more authentic crisis-feelings than armies in the sky" (Kermode 93–94). This book can make no claims as to how people in the seventeenth century may have behaved under the eschatological terror promised by *Revelations*, however, what is different is that our postmodern cataclysm is man-made. The constructed binary between faith and science has probably never been so pronounced as it is now, with supremely dogmatic evangelists on either side creating an entrenched division as never before. The analysis of *Strangelove* in the previous chapter, nonetheless, brought to light the faith in, and deference shown to technology and the auspices of science by the elites and technocrats in power at the height of the Cold War. We, in the postindustrial west, live in a time in which the struggle to find and affix meaning to our lives is possibly our greatest challenge. For many, the apparent logical fortitude of science, and the promise that technology will improve our lives is the only rational foundation upon which to build meaning. The imperative for those in power to defer to scientific modes, that is to say, capitalist economic modes of organization ahead of all faith-based, abstract or irrational considerations appears to be inescapable.

As was argued in the previous chapter, many ancient vestiges of religious feeling, in particular Christian doctrines of faith in a higher immutable source, have been transmuted on to the ostensibly secular spheres of science and technology. The Bomb's mysteriousness and immutable logic powerfully embody the same apocalyptic Christian awe felt by those in the past towards the coming "armies in the skies" (*Ibid*). Discussing America's nuclear theology in *Nuclear Madness: Religion and the Psychology of the Nuclear Age*, Ira Chernus argues that the mixture of dread and awe elicited by the Bomb creates a form of distorted religious feeling. The sub textual argument of *End Zone* and *Crash*, therefore, is that this religious distortion extends beyond the Bomb to include all technology, because technology, science and the cold numerals of market economics are the only sources of certainty in a postmodern era in which meaning is always fractured, nebulous or eternally deferred. Gary Harkness's spiritual desire for simplification of meaning in *End Zone* and James Ballard's immersion into the technological apocalypse called "autogeddon" in *Crash*, elucidate an apocalyptic paranoia less immediate, but more culturally entrenched, than that of the Cold War films discussed in the previous chapter. The irony of their spiritual seeking is that their journeys are death-bound and sacrificial, offerings to the technological god. The protagonists of *Crash* seek to disperse their energy into the universe in violent physical synthesis with technology, acts that can be endlessly reproduced in photographic images. Harkness seeks enlightenment in the nuclear jargon of the Cold War and in the sport that is perfect for a world ruled by the Bomb, a sport of systemic, patterned and quantifiable violence. In a stricter thematic sense, *End Zone* is closer to *Strangelove*, as it is concerned with the specific subject of nuclear apocalypse in Cold War America. As such, it concerns itself with language and the production of meaning in a world shadowed by the looming logic of the Bomb. *Strangelove* touches upon these linguistic aspects with its satire of the technocratic terminology and nuclear gibberish, as exemplified in its parodying of passages from Kahn's *On Thermonuclear War*. *End Zone* expands upon this theme with perfectly pitched satirical emulations of official deterrence jargon. As Dewey notes, DeLillo deftly captures the "miasma of military jargon and the chilling apocalyptic euphemisms of nukespeak; the pornography of motivational clichés; the sculptured eloquence of classroom lectures; the fine-spun gobbledygook of public relations" (56).

Crash, on the other hand, is concerned with technological and instrumental dehumanization: how we adapt, or not, to life in an environment that is changing at an exponential rate. Its concern with the apocalyptic does not directly refer to nuclear fears, but to the *Eros* and *Thanatos* of our relationship with technology in the postnuclear era. *Crash* presents the car as both provider of fantasies of transcendence, and as technology's surrogate womb, thus it is an embodiment of all of our libidinal and destructive technological urges.

End Zone's Linguistic Satire

End Zone is the story of Gary Harkness's spiritual search for a fixed and stable sense of meaning in the proto-apocalyptic atmosphere of 1970s Cold War America.[5] What Harkness cannot find in his parents, in education, in quotidian routines, he seeks out in the West Texas desert at "Logos" College, where, as the name suggests (being the Latin for "word"), he hopes that signifier and signified become one, where meaning will be fixed and all the terror of uncertainty and of death will be banished. In the brutal simplicity of the desert and the calculated violence of American Football, Harkness wishes to shed all the psychoses and neurotic complexities of postnuclear life. "We practiced in the undulating heat with nothing to sustain us but the conviction that things here were simple" (4).

As narrator of his tale, Harkness begins by sketching out the details leading up to his ascetic rejection of the corrupted world. He recounts his compliance with his father's wishes for him by excelling at an early age as a football player. Harkness quickly makes it clear, however, that his world and the world his father occupies are radically different places. The truths and maxims of his father's heyday are now fully obsolete under the Cold War's technically and logically perfect insanity. "He believed in the idea that a simple but lasting reward, something just short of a presidential handshake, awaited the extra effort, the preserving act of a tired man. Backbone, will, mental toughness, desire—these were his themes, the qualities that insured success. He was a pharmaceutical salesman with a lazy son" (16). The source of the radical difference between Harkness and his father, and their respective paradigms, is linguistic. Language is simple and monolithic for his father; there are words attached to their meanings and that is simply that. For Harkness signification has drifted away from its former signifiers and the *terra firma* in which his father's beliefs are rooted is barren with meaninglessness. This linguistic schism is summed up beautifully in the sign his father hangs on the wall of the fourteen year old Harkness's bedroom to motivate him: "When the going gets tough, the tough get going":

> I looked at this sign for three years (roughly from ages fourteen to seventeen) before I began to perceive a certain beauty in it. The sentiment of course had small appeal but it seemed that beauty flew from the words themselves, the letters, consonants swallowing vowels, aggression and tenderness, a semi-self re-creation from line to line, word to word, letter to letter. All meaning faded. The words became pictures. It was a sinister thing to discover at such an age, that words can escape their meanings. A strange beauty that sign began to express [17].

This passage encapsulates the radical unreliability of language, its corruptibility, its performativity and its numinous beauty. As such, it reflects DeLillo's own views on language, his sense of awe towards the power and beauty of language that is evident across his entire *oeuvre*. In *End Zone* DeLillo uses his linguistic skill to subvert official nuclear jargon—language is, after all beyond ownership, infinitely commutable, a shared medium of human existence for the brief time that we share existence. The adolescent Harkness comes to understand the disconnection between signifier and signified, and it terrifies him. *End Zone* sees the college-age Harkness's quest for linguistic and ontological fixity, which after a few failed attempts in various colleges, culminates in his ascetic journey to Logos. At Logos, he searches among the patterns of carefully orchestrated violence in American football and among the technical argots of nuclear war for something real to which he should dedicate his life. In his untethered state of existential terror, he

II. End Zone and Crash

turns to the language systems that purport certainty, based upon the immutable laws of science, of quantifiable proof. The certainty that nuclear weapons signify, however, is death. What Harkness fails to see, initially, is the post-structuralist insight that languages serve only the systems from which they stem. In other words, nuclear technical jargon purports a scientific certainty—countless permutations of war and post-war situations—that when distilled down to its essence ultimately signifies potential mass and unaccountable death, the death of meaning itself. Harkness, as is discussed below, is too worldly and smart to become embroiled in the jargon of economics, as he knows the signifiers and signified in those textbooks drift in estranged realms of thinking, but he cannot escape the all-powerful logic of the Bomb. Harkness, then, works effectively as DeLillo's Trojan horse into the center of nuclear jargon and by extension into all scientific language that tries to claim certainty. As such *End Zone* is almost uniquely clear and insightful in its poststructuralist critique of American culture. The linguistic systems of (Cold War derived) scientific management and economics dominate the postnuclear era, and the reductive element of their claim to certainty is a direct attack on language itself. For DeLillo, this is an attack on the palate of human experience itself, and his job is to reclaim language from these repressive regimes by subverting and critiquing them.

Following failed attempts to play football at four different colleges, Harkness finally ends up at Logos "[b]eing made to lead a simple life" under the guidance of head coach Emmet Creed, who has "became famous for creating order out of chaos" (59).[6] Harkness recounts being expelled from the first college, Syracuse University, after barricading himself in a room for two days with a girl named Lippy Margolis. "She wanted to hide from the world and I volunteered to help her. For a day and a night we read to each other from a textbook on economics. She seemed calmed by the incoherent doctrines set forth on those pages" (18). DeLillo's choice of the science of economics is a pointed one. The broader subject of economics is one of the most dogmatic and vague public discourses. The marketplace, the electronically manifested and seemingly autonomous nebulae of trade to which most humans on the planet are beholden, is impenetrably and recalcitrantly unpredictable. It remains so despite attempts going back hundreds of years to make it rationally calculable, beginning with Smith's brutally simplified *homo economicus* model, and culminating in the detachment of capital from productive value, in order, seemingly, for the market to find its own natural equilibrium. A few simplistic rules about human nature and a vast battery of computational power underlie innumerable economics textbooks and economic opinions. The cyber-market is a system powered by a combination of millions of individual human decisions and an infinitesimal number of computational decisions, that at times may produce radical, atomic randomness or others may coalesce into critical-mass sweeps, the dynamics of which, are barely understood. Economics textbooks promise a certainty that clearly does not exist, not in the field of economics, or any other offshoot of teleological Enlightenment thinking. What bubbles away beneath the thin veil of certainty for Harkness and his girlfriend is the all-pervasive terror of blankness, of meaninglessness, of nuclear armageddon. Lippy Margolis seeks comfort in the words of the textbook that promises certainty, fixity of meaning and predictability. Harkness is a keen receiver of this kind of terror, but while too smart to believe in the book's claims to certitude, he nevertheless sympathizes with her stand against the world. "When I was sure I had changed the course of her life for the better, I opened the door" (18).

Harkness's second denial of the postnuclear world happens at Penn State University. His neurotic descent this time is a reaction against the spirit-killing ubiquity of the simulacrum, a vacuous and objectified mechanization of the body, whereby the indistinguishability of day to day routine will eventually destroy the human soul:

> I had not yet learned to appreciate the slowly gliding drift of identical things; chunks of time spun past me like meteorites in a universe predicated on repetition. For weeks the cool weather was unvarying; the girls wore knee-high stockings; a small red plane passed over the practice field every afternoon at the same time…. I tripped on the same step on the same staircase on three successive days. After this I stopped going to practice [18].

Interestingly, Harkness, in this instance rejects routine and simplicity for their own sake as spiritually deadly, yet he ultimately ends up at Logos pursuing a deeper meaning in an ascetic suffering of routine and simplicity. At Penn State, Harkness rejects endless repetition and discipline without any recourse to a deeper meaning or fulfillment, telling his coach "it could not be truly attractive unless it meant oneness with God or the universe or some equally redoubtable super-phenomenon" (19). He rejects routine without spirituality as a mechanization of society and he turns his back on the world again, saying, "we were becoming a nation devoted to human xerography" (19). As well as foreshadowing Baudrillard's essay "Xerox and Infinity" (1990), an invective against social mechanization by the means of scientific management and technology, this comment also invokes Foucauldian concepts of

II. End Zone *and* Crash

the molding and shaping of individuals into obedient workers to operate the cogs of postmodern industry. In this sense, it also invokes the Frankfurt School rejection of positivism as is summed up by Horkheimer: "All life today tends to be increasingly subjected to rationalization and planning.... The individual's self-preservation presupposes his adjustment to the requirements for the preservation of the system" (Horkheimer 143).

After Penn State, Harkness goes home to his parents in upstate New York and ironically falls into a blank routine far more depthless and aimless than the earlier college routine that had alienated him. He states, rather vaguely, that "in late Spring, a word appeared all over town. MILITARIZE" (20). This detail seems to snap Harkness out of his aimless catatonia and he enrolls in Miami University where "[r]epetition gave way to the beginnings of simplicity" (20). Again, Harkness has to leave. "It started with a book, an immense volume about the possibilities of nuclear war—assigned reading for a course I was taking in *modes of disaster technology*" (20).[7] DeLillo is undoubtedly slyly alluding to the tomes of Herman Kahn that sought to reify the metaphysical pornography of a thermonuclear conflict in technical jargon, mathematics and graphs. Kahn, as discussed in the previous chapter, developed a powerful political currency in the RAND Corporation and other corridors of power with his nuclear war manuals *On Thermonuclear War* and *Thinking the Unthinkable*. DeLillo captures the Freudian blend of *Eros* and *Thanatos* that went right to the core of America's Cold War technocratic and technological jousting—and no less the implied sadism in the approach of the technocrats—with an acerbic and expertly pitched mimicry of the nuclear jargon and the exposition through Harkness's imagination of what this vacuous jargon might mean in a real nuclear war. "The problem was simple and terrible," Harkness says, explaining the lead up to this particular breakdown, "I enjoyed the book." The earlier part of the passage presages Harkness's ascetic urges in his desire for a reset-to-zero, the apocalyptic desire for simplification of meaning via the destruction of the world and its irretrievable complexities. The passage also suggests the pornographic pleasure of destruction, of the rending and burning of flesh, that resides in Harkness, in Kahn and the nuclear techno-warriors that *Strangelove* satirizes, maybe, in the human psyche:

> Carbon 14 and strontium 90. Escalation ladder and subcrisis situation. Titan, spartan, Poseidon. People burned and unable to breathe. People being excavated from doomed cities. People diseased and starving. Two hundred thousand bodies decomposing on the roads outside Chicago.... Pleasure in the contemplation of millions dying and

dead. I became fascinated by words and phrases like thermal hurricane, overkill, circular error probability, post-attack environment, stark deterrence, dose-rate contours, kill-ratio, spasm war. Pleasure in these words. They were extremely effective, I thought, whispering shyly of cycles of destruction so great that the language of past world wars became laughable, the wars themselves somewhat naïve [20–21].

In the twentieth century, the advent of nuclear technology and technocracy brought many of the Enlightenment ideas of mechanical rationalization into being in the social sphere that up to that point had not been realized. As argued in the previous chapter, the existence of such a destructive force as the atom, and later hydrogen bombs, in the eyes of the political elite (particularly Robert McNamara), necessitated a new kind of reason, an *uber-rational* approach. Out of this necessity, primarily from the offices of the RAND Corporation, came Game Theoretical deterrence strategies, and later economic strategies that were based upon the same principles. The Enlightenment goal to secularize the social sphere was ostensibly fulfilled in the mid-twentieth centur but, of course, this rationalization of society came about under the auspices of the Bomb and American apocalyptic awe was merely transferred from "armies in the sky" to the terrible and mysterious power of nuclear war. For Harkness, the language of the "past world wars" is naive because it purported the idea of dying for world peace, freedom, honor, and other spiritual and faith-based intangibles. The secular apocalypse promised by a nuclear conflict had all the terrible religious awe of past apocalypses but without their spiritual meanings. This paradox is what drives Harkness's ascetic tail-chasing and his vacillation between acceptance/rejection of the manifestos of technique. For DeLillo, Harkness's problem is emblematic: the spiritual, philosophical and cultural conundrum of the postnuclear age.

The sadistic pleasure Harkness guiltily feels in obsessing over the nuclear war tomes is deeply bound up in the language used to describe mass death. The promise of certainty that the language conveys is founded upon the technological power that it describes, which is the power to bring death. The language would be euphemistic technical gobbledygook if it weren't for the technological reality of which it "whispers shyly" (*EZ*, 21). In other words, Harkness is awed by the power of this nuclear argot to evoke meaning. He revels in the pornographic suffering that half veils the sexual element of a sumptuary mass-expenditure of human energy. The Cold War, as Baudrillard argues in "The Beaubourg Effect," became an inverted technical exercise for the sake of technique itself. The secular technological apocalypse the Cold War promised did not speak to any spiritual aspect of human life as earlier apocalypses had; it was purely autotelic and contained no deeper meaning than the awesome technical power it embodied, and the language that imagines that technical power. The result of this is a terrible fracturing of meaning, a postmodern rootlessness, with which Harkness struggles to come to terms. This is the reason Harkness cannot help but fetishize the nuclear jargon he finds in the textbooks, despite the fact that it depresses him terribly. These words have implications, they have meaning, they imply the sex of death—what he, and the rest of the human race are both drawn to and terrified of.

The technical language of nuclear war is thus at the same time both meaningful and meaningless.[8] The logical purity of nuclear war lies in its potential to simplify all complexity by destroying meaning. Therein lies the paradox at the heart of the ascetic-linguistic urge towards apocalypse: the source of all invested meaning in the world could be erased.[9]

The continued existence in the world of such a destroyer-of-meaning, arguably, condemns all future narratives and meanings to the status of pre-dead. The jargon that describes this cataclysm of meaning is itself void of meaning. DeLillo attacks this monstrous linguistic abomination by reclaiming language's tendency to work against the technology of war, including its jargon. Osteen cites Jonathan Schell's work of creative nonfiction, *The Fate of the Earth* (1982) to surmise this nuclear apocalyptic conundrum. Schell's text illuminates the paradox that killing all the world's people kills death itself, as there is nobody left to die, which in turn kills meaning as there is nobody left to ascribe and narrativize experience: "In this sense, the jargon of nuclear war does accurately signify the results of using nuclear weapons: both jargon and weapons murder meaning. Hence the voiding of complexity and meaning potentially caused by nuclear war is perfectly represented by the sterile language of nuclear strategy" (Osteen 39).

The effect of this rootless postnuclear, (postmodern) recourse to technique and game-playing—the endless interchangeability of one reality for another within the quantifiable and technically rational capitalist scheme—Robert L. Caserio argues, may be causing the death of shared meanings and narratives. Writing about Ballard in his essay "Mobility and Masochism: Christine Brooke-Rose and J.G. Ballard," Caserio argues that "[p]ostnuclear history, the productive agent of postmodern fantasy, is pre-deceased.[10] Ballard's disambiguation of his fantasy via his grim determination of the historical present reveals postmodernism to be postmortemism" (Caserio 307). This assertion applies readily to the apocalyptic aspects of both of novels discussed here.[11]

The Bomb, for these reasons, is the terminus of logical perfectibility in technological terms. While nuclear apocalypse may be unlikely, the Bomb's true power resides in its pre-destruction of narrative. What is left is neoliberal capitalism's pseudo-scientific promise of technical certainty; only what is technically achievable and what can be materially quantified is of value in a world of pre-dead myths and narratives. Thus, the terrifying auspices of technology's destructive power are overlain with its ameliorative effect, its promise of certainty, of mathematical and mechanical immutability. Osteen elaborates the effect this has on the technocrats who use and abide in this logic, the effect that also appears to seduce Harkness:

> The habit of thinking in jargon encourages them to conceive of war as a perfect, rule-bound structure, occurring within white lines that demarcate the thinkable from the unthinkable. This, then, is how jargon itself is a weapon: the violence it does to meaning, and the simplification it effects on morality and responsibility, harden the mind to accept, even welcome, apocalypse [Osteen 41].

Thus, *End Zone* expands upon *Strangelove*'s satire of the almost blasé attitude to nuclear war held by the bunker-bound military, technocratic and political elite in the film. The speech extolling the chauvinistic pleasures of underground life by the doctor himself exposes the degree to which the illusion of technical precision and cleanliness had infiltrated the mindset of America's technocratic elite. Osteen continues: "In this way the ascetic desire for purity mushrooms into a form of fascism that permits atrocity. Imagining nuclear holocaust as a game makes it more likely to occur; once framed, it seems more manageable and desirable. Nuclear war becomes merely another fiction with a preconceived end" (41).

    Harkness continues to read more nuclear manuals until he becomes too depressed to continue at Miami University. He returns home again to his room, his parents, and senseless apathy. That is until the prospect of the Vietnam draft surfaces, and he allows his father to pull some strings with a former classmate who is an influential alumnus of Michigan State. "Negotiations were held and I was granted an interview with two subalterns of the athletic department, types familiar to football and other paramilitary complexes, the square-jawed bedrock of the corporation" (22). Harkness manages to convince them that he is ready to take orders. The following college year, as he tells it, he was "leading the freshman squad in touchdowns, yards gained rushing, and platitudes," until, "in a game against the Indiana freshmen, I was one of three players converging on a safetyman who had just intercepted a pass. We seemed to hit him simultaneously. He died the next day and I went home that evening" (22). After seven weeks in his room shuffling a deck

II. End Zone *and* Crash

of cards Harkness receives a phone call from Logos head coach Emmet Creed, and Harkness is tempted to the desert because, he says, "I had discovered a very simple truth. My life meant nothing without football" (22).

Harkness refers to football in the above passage as a "paramilitary complex," yet admits at the end that his life is meaningless without it. Harkness's ambivalence regarding the paramilitary complexes of nuclear war, deterrence jargon and American football embodies the paradox of postnuclear instrumentalism—the promise of methodical rationalism at the cost of predeceased or voided narratives. The instrumental complexes have a narcotic effect on Harkness. His repulsion toward the senselessness of the deaths they convey—the death of the Indiana safetyman, his own, the "two hundred thousand bodies decomposing on the roads outside Chicago"—is overcome by the totality of the system and the totalitarianism of its systematic rationality. Harkness surrenders to football, to the desert, to simplification, to the playing out of nuclear war games with Major Staley and to Creed's brutal instructions.

DeLillo animates Harkness's time at Logos, nonetheless, with a helping of absurdist humor and no little sympathy for his plight, if not his choices. Harkness's spiritual quest for meaning is emblematic of the difficulty of living in the current age, after all, and this very seeking is at the core of every DeLillo novel written to date. In *White Noise* Jack Gladney vainly scavenges the fragments of a media-saturated consumer-plantation America for a deeper meaning to his life, to alleviate his fear of death, the full stop at the end of a life lived on the surface of things. Lee Oswald seeks a higher purpose in Marxist revolutionary fantasies in *Libra*. Eric Packer, the billionaire investment banker of *Cosmopolis*, deliberately throws away his fortune. Packer's is a life's energy dedicated to achieving metamorphosis. He seeks to escape the messiness, the grime, the desire and the unaccountability of corporeality and transform into cyber-technology's promised ideal of perfection and certitude. Packer unknowingly seeks a connection with fellow human beings but searches for a sublime unity in the mechanics of free-market acquisition, his discovery of the vacuity and virtuality of cyber-capitalism's purpose leads to his disintegration as a person.

In the case of both novels, connection with other persons on a subliminal or empathetic level is not possible if we merge with an instrument that only seeks its own growth, or a technology that can express much more powerfully than any other, latent desires to destroy ourselves. Both Ballard and DeLillo, however, seek to create new narratives, new stories, outside of the pre-deceased nuclear narratives, where we can imagine a life lived imaginatively, together.

Patriarchal Priests, Masculine Logic and the Nuclear Word as "Shit" in *End Zone*

Harkness's struggle is emblematic of the philosophical problem that is probably as old as human self-awareness. It has been framed in philosophical discourse as the empirical versus metaphysical. The standoff between positivism and irrationalism in the twentieth century reframes the divergence in a way that is more up to date with modern scientific and technological achievements. The divergence, if one will allow the simplification, can be distilled down to the human need to categorize and rationalize, on the one hand, and on the other the quest for a numinousness, a *summum bonum*, and an acceptance of the unknown and possibly the unknowable.[12] If one permits a further simplification, what underpins both aspects in psychological terms are different approaches to the fear of mortality. Empiricism—what can only be verified in the material world—precludes the existence of God, and so without scientific rigor, rationalism, and a systemic approach to life we are left only with a world of chaos. For metaphysics, the fear is that life lived for its own sake is not meaningful enough and so there must be more to it than meets the eye.

The former aspect is embodied in the novel by a trio of patriarchal figures in Harkness's life, beginning with his actual father, who believed in the insentient safety of hard work. "It paid, in his view, to follow the simplest, most pioneer of rhythms—the eternal work cycle, the blood-hunt for bear and deer, the mellow rocking of chairs as screen doors swing open and bang shut in the gathering fragments of summer's sulky dusk. Beyond these latitudes lay nothing but chaos" (17). DeLillo depicts a postmodern masculinity that is couched in terms of efficiency and ruthlessness. This postnuclear definition of masculinity was investigated in the previous chapter's discussion of *Strangelove* and the SAC movies, however, *End Zone* interrogates this technical masculinity in closer detail, suggesting that it draws on an ancient potency as insulation against mortality's looming specter. Harkness's father hides from mortality in the prescribed conformity of a 1950s American masculinity where hard work and toeing the line were paramount, as is personified by the sign he hangs in Gary's room, and his favorite motivational cliché,

II. End Zone *and* Crash

"[s]uck in that gut and go harder" (16). The second of Harkness's patriarchal mentors is Emmet Creed. Creed is a mysterious figure in the novel, monomaniacal and hovering at the fringes of the narrative, watching the football practice from a tower overlooking the field. Harkness describes him as "a landlocked Ahab who paced and raged, who was unfolding his life toward a single moment" (52). Creed espouses the masculine angular logic of American Football. Its inherent violence harks back to an older conception of male potency, tribal violence and the violence of the hunt. The violence of American Football, however, is sublimated through instrumental rationalism. This violence is caged and made obedient, stripped of its radicalism or the ancient liberty it implies—it is de-libidinized by its virtualization and mechanized to meet the requirements of technology's totalizing sign, the Bomb. Harkness's roommate Anatole Bloomberg provides a useful description of Creed's assistant coach Brian Tweego, equally applicable to Creed, in a perfect (if deeply ironic) summation of nuclear instrumentalism: "I respect Tweego in a way. He thinks in one direction, straight ahead. He just aims and fires. He has a ruthlessness of mind. That's something I respect. I think it's a distinctly modern characteristic. The systems planner. The management consultant. The nuclear strategist. It's a question of fantastic single-mindedness" (47).

Masculine violence, and masculine, patriarchal logic were separated from their primal and chaotic elements and reconceived as mechanistic and ruthlessly rational during the Cold War. "Football is a complex of systems," Creed tells Harkness. "It's like no other sport. When the game is played properly, it's an interlocking of a number of systems. The individual. The small cluster he's part of. The larger unit, the eleven" (194). Creed's pep talk to Harkness espouses an ascetic value in self-sacrifice, fasting, purity and so on. The Sioux, Creed tells Harkness, purified themselves through fasting and solitude, deepening the irony of this harking back to a truer masculinity. Creed is trying to imbue the technical exercise that is American Football with an ascetic spiritual element. Harkness is drawn to Creed's proselytizing because he knows American Football is the sublimated violence of nuclear war in miniature. By immersing himself in the machinations of death he hopes to immunize himself from the fear of both his own death and of the apocalypse.

The third, and most seductive of Harkness's conformist patriarchal priests is Major Staley. Harkness meets Staley in his motel room in the desert, where Staley, in turn, extemporizes on his philosophical views about the theology of the bomb; the probability of a limited, rational nuclear war; the technological primacy of modern warfare and the resulting diminishment of masculine warrior values. These extemporizations are presented by DeLillo as long quoted tracts in stand-alone paragraphs that are interspersed with one-line statements such as "I've had a checkered career at best," and "Nagasaki was an embarrassment to the art of war" (79–80). These contrary interjections reveal both Staley's ambivalence to the war complex that gives him currency, and the general mixture of awe and horror that the weapons evoke. The philosophical vignettes are also interspersed with paragraphs that explain in highly technical detail the effects of nuclear weapons, diegetically, it must be assumed, for Harkness's benefit, but in textual terms an opportunity for DeLillo to both horrify/titillate the reader as well to disarm the official language. It is the ambivalence of Staley's thinking that must draw Harkness to him. Harkness seeks a resolution of the conflict within him between conformity, systematization, simplification and the search for the spiritual meaning of his life. Staley's speech expounding the probability of nuclear war fought on a rational basis represents the belief in control, in measurement, in accuracy and rationality. It is the masculinity of the machine-man, an angular logic:

> I think what'll happen in the not-too-distant future is that we'll have humane wars. Each side agrees to use clean bombs. And each side agrees to limit the amount of megatons *he* uses. In other words we'll get together with them beforehand and there'll be an agreement that if the issue can't be settled, whatever the issue might be, then let's make certain we keep our war as relatively humane as possible [78, emphasis added].

This part of Staley's speech is reminiscent of the Kennedy administration's Flexible Response doctrine and later Robert McNamara's No-Cities doctrine, both of which called for rationality and restraint in the event of nuclear war. The idea that a conflict between two global powers that had the combined firepower to annihilate the planet would be enacted according to rules of limitation fomented a ludicrous and dangerous reality. The strategies were replaced eventually by the MAD doctrine. Staley continues to extol the fantasy of control as his speech becomes decidedly Kahn-esque: "People close their minds. They think nuclear war has to be insensate, both sides pushing all the buttons and the whole thing is over in two hours. In reality it's likely to be very deliberate, very cautious, a kind of thing that's almost fought in slow motion" (79). Staley's fantasy of control reflects the same arrogant technocratic disconnection from reality that *Strangelove*'s War Room setting satirizes. The idea that technology and its adjuncts are rational and thus circumvent human irrationality is shot through with acerbic irony by DeLillo, in a manner that

II. *End Zone* and *Crash*

recalls *Strangelove*'s sarcastic illustration of how the doomsday device circumvents "human meddling." "There'd be all sorts of controls," Staley says. "You'd practically have a referee and a timekeeper. Then it would be over and you'd make your damage assessment" (79). Like Buck Turgidson and the real-life figures for which they are avatars, Staley calculates the enormous loss of human life in terms of numbers, and like Buck, puts the optimistic slant on a winnable nuclear war. "We wouldn't be the same strong industrial society after one thousand megs but our cities would still be standing and the mortality rate would be in the fairly low percentiles, about eight to twelve percent" (79).[13]

Staley, however, is ambivalent regarding this machine-masculinity, as is Harkness. His next speech laments the disappearance of an older, purer form of masculinity, lost to the vagaries of the techno-age of warfare:

> War is the ultimate realization of modern technology. For centuries men have tested themselves at war. War was the final test, the great experience, the privilege, the honor, the self-sacrifice or what have you, the absolute ultimate determination of what kind of man you were. War was the great challenge and the great evaluator. It told you how much you were worth. But it's different today. Few men want to go off and fight. We prove ourselves, our manhood, in other ways, in making money, in skydiving, in hunting mountain lions with bow and arrow, in acquiring one kind of power or another [80].

Staley is lamenting the loss of the sense of purpose and meaning that went with old-fashioned wars. Masculinity was proved in primitive ways, physical ways, for passionate reasons like territory and survival. Concepts of passion, like honor, bravery, and patriotism are unquantifiable factors; they do not lend themselves to efficiency. These human qualities have been excised by the prescription of market-based quantification. Passionate and ideological approaches to war have come to be deemed as unquantifiable, thus irrelevant and obsolete. Staley has made a career from the currency this virtual war has provided—where physical conflict is not even necessary in what is simply a technical exercise—but laments the sense of purposelessness and meaninglessness it manifests: "Today we can say that war is a test of opposing technologies.... War has always told men what they are capable of under stress. Now it informs the machines.... It's better to be efficient than brave" (80–81). The virtual war that Staley describes is an esoteric system. It is an exercise in technique that is closely related to that described some years later by Baudrillard in his essay "The Precession of Simulacra"; a war fought not against an ideological enemy, but as this book argues, against the perceived chaos and uncertainty generated by people.[14]

The placating effect of Staley's reassuring discourse on technological rationality is very short lived for Harkness. After this first meeting with Staley, Harkness walks back to the college, pleased with the encounter. "I counted cadence for a few beats in a pleasantly regimental voice, nonchalant and Southern" (84). He wonders if he'll be able to find a painted rock he had found in the desert previously on one of his miniature ascetic sojourns, "[i]t was important at that moment to come upon something that could be defined in one sense only, something not probable or variable, a thing unalterably itself" (85). Harkness wants to reinforce Staley's words, the assurance of nuclear rationality, with seeing an object whose meaning is fixed firmly to its linguistic signifier to prove that solid ground does exist, that there is an immutable truth. The object he encounters, however, is a mound of feces. "Then I saw something that terrified me. I stood absolutely still, as if motion might impede my understanding of this moment. It was three yards in front of me, excrement, a low mound of it, simple shit, nothing more, yet strange and vile in this wilderness, *perhaps the one thing that did not betray its definition*" (85 emphasis added). The shit simply reminds him that perhaps the only truth that is universal and immutable is the truth of death, the very truth that Gary has been in denial of, the very truth of which Staley, and nuclear language and rationality also denies. Language and meaning will terminate in death, the nuclear apocalypse will kill all the dizzying complexities of life and this is the unacceptable truth that Gary is trying to deny. Shit, as signifying death, is "not probable or variable," it is "a thing unalterably itself," and Staley's words, and all the words of nuclear rationalization, technocracy and political consensus-making are, by implication, shit. Harkness (DeLillo) goes through six different terms for organic waste, defining each in terms of their implication of a void:

> There was the graven art of a curse in that sight. It was overwhelming, a terminal act, nullity in every word, shit, as of dogs squatting near partly eaten bodies, rot repeating itself; defecation, as of old women in nursing homes fouling their beds; feces, as of specimen, sample analysis, diagnosis, bleak assessments of disease in the bowels; dung, as of dry straw erupting with microscopic eggs; excrement, as of final matter voided, the chemical stink of self discontinued; offal, as of butchered animals' intestines slick with shit and blood; shit everywhere, shit in life cycle, shit as earth as food as shit, wise men sitting impassively in shit, armies retreating in that stench, shit as history, holy men praying to shit, scientists tasting it, volumes to be compiled on color and texture and scent, shit's infinite treachery, everywhere this whisper of inexistence [85].

This passage of the book is the clearest convergence between DeLillo and Baudrillard's semiotic thinking. As Wilcox states, "[f]or both, death is the

II. End Zone and Crash

ultimate signified, the single natural event which ultimately cannot be subsumed into simulacra, models and codes" (353). Wilcox cites Baudrillard's *Symbolic Exchange and Death* as a work that bears much relevance to DeLillo's writing, but it is most apposite in *End Zone* and DeLillo's treatment of the American Cold War's semiotic instrument: "Perhaps only death, the reversibility of death is of a higher order than the code. Only symbolic mediations of contemporary society deprive the individual of an intimate relation with death, with the result that society is haunted by the fear of mortality" (*Symbolic Exchange* 104). This conception of the fear of mortality is what haunts Harkness. He undertakes his spiritual search for meaning in a quest for a semiotic purity and is thus drawn to the end of meaning, deathward by the terminal semiology of nuclear jargon. The nuclear bombs, in a deeply contradictory manner, through the voiding of meaning, thereby embody a form of theology. This contradiction is the essence of what is tearing Gary apart—the nuclear terminology, the world's dehumanization via instrumental totality is a linguistic heart of darkness into which Gary throws himself, his saintly quest to find a true meaning beneath the false word.

The "Theology" of the Bomb in *End Zone*

The comforting certainty provided by science and the assuming of miraculous interventions in human life could, in the past, only be received through faith in God. The most awesome of technological achievements are not fully understood by any one person; they are the coalescence of a vast span of human ability. The workings of complex technology remain a mystery to the vast majority of people. In this way, technology is becoming more miraculous as time goes by, with the power to create or modify the human organism now at hand. The ostensibly secular realms of science and technology are very often dogmatically set in opposition to religion, which, in a twist of irony is usually most vociferously proclaimed by the very proponents who espouse their utopian potential. This culturally pervasive notion of technological and scientific progress is, of course, a teleological one bound up in the utopian idea that humanity is heading towards perfectibility. The contradiction inherent in this belief is again personified in the existence of nuclear weapons. Human beings have been more successful at developing death-making than life-giving technology.[15] In this transference of religious faith, the bringer of the apocalypse is no longer God (in a denotative sense), it is post-nuclear technology, and in its destructive power and its miraculous achievements lie the fear and aew required for worship. The previous chapter reveals the religious aspects of the deference shown to the machine's mysterious power by those in the War Room in *Dr. Strangelove*. In *End Zone* the theology of the bomb is expounded by Staley, who teaches "Aspects of Modern War" at Logos. The narrator, Harkness, explains the source of Staley's beliefs: "[h]is father was the school's most famous alumnus, a three-letter man and a war hero, one of the crew on the Nagasaki mission" (69).

Prior to the excrement episode turning Harkness's faith in the nuclear word to shit, Staley mesmerizes him with a missive extolling the theology of the hydrogen bomb. It is his first in a number of speeches to Harkness, which initially vacillate between faith in mechanical rationality and fear of technology's overwhelming power. Staley's reticence, however, becomes less pronounced with each speech and the last five of Staley's disembodied paragraphs are highly technical descriptions of the aftermath of nuclear war, descending into a jargonistic miasma of telling the untellable, with sentences such as "[t]here's a factor-four discrimination against strontium in the human body" (83). This recourse to jargon is addressed directly by Staley, almost apologetically when he says, "I don't make up the words, Gary. They don't explain, they don't clarify, they don't express. They're painkillers. Everything becomes abstract. I admit it's fascinating in a way. I also admit the problem goes deeper than just saying some crypto-Goebbels in the Pentagon is distorting the language" (80). Staley's offhand critique, here, highlights the complexity of how a word or entire jargon comes into existence. There must be consensus and agreement, and those who use this language must be invested in it. Staley's comments reveal the paradox in nuclear jargon. Every last person on earth is invested in the possibility of nuclear war, yet this argot was/is circulated by a very small group of technocrats and politicians who derive huge power from this new knowledge. Staley's musings also highlight that the words are quite meaningless, as they attempt to signify what is fundamentally unknowable, what may, in fact, be the end of all meaning. Those for whom nuclear jargon was a source of currency, then, traded on being experts in the fundamentally unknowable. Moreover, this was carried out in a way that had to necessarily remain esoteric in order that their power not be diluted.

Staley's propounding of the need to control language is in a sense a scriptural process. Who controls the onomastic process wields the power of what is named, and the public must accept the official doctrine. Upon coming into existence, the Bomb had subjugated its creator species under the awe of its

II. End Zone *and* Crash

power, and so those in officialdom had to learn to speak the Bomb's language in order not to control it (it was arguably already out of human control the moment the atom bomb came into existence) but to channel its subjugating power. The currency of power created by such an object was immense, and thus was seized upon in the early days by the nuclear priests of the RAND Corporation like Kahn, Albert Wohlstetter, Thomas Schelling, Alain Enthoven and others. Those who understood the Bomb's language, the impossibly complex mathematical permutations of deterrence strategies, began to wield some of its enormous true power. The complex formulae issued forth from the Bomb's destructive essence, of course, assumed the fundamental doctrine of the underlying capitalist ideology, that of self-interested gain. The fearful theology of the Bomb, then, was that of maximal quantifiable control, the assumed natural order of the so-called free market. It's apocalypse, it can be argued, is the accelerated attempt since the end of the Cold War by various cabals of elite American power to remake the world according to evermore radical strains of neoliberal capitalism.

This frontier attitude to America's arsenal of nuclear weapons is bound up in the millenarian myth of apocalyptic regeneration. The removal of the heathens, who occupied the land, in order that God's elect could facilitate the dawning of Eden, was the first instance of regenerative violence in America's conception of itself. Richard Slotkin argues, as will be discussed in further detail, that the apologue of regenerative violence has remained at the core of American mythology despite its obsolescence. A core argument of this book, following on from Slotkin's insights, is that the American response to the Bomb (the American sense of the apocalyptic) is tied up in this mythology in a number of ways. The nuclear apocalypse has remained religious, despite its secularization, despite the removal of ideology and the removal of faith.

Staley elaborates this transference of worship from God, the sometimes smiteful, sometimes loving supreme being who resides in heaven, to the technological signifier of God, an almighty and mysterious power that has sucked up all our awe and terror like a spiraling vortex:

> There's a kind of theology at work here. The bombs are a kind of god. As his power grows, our fear naturally increases. I get as apprehensive as anyone else, maybe more so. We have too many bombs. There's a kind of theology of fear that comes out of this. We begin to capitulate to the overwhelming presence. It's so powerful. It dwarfs us so much. We say let the god have his way. He's so much more powerful than we are. Let it happen, whatever he ordains. It used to be that the gods punished men by using the forces of nature against them or by arousing them to take up their weapons and destroy each other. Now god is the force of nature itself, the fusion of tritium and deuterium.

> Now he's the weapon. So maybe we went too far in creating a being of omnipotent power. All this hardware. The big danger is that we'll surrender to a sense of inevitability and start flinging mud all over the planet [78].

Man has created God, in a literal sense, out of technology and man must obey this God or be destroyed. Its scripture preaches efficiency, productivity, ruthless (masculine) rationality, the tutelage of conformity preached by the trio of patriarchal priests. Harkness's ascetic journey is a linguistic one; constantly seeking reification of meaning in words, in nomenclature, in neologism, in skewed technical gibberish, in poetry and so on: "To begin to reword the overflowing world. To subtract and disjoin. To recite the alphabet. To make elemental lists. To call something by its name and need no other sound" (86).

The novel ends with a last vain ascetic gesture by Harkness, a hunger strike against something he has not named. He is trapped in the linguistic nebula of nuclear efficiency, he has found no spiritual *summum bonum* and his last gesture is his final rebellion in the novel against the plotted, planned and efficiently mapped movement towards the end zone. The novel, however, is narrated by Harkness in the past tense. DeLillo subverts the melodrama of his death, and the typical apocalyptic endings to nuclear fiction with the inference that Harkness found a way out of his trap—through the very act of narrativizing his tale.

In the epigraph to this chapter DeLillo's quotation implies that the machinations of official language, nuclear language and the theology of capitalist efficiency are destroyers of meaning, but in our art and our narratives we can reclaim and reinvest language with human meaning. In his essay "'It is Only a Statement of the Power of What Comes After': Atomic Nostalgia and the Ends of Postmodernism," Daniel Grausam analyses the theological and narratological aspects of DeLillo's (and Richard Powers's) novels. "Storytelling," he writes, "may have no direct agency in the world, yet a world without storytelling has given up on the possibility of an alternative history or organization of social reality" (10–11). Grausam signals the complex spiritual questing in DeLillo's novels, not a religious view of language but a belief in its numinous and moral power. This power derives from its potential to expose the argots of mechanized logic, the Cold War's modeling systems, which moved the idea of people as self-interested automotons into the heart of the capitalist system. Language must be used to defend against that which tends to destroy the stories and narratives that bind and connect people. DeLillo is aware that this postnuclear tendency towards the excision of indeterminate factors, passionate, human abstractions, particularly in the realm of the social sciences, is directly antithetical to language and its conveyance of the human ability to imagine ourselves. For this reason, *End Zone*'s tale of Harkness's struggle for meaning under the auspices of the Bomb's void is an act of resistance. What sets him apart ultimately from Baudrillard is DeLillo's belief in the power of language to break free of its confinement. Despite its availability to the capitalist apparatus, and perhaps precisely because of its maddening indeterminacy, fluidity and abstraction DeLillo claims language and the imaginative possibility it enables for narratives of a collective and binding purpose as the only possible way humans will survive our creations in the postnuclear world.

Violence Without Regeneration in *End Zone*

As discussed, the theological facet of America's relationship with postnuclear technology and in particular its apocalyptic element, goes to the heart of American mythology. It is bound up in the formative Utopianism of the early settlers' use of technique, commerce and violence, to hue Eden from the wilderness. Bercovitch argues this point extensively in *The Puritan Origins of the American Self* (1975), while Slotkin critiques the myth of regenerative violence that, he argues, is recapitulated throughout American culture. The utilitarian American attitude to nuclear weapons is paradoxical in the sense that there is no regenerative aspect to total annihilation. In *End Zone*, Harkness comes to realize that the only certainty and the only narrative provided by the mechanized rationality and its political and social systems in the postnuclear world is that of death. Similarly, in this regard, the protagonists of *Crash* seek to transcend their corporeal forms, to reimagine their bodies in new technological forms via the staging of miniature violent apocalypses. These acts are death-bound, however, with only a hollow technological possibility of regeneration.

In *Gunfighter Nation: The Myth of the Frontier in Twentieth Century America* Slotkin analyses modern filmic and literary reconstitutions of America's formative mythologies. Discussing a selection of middle-twentieth-century Westerns in terms of their thematic relationships with the politics of their times, Slotkin argues that American mythology consistently adopts the narrative of freedom gained through revolutionary violence. Made sacred in the constitutional right to bear arms against tyrannical governments, violence becomes a political purifier, a way to solve problems of injustice, to protect freedom and so forth, and is thus, Slotkin argues, integral to America's exceptionalist mythology. Revolutionary violence is deeply bound up in Christian notions of utopia. Outbursts of revolutionary violence (not just in America, as this thinking resides in Enlightenment utopianism), are predicated on the belief that once the source of tyranny or injustice is removed a perfect society may be born. As the French Revolution's orgy of beheading reveals, however, violence usually begets violence—and one tyranny is replaced with another. In this sense, outbursts of revolutionary American violence are miniature apocalypses. They are founded on the same religious teleological notions, and seek the same kind of reset-to-zero that underpins the apocalypse.[16] If one considers the formative violence that forged the United States—the slow extermination of the natives who were not deemed part of God's plan for the dawning Utopia—the contradiction inherent in this revolutionary violence becomes clearer. The contradiction also resides in the earlier conception of Christian apocalypse, the belief that in order to create perfection the imperfect must first be destroyed. Dr. Strangelove's proselytizing monologue extolling post-apocalyptic mineshaft life suggests a better-bred human will emerge after the radioactivity has subsided. Violence is also seen as transformative by Vaughan and Seagrave's pursuit of a perfect death in *Crash*: both believe it is the only way to truly commune with the world and other people.[17] The contradiction inherent in nuclear war is, clearly, the greatest of all. The American mythological view of a nuclear apocalypse, according to Slotkin's thesis, is a possibility to remake the imperfect. The Bomb will produce a cataclysmic outburst of revolutionary violence that will reset-to-zero the entirety of human civilization and kill all death by killing all life. The transcendent element of the millenarian apocalypse, however, is lost in this form.

    Harkness's relationship with Myna epitomizes his need to believe in the regenerative violence of nuclear war. Myna, he recounts, had a penchant for wearing a bright orange dress with a mushroom cloud appliqued on the front. Myna is overweight at 165 pounds, and so in the fullness of her body resembles an ancient fertility Goddess and also emanates the sense of an explosion. The veritable explosion of life and fertility that Myna embodies represents for Harkness the possibility that a nuclear apocalypse might be a regenerative life-giver. Harkness mythologizes Myna—to suit his own psychological proclivities, to sooth what is causing his anguish—as a fertile nature-mother, harking back to the most ancient of human myths of destruction and rebirth,

II. End Zone and Crash

and the Christian apocalyptic myth of Armageddon and Heaven's dawning. In other words, Myna becomes the conduit for Harkness's desire for redemption from the totality of nuclear war and his own paralysis.

Harkness is a creation for DeLillo and the reader to explore the American apotheosizing of nuclear violence. He is drawn to the "paramilitary complexes" of American Football, nuclear jargon and war games but comes to accept finally, that there is no regenerative element in either the jargon or the unknown void nuclear war may bring about. The jargon is a dead language, it is pre-deceased by the totalizing logic of the Bomb's reality, and so offers none of the technical assurance it espouses. There is no regenerative element either, in the violence of nuclear war, as a potential escalation and all-out nuclear war between the superpowers could, in actuality, mean the end of human life on earth. Slotkin argues in *Gunfighter Nation* that the frontier myth of regenerative violence is no longer tenable in an America whose space (both physical and cognitive) is almost fully colonized by the manifestations of neoliberal capitalism. DeLillo's poststructuralist tendencies to view language as inherently political sees *End Zone* interrogate the transcendent and violent (theological) aspects of American Cold War technique, ultimately showing it to be dangerously paradoxical. In *End Zone* and in much of his life's work to date, then, DeLillo is arguing a closely related point to that which Slotkin makes: that American mythology is being unraveled by its own logical contradictions. The American mythology of purifying violence has reached a logical terminus under the sign of the Bomb, from which it cannot recover. Much like Baudrillard's thesis in "The Precession of Simulacra," *End Zone* depicts a politico-linguistic system whose only justification is its own technique. The existence of world-annihilating nuclear weapons systems stands totem-like as incontrovertible proof that human considerations are secondary to the requirements of the system. Thus Harkness's ascetic journey into the nuclear linguistic heart of darkness fails to reveal to him a deeper truth or purpose for his life but succeeds in highlighting the gaping hole at the heart of postnuclear American mythology. As has been discussed in the "Patriarchal Priests" section, Major Staley's philosophical ponderings over modern warfare seem now like very prescient critiques of the two Gulf Wars and recent conflicts in which drones are commonly used to kill from thousands of miles away. Staley's opinion that postmodern warfare is just an exercise in technological supremacy, with little to do, in reality, with ideology, is very closely related to Baudrillard's summations of recent American wars as thoroughly fragmented, sublimated and as he argues, simply virtual.[18]

Harkness's three hundred pound Jewish roommate Anatole Bloomberg, one of the cast of football players in the novel whom David Cowart describes as "verbal grotesques," rhapsodizes in an apparent stream-of-consciousness outburst, apropos of nothing, on the philosophical nous of war and destruction. Some of the passage, which spans two pages, is deliberately obtuse, giving the sense that DeLillo, as he does in a much more sustained manner in his later apocalyptic satire *White Noise*, is delighting in the subversive element of language's indeterminacy and in mocking the absurdities of our current postnuclear era. Through this linguistic ludic web, however, emerges an intellectual seriousness, which is DeLillo at his most crystalline and perceptive. Bloomberg, sitting at a long table in the dining room with Harkness and two others begins the oration:

> In our silence and terror we may steer our technology toward the metaphysical, toward some unimaginable weapon able to pierce spiritual barriers, to maim or kill whatever dark presence envelopes the world.... We all know that life, happiness, fulfillment come surging out of particular forms of destructiveness. The moral system is enriched by violence put to positive use. But as the capacity for violence grows in the world, the regenerative effects of specific violent episodes become less significant. The capacity overwhelms everything. The mere potential of one form of violence eclipses the actuality of other forms [210].

The yearning for a metaphysical weapon is the yearning for the transcendence that the technical apocalypse seems to preclude. The regenerative element in America's mythological violence is nullified by the mortal shadow cast over narrative, meaning and language by nuclear war's totalizing logic, by the sheer abysmal void it precipitates. Sublimity is excised from this conception of apocalypse, thus Bloomberg's fantasizing about a metaphysical weapon that can kill "the dark presence that envelops the world." Harkness vacillates throughout the novel between the comfort of systems, of agreed upon rationalizations of one facet of life in late capitalist America or another, and the search for sublimity, for the poetic and numinous life that cannot be reduced to materialism.

American Football and Game Theory in *End Zone*

DeLillo's novel makes the clear point that the violence of American Football is sublimated through mechanization in precisely the same way as it was in the Cold War's systemic logic. American Football consists of carefully organized outbursts of violent energy, but the game is always reset to the sys-

II. End Zone *and* Crash

tematic pattern. The American Cold War was also couched within the conceptual framework of a game by those in RAND, who used Game Theory as a basis to enact the permutations of deterrence and the escalations that followed if war were to break out. A war game could be reset-to-zero in an instant, regardless of its outcome. The technocrats at RAND became so enthralled by the logical beauty of Game Theory that they forgot its application and it became an autotelic system detached from reality and the needs of humanity. It became a game world that could be reset and played over and over, a technical exercise where human judgment was substituted with mechanical calculation. This became the Bomb's logic, its scripture—the logic of efficiency, of productivity, of mechanical calculation, of ruthlessness—the logic of postnuclear neoliberal capitalism.

Logos win all their games easily, but the whole season revolves around a game against West Centrex Biotechnical, a team that is described at various times by Logos players as efficient and ruthless, like unstoppable cyborgs.[19] Chapter nineteen, the lengthiest chapter in the book, taking up the entirety of Part Two, describes Logos' loss to West Centrex through Harkness's blissful and sometimes sublime interpretation. Harkness is happy when life is reduced to simple warrior rules, the violence that harks back to primitive passions.

What is most pertinent here, however, is Harkness's (or an omniscient narrator, it is never made absolutely clear) interjection in parenthesis at the start of the description. This parenthetical interjection extols the virtues of the "exemplary spectator" (107). The first objective of the parenthetical passage is to deny the trite analogy between American Football and war. The opening paragraph refers reflexively to the "author" (ostensibly Harkness, but playfully and self-reflexively to DeLillo too), who is not "willing to risk death by analogy in their public discussions of the resemblance between football and war" (107). Quoting Logos' Professor of "Exobiology" Alan Zapalac, the narrator states that the exemplary spectator has little interest in these analogies: "I reject the notion of football as warfare. Warfare is warfare. We don't need substitutes because we've got the real thing" (107). DeLillo is being sly, in this instance, perhaps forewarning against unsophisticated interpretations of the analogy. There is no doubt the book creates an analogy between football and war, but a very specific kind of war, a virtual war, fought with technique, within a specific game paradigm, namely, the Cold War. The analogy between American Football and Cold War technique, what the sport reveals about the culture that adores it, runs much deeper than simple sport—as—war analogies: it speaks directly to the prevailing logic of the time, the ruthless efficiency required to live under the sign of late capitalist technique. The exemplary spectator understands this connection and embraces its power. The following extract, however, indicates that the "exemplary spectator" is not the exemplary reader, that the exemplary spectator is in fact radically conformist. DeLillo is exploring the attraction of conformity to the "theology of the bomb," and in so doing is perhaps luring the reader into agreeing with the sentiment, before exposing it as quasi-fascist. To accept that flawed systems are preferable to chaos is a perfectly acceptable rationalization of the modern world, however, as the passage suggests, the dictates of logical cleanliness and efficiency quickly and easily shift to a totalitarian rationality. This criticism goes to the heart of modern day neoliberal capitalism:

> The exemplary spectator is the person who understands that sport is a benign illusion, the illusion that order is possible. It is a form of society that is rat-free and without harm to the unborn; that is organized so that everyone follows the same rules; that is electronically controlled, thus reducing human error and benefiting industry; that roots out the inefficient and penalizes the guilty; that tends always to move toward perfection [107–08].

The exemplary spectator, then, does not lust after violence in muted forms; she or he seeks the very checks and balances that de-libidinize that violence. The exemplary spectator is the nuclear technocrat made civilian—the person who knows that the masses of checks, balances, details, controls and systems in everyday life may amount to a mere *illusion* of control, but nevertheless understands the need for this illusion in the interests of *productivity*. There is technique and rationality, or there is chaos, as Gary's father, Creed and Staley believe. The exemplary spectator understands the benign illusion as the only insulation from chaos and meaninglessness: "The exemplary spectator has his occasional lusts, but not for warfare, hardly at all for that. No, it's details he needs—impressions, colors, statistics, patterns, mysteries, numbers, idioms, symbols. Football, more than any other sports, fulfills this need" (108). Thus, in a postnuclear world overshadowed by the secular apocalypse, where spiritual meaning has been displaced by the power of our own technologies, the rules and modular logic of the game must be used to affix our existence to the corporeal business of living.

The game is technique and technique is the game. The logic of late capitalism, as is argued by two important theorists of our cultural epoch, Jameson and Baudrillard, is an autotelic system, self-referential, self-sustaining, played, like nuclear wargames on the basis of strict rational rules. The system is contradictory however, as it is based upon a vestigial sense of the apocalyptic,

II. End Zone *and* Crash

the notion of a reset-to-zero. It is a recapitulation of the myth of millennial apocalypse, and the more ancient cycle of death-and-rebirth, in secular and technical form. The death tolls of the Randian war games, Kahn's tomes, all of the projections and configurations of war mapped out by the nuclear technocrats were simply quantifications, figuring only in the logic of the game as a means to measure victory. Similarly, Baudrillard argues that all the human suffering that amasses as a side-effect of capital acquisition remains unquantified, unquantifiable, and irrelevant to the game, that is of course, leaving out the human suffering from which profit is directly made. Neither can a nuclear holocaust be reset-to-zero, nor can the drastic social imbalances caused by skewed capitalist acquisitiveness be reversed and reset-to-zero once the game has been won or lost.

DeLillo plays with the notion of nuclear war as a game directly in chapter twenty-nine of *End Zone*, which sees Gary playing a war game of Major Staley's design in his motel room. Staley begins by telling Gary that the problem with war games "whether they are being played at the Pentagon, at NORAD or Fort Belvoir, at a university or think tank, was the obvious awareness on the parts of all participants that this wasn't the real thing" (214). The problem, Staley cites, is that the emotions of a real situation of such stress can never be elicited in a game situation. Human emotions are passionate, unquantifiable and irrational—they have no place within the autotelic rules of the game—yet they may in fact be the most decisive motivators of human decisions in an actual war situation. Despite this dry, detached, sterile and emotionless game scenario however, the ensuing game between Staley and Gary ends in global cataclysm after merely twelve moves. Before the two begin to play, Staley outlines the game's context, which is based upon the real Cold War flashpoints and tensions in exacting detail. Only after the context is defined at length can Gary begin to participate in the game, with Staley's fetishization of the war game's details becoming abundantly clear: "Before we started, he said he was working on a totally simulated world situation— seven major nations of his own making.., fairly complete demographic, economic, social, religious, racial and meteorological characteristics for each nation" (218). Despite Staley's disparaging preamble about the veracity of war games he has clearly become absorbed in the (realistic) details of a game fantasy of his own creation. Harkness is less than enthused by the prospect of the game as he watches Staley meticulously detail the game's pre-war stage: "I had trouble finding any particular pattern but I could tell quite easily how much time and work he had put into the project. It seemed almost sad. I was hardly a competent enemy" (217). Harkness's reticence stems from his belief that his motivations are different from Staley's. Harkness's journey is an ascetic one that is in dialogue with the spiritual elements of American apocalyptic mythology, one that is seeking a deeper meaning at the heart of the new doctrines of the apocalyptic: "I had no experience in this sort of thing. I had been plagued by joyous visions of apocalypse but I was not at all familiar with the professional manipulations, both diplomatic and military, which might normally precede any kind of large scale destruction" (217–18). The game, however, begins to seduce him. DeLillo maps out the game in clipped declarative sentences, each of the twelve steps containing a few sentences each. It is a style that emulates nuclear jargon, yet its brevity is also deadpan and underscored with the black irony DeLillo employs elsewhere in the novel and in *White Noise*: "The city-busting begins. Selected population centers within COMRUS borders are hit by Minutemen 3 ICBMs carrying MIRV warheads" (219).[20] The game ends abruptly with spasm response, and Staley's phone ringing. Staley stares at the object unknowingly. In this passage DeLillo uses the game motif to subvert traditional nuclear holocaust fiction. The deadpan and abrupt description of the game's destructive ending and Staley's reaction to the phone call are reminiscent of novels such as Pat Frank's *Alas Babylon* (1959) and Burdick and Wheeler's *Fail-Safe*, both of which feature much telephonic drama surrounding the nuclear event.

The narrative rejoins Gary in the final chapter more listless and lost than ever. Myna returns after Christmas "many pounds lighter," which Harkness finds difficult to accept (221). He turns to the African American star of the football team, Taft Robinson, for spiritual sustenance. Robinson is monomaniacal and lives alone in a bare room. He and Harkness finally have a conversation, which reveals Robinson to be not quite the oracle he had hoped, and the novel ends with Harkness's hunger strike and the words "[i]n the end they had to carry me to the infirmary and feed me through plastic tubes" (236). The ending is not cheerful but not apocalyptic. The final two words "plastic tubes" evoke a sense of the futile nature of Harkness's journey. Instead of a singular revelation, or a holy vision, his ascetic journey leads him to be force-fed through the most mundane of common modern materials, cheap, disposable, polluting plastic. The ending may seem hopeless until the reader remembers that Harkness has narrated his own tale.

DeLillo, in the penultimate chapter, has drawn the reader back again to the idea of the "exemplary spectator." If the logic of war as a game and games as war is reversible in a virtualized world where technique is the primary element, it can be read that the exemplary spectator is the citizen who sees all possible scenarios as a game. The exemplary spectator understands that control is a benign illusion, but that the logic of the game demands certain mechanical responses that are prescribed from on high—from the Bomb's scripture of quantified rationality and productivity towards the endless requirement for growth. In the theological sense of the Bomb, the game motif is a formal method of prayer. The Game model of capitalist acquisition has permeated to the core of America's political economy (in particular), it calls for growth, consolidation, strategy, ruthless rationality—it is instrumentalism made social. This and many other aspects of the American Game-paradigm are detailed in the recent television series *The Wire*, which is discussed in the following chapter. DeLillo, however, has probably been the most insightful contemporary American author of the manner in which scientism has been reified in American social organization and culture. *End Zone* is perhaps unfairly neglected by the overall critical appraisal of DeLillo's *oeuvre*. It is a novel of great prescience and is hugely relevant to our cultural epoch, as is hopefully illuminated by this chapter. Without the benefit of a time span to facilitate the unfurling of history, DeLillo produced the highly insightful American football/game model nuclear allegory that is *End Zone*, long before the game model had fully insinuated into the cultural mechanism.[21]

The Apocalypse Filmed, Photographed, Cut Up, Miniaturized and Multiplied in *Crash*

End Zone illuminates the religious, teleological and semiotic elements of postnuclear capitalism. *Crash*, on the other hand, imagines the physical violence in which we seem to willingly partake as offerings to the new god that rules our world. *Crash* attends more to our corporeal immersion in technology and imagines how this may change us both physically and psychologically, yet both novels essentially entail spiritual quests for meaning in an instrumentalized world. There are no direct references to nuclear war or nuclear technology in the novel, just the occasional mention of "autogeddon," which nevertheless references both the technological (automobile) and older religious (Armageddon) elements of apocalypse. The term also conjures the association of car crashes with auto-eroticism, and of course, autoerotic death. Without directly referencing nuclear apocalypse, Ballard nonetheless posits the ultimate and holiest of transcendences the crash cultists seek in violent technological death.

In his much-referenced essay "The Transvaluation of Utopia," Wagar argues that Ballard is a utopian writer. He does this by splitting concepts of utopia into "naturalist" and "idealist." (76).[22] "These two great rivers of utopian dreaming flow through the history of ideas," Wagar writes, and "have contended with each other for thousands of years in every philosophical arena in the world" (56). The naturalist current of utopian thought is very much bound up in Enlightenment thinking. The idea that a practical application of the laws of the universe will bring about a perfect society is at the core of Newton, Comte, and Smith, those Enlightenment thinkers whose influence has been most prevalent in the secular rationalization of the Western world. The idealism that denies this instrumental view of the world can be found in Platonism, mysticism and modern and postmodern irrationalism. Ballard's writing, Wagar argues, belongs with an irrationalist tradition of utopian writers such as Nietzsche, Shaw, Aldous Huxley, Teilhard de Chardin, C.S. Lewis and William Burroughs. His definition of the group of crash cultists in the novel as an irrationalist "utopian cell" is accurate to the extent that their utopianism is necessarily death-bound and that their response to the psychopathology of industrialized 20th century life is similarly psychopathological: "The point, again, is simply to transcend reality, including the technological landscape of the late 20th century, by passing *through* it rather than *around* it. Ballard's way out of the world is through the world, through all its muck and madness, as in the lives of many saints in Christian hagiography" (64). The group has found a way to ritualize the technological, to embrace the world as it is and to ritualize its mythologies according to those most ancient—death and rebirth, destroying the imperfect to make way for the perfect. The (dystopian) utopia imagined in *Crash* sees the emergence of what could be deemed a techno-dysmorphic group, whose bodies are cut up in staged acts of violent automobile communion and put back together in new configurations that obey the prevailing logic of the camera, the television program or movie. The effect of both the car and camera, in the realm of Ballard's *Crash* is that of pornography—in the filmed autoerotic vehicular death there are multiple angles, cut and edited, often fixated on a single body part, its functionality, its disembodied mechanical auto(nomous) eroticism. *Crash*'s Ballard narrates the tale of he and his wife Catherine's induction into the group—following Ballard's involvement in a crash—that believes in the transformative holiness of violent car accidents. The group is made up of the aforementioned Ballard and his wife; the leader Dr. Robert Vaughan, a kind of psychotic Dean Moriarty; Colin Seagrave, an automobile

II. End Zone *and* Crash

stuntman, and his wife, Vera; Gabrielle, their friend, a mutilated woman in a leg brace; and Helen Remington, the passenger and widow of the man who died in Ballard's accident. Throughout the narrative, members of the group perform violent crash rituals that adhere to the logic of film's cut and edit process, most significantly that of pornography in its fixation on specific body parts. In interviews J. G. Ballard has repeatedly referenced his belief in the influence of this logic on the mechanized world, particularly in visual media and advertising:

> [S]cience is moving into an area where its obsessions begin to *isolate completely* its subject under the lens of its microscope, away from its links with the rest of nature. This is always the risk with science as a whole. The pornographic imagination detaches certain parts of the human anatomy from the human being and becomes obsessively focused on the breast or the genitalia, or what have you. That sort of obsession with what I call *quantified functions* is what lies at the core of science; there is a shedding of all responsibility by the scientist who is just *looking* at a particular subject with a tendency to ignore the contingent links [Lewis 29, original italics].

The effect of pornography in its filmed forms is to dismember the body according to the logic of the camera angle, the close up, and the edit. The transcendence the crash group is trying to achieve involves a reconfiguration of the body according to this logic, according to the cut-up and re-edit techniques of fetishized body parts in television advertising and other forms of pornography.

The opening page of the novel has Ballard recounting the violent circumstances of Vaughan's death. Vaughan, Ballard tells the reader, had been attempting to crash into Elizabeth Taylor's limousine in a most carefully detailed, filmed and fatal union. Vaughan seeks to reverse the *petit mort*, to liken death to the ultimate simultaneous orgasm with Taylor, releasing and comingling their energy together into the ether. Crucially, the act is filmed, and so becomes a cinematic scripture of spectacular violence. Ballard tells the reader that Vaughan instead, however, jumped a flyover ramp and landed on a bus full of airline passengers. This is perhaps Vaughan's only true car accident in the novel, despite, as Ballard tells us, the rehearsals of the moment Vaughan had been staging for weeks beforehand "with the devotion of an Earl Marshal" (1):

> The walls of his apartment near the film studios at Shepperton were covered with the photographs he had taken through his zoom lens each morning as she left her hotel in London, from the pedestrian bridges above the westbound motorways, and from the roof of the multi-story car-park at the studios. The magnified details of her knees

and hands, of the inner surface of her thighs and the left apex of her mouth.... At his apartment I watched him matching the details of her body with the photographs of grotesque wounds in a textbook of plastic surgery [1].

Elizabeth Taylor is referred to thereafter in the novel as the actress to denote the value of her commodification in exchangeable terms. In its treatment of her, *Crash* makes it clear that her value is not intrinsic; it emanates from her celebrity status, from the Debordian logic of her infinitely available image. Vaughan's wish to smash his body together with Taylor's via their dream machines—the car and camera, which have the power to transform and create new corporeal forms for the world to come—must crucially adhere to the spectacular logic of the filmed event in order for it to become a communal act of transcendence. Ballard eroticizes the spectacle of Vaughan and Taylor's violent union through the pornographic logic of dismemberment. Vaughan and the rest must pass through the "muck and the madness" of the world by immersing in its logic of violence and instrumentalism, the logic of the Bomb—only in this way can its regenerative promise be unlocked, the apocalyptic myth of reset-to-zero. Vaughan attempts to transcend the quotidian horrors of the postmodern world by fusing his energy for all eternity with Elizabeth Taylor's. The act must be carried out via the ubiquitous technologies of car and camera; technologies that reflect and channel the latent violence of human mechanization in the late twentieth-century, whilst also speaking to deep seated psychic desires to transcend the body. It is not the value of Taylor's inherent energy that Vaughan seeks; instead he recognizes her submission to dismemberment by camera, her willingness to be re-cut and re-edited and to become consumable. The latent pornographic violence of the camera is manifest in the car's potential to physically re-cut and re-edit. The physical editing of their dying bodies must be accompanied by the camera's capturing of the spectacle, in order that it become accessible to the simulacrous logic of late capitalism, in order that it become endlessly reproducible and infinitely distributed. In the inevitable re-editing of the photographs that would be taken, the mechanized eroticism of the dismemberment could be shared by all throughout time:

> In his vision of a car-crash with the actress, Vaughan was obsessed by many wounds and impacts—by the dying chromium and collapsing bulkheads of their two cars meeting head-on in complex collisions endlessly repeated in slow-motion films, by the identical wounds inflicted on their bodies, by the *image* of windshield glass frosting around her face as she broke its tinted surface like a death-born Aphrodite [2, emphasis added].

II. End Zone *and* Crash

Vaughan understands our complicity in spectacular violence as a bloodlust that manifests in everyday life in the car crash but goes unacknowledged by a morality that has been rendered obsolete by the conditions of the late twentieth-century. Ballard's group may be extremists, but for this reason their actions offer an insightful critique of everyday violence in the postindustrial world, enacted under the shadow of the great technological totem. We willingly interact with this technology, which is individually highly dangerous and collectively catastrophic. *Crash* posits a possible answer to the question: why do we participate; why do we offer ourselves willingly to the slaughter? The protagonists of *Crash* simply take the logic of the car crash to its extreme, suggesting that our everyday willingness towards this kind of violence is a manifestation of subconscious desires. Technology, after all, is no more than an extension of our corporeal, cerebral and sensorial selves, thus is naturally charged with what is latent in us subconsciously. There are certainly libidinal elements inbuilt into our technology—the automobile bears this out—and there are also undoubtedly spiritual/mythological elements inbuilt, as discussed, in its utopian and apocalyptic potential. Vaughan and the others are attempting to tap into the subconscious and mythological elements of the technology that rules us. Teleological and utopian mythology is now overlain with the transformative and miraculous power of postnuclear technology, it is secularized, subject to humanism and this powerful combination drives our faith in Western scientism. The trajectory of recent science and technology has seen a move away from the physical world, into a virtual and networked one. It has also moved very perceptively towards the mechanically enhanced, cyborg idea of the human body. This move implies the transcendence of the corporeal, of the obsolete vessel that is messy, fluidic, asymmetrical and subject to temporal decay. In his prescience, Ballard understood that technology was moving away from the realm of the physical and toward the virtual, away from the truth of unenhanced organic human life and most possibly towards the long-held fantasy of transcendence of the flesh. As technology is intrinsically laden with the baser aspects of our unresolved subconscious desires, the transcendence that awaits us, according to Ballard's thinking, is a febrile and violent dehumanized nightmare.

DeLillo's novel *Cosmopolis* (2003) in this way follows on from Ballard's warning only with the updated technological systems of cyber-capitalism. Eric Packer seeks to shed his body and meld fully with the informational pulse and rhythm of the cyber-market but fails to understand that true communion with the *lifeforce* means an acknowledgment of the radically unknowable. In DeLillo's novel, the loneliness of radical individualism and the airless certainty of scientism precludes the acceptance of nature and the acceptance of the passing of life needed to give a deeper meaning to the transcendence of the body.

In *Crash* we see the terminally disaffected Ballard and his wife seek a new kind of communion, a new kind of authenticity by immersing themselves in technology's transgressive, violent element. The naturalist or rationalist utopian imagines a world of order and quantifiability, while the irrationalist sees that mythology (narratives of ourselves) and libidinal drives are intrinsic in human social agency. Violence, even in our ostensibly benign technology, is barely latent—as technology has been imbued with all of the foibles of our collective subconscious and our mythologies. There is a tendency in us, perhaps, to unthinkingly assume that logic is a law of the universe, somehow existing outside of our machinations, and not subject to the limitations of our sensory, cognitive (and political) ability as a species. The rationalization of the social world according to Cold War market-based quantification models has not resulted in greater efficiency or functionality, it has instead meant that we understand our postnuclear technology and neoliberal scientism in terms of the teleological, apocalyptic and tribal-libidinal mythology that transferred to the Bomb. Thus, in *Crash*, the ritual acts, the car crashes that seek transcendence and communion are not enacted via moribund theistic narratives but via technology, a new conduit for human libidinal latency, miracles and regenerative apocalypses.

Freud, the Death Wish and "Autogeddon"

The car was already old technology when Ballard began to write "Crash," the section of *The Atrocity Exhibition* (1970) that he was subsequently to expand into a full novel. "Throughout *Crash*," Ballard wrote in his introduction, "I have used the car not only as a sexual image, but as a total metaphor for man's life in today's society" (Introduction). In spite of its age, and unlike the general exponentially increasing rates of obsolescence in the technological realm, the car is still pivotal to our technological lives, and in a number of ways is emblematic of our relationship with all of technology in psychological and mythological terms. It is a technology that we physically occupy, as vast chronological slabs of human existence are lived *autocentrically*. It is technology's surrogate womb, and it thus evokes amniotic feelings of comfort, isolation, a surrender to powerful locomotion, protection and safety. The car's mythological status as a dream machine, a facilitator of freedom and limitless mobility spans post-industrial culture—its presentation in advertising and marketing as both priapic and yonic is a process that is almost as old as the motor car itself and has entered the pop lexicon of how cars are perceived. To this end the automobile acts as a psychic bridge connecting deep-seated unconscious desires and American capitalism, specifically, its myths pertaining to the seeking of individual freedom. Expressions of automotive transcendence and individualism in American culture span everything from *On the Road* to *Pimp My Ride* and much in between.[23]

Critics such as Robert L. Caserio, Wagar, Nick Davis and Dennis Foster have made explicit the Freudian and psychoanalytical aspects of *Crash*'s eroticization of violence. As Caserio points out, "Ballard has said that he devoured Freud in his adolescent years, and that consequently he set out on a medical career to become a psychoanalyst" (302). Caserio is quick to note, however, that Ballard's application of Freud (to Vaughan) is not straightforward, vacillating, as he sees it, between "earnest application of Freud ... parody of Freud; and "pop" stylization of Freud (something between endorsement and subversion)" (303).

In his essay "Mobility and Masochism: Christine Brooke-Rose and J.G. Ballard," Caserio looks at masochism as a creative and restorative force. He bases his thesis on Freud's "The Economic Problem of Masochism" (1924) and Jean Laplanche's development of Freud's essay. In Caserio's conception, Vaughan and the rest of the cell are bound to immobility by their obsession, "for Vaughan wants to limit the meaning of what he plots, and to see desire stilled by consummation" (Caserio 302). The creative power of immobility, for Caserio, stems from a formative moment in childhood in which vital pleasure stills the child's movement. The rejoining of passivity with intense pleasure later in adulthood subconsciously mingles feelings of suffering with eroticism. Thus, writes Caserio, "Vaughan has made himself the delegate of Eros to convince highway victims that the roadside slaughter really represents death's binding and defeat by love" (302). The ultimate consumption of desire, however, in Vaughan's case, is an erotic release—a sumptuary expenditure of his life's energy, to be reconstituted from the altar of technology and consumed via the resulting spectacular images into infinity. Vaughan's obsession may be to "still desire" as Caserio contends, in a tendency "to totalize the meaning of vehicular casualty," but the crash cult's quest for an irrationalist utopia is death-bound, like all ideas of transcendence and utopia (302). What is ultimately implied in notions of total freedom and the breaking of the bonds of physicality is death's release from the confines of the organism. Their quest is utopian in the sense that they seek an ultimate communion, a co-mingling with universal energy, and they do so through the physical and mythological tenets of what is most powerful and ubiquitous in modern human life.

In *Civilization and Its Discontents* (1930) Freud proposes that the religious feeling of connectedness or oneness with all life is rooted in the formative period of infancy in which individual subjectivity is yet to be formed. In the womb and in infancy, the child has yet to distinguish herself from her mother or any other object she encounters, thus in this idful state is connected to all things and beings. A vestige of this infant feeling of connectedness remains for some into adulthood, Freud speculated, producing the religious, or what he termed oceanic feeling. Male intercourse, for Freud, is an expression to some extent of an Oedipal desire to return to the womb. Thus, the experimentations of Ballard's crash cult at the limits of our intersection with everyday technology are Freudian. The death instinct, in Freudian terms, then, is counter-intuitive in that it is an expression of the desire in adults to return to the womb, which is a desire to return to the feeling of oneness and connection to all living energy, that was once felt. Vaughan, Ballard, Seagrave and the others wish to achieve transcendence of their flat virtual world, of the limiting physical and metaphysical dimensions of their living bodies through the regenerative violence of technology's womb.

Setting aside Ballard's glib use of Freudian theory, what Foster in particular has revealed about Ballard's infantilization post-crash is of particular pertinence. The opening chapter of the novel, as mentioned, details Vaughan's plans for Elizabeth Taylor, as well a plethora of erotic crash fantasies Vaughan has envisaged including one involving Ronald Reagan, whose relevance is discussed below. Chapter two details Ballard's crash; the instantaneous altering of the bodies of the three people by the collapsing structures of the cars; the spectacle viewed and absorbed by Ballard, Helen Remington, and the onlookers of the instant death of Remington's husband, the ejection of bodily fluids and the total helplessness of the two; Ballard's delivery from the chrysalis of his wrecked car by the fire and ambulance crew, and his comportment to the incubating sterility of hospital. The tone of Ballard's prose is lysergic-apocalyptic; Ballard's rebirth and delivery unto the bosom of technology is iridescent with latent and manifest violence. In the infantilizing process of Ballard's hospital recovery, he notes of his wife and the nurses that "all these women around me seemed to attend only to my most infantile

II. End Zone *and* Crash

zones ... these starched women in all their roles reminded me of those who attended my childhood, commissionaires guarding my orifices" (22). Ballard is immobilized, and his second infancy is ministered by the "commissionaires of his orifices" under the auspices of medical science: "In his second childhood, he has new orifices in his knees and scalp, through which pus drains. Generally the adult abandons infantile zones of need and pleasure—those of polymorphously perverse sexuality—but in their new configuration, linked to crash wounds, they constitute the reborn sexual bodies of Vaughan's photographed victims" (Foster 525).

Ballard's infantilization, his "stilled movement," reorganizes his Oedipal desires around the technology that tends to his immobile body. It opens to him a new techno-sexuality that is as diffuse as the means of technology themselves. In other words, where technology invades flesh, any flesh, there is erotic potential. Ballard's rebirth into the realm of totalized techno-logic opens him to a potentially limitless eroticization of his object-world. The outcome of the mechanical objectification of the human body is an omnipresent pornogrification wherever flesh and technology interact.

The mechanized logic of pornography—the endless hyperrealizing effect of the camera and car in the age of commercial propaganda, and the infantilizing effect that the instant gratification of any and all desires has on the individual—is externalized in the reborn Ballard. In this way, the reborn Ballard embodies the replacement of Christianity's phallic order with the phallic order of technology's god and, thus, the atomized diffusion of (violent) eroticism throughout the technological hyperreality: "This obsession with the sexual possibilities of everything around me had been jerked loose from my mind by the crash.... The crash between our two cars was a model of some ultimate and yet undreamt sexual union" (19). When Ballard meets Gabrielle for the first time, Vaughan shows him a photo-journal of her violent transformation into a re-edited being—a quasi-cyborg whose chromium cane and back-brace act as conduits for her technologically diffused sexuality:

> Without thinking, I visualized a series of imaginary pictures I might take of her: in various sexual acts, her legs supported by sections of complex machine tools, pulleys and trestles; with her physical education instructor, coaxing this conventional young man into the new parameters of her body, developing a sexual expertise that would be an exact analogue of the other skills created by the multiplying technologies of the twentieth century [79–80].

For Ballard the author, sexual repression gives way to the sexualization of everything under the new order. The new technologically diffuse sexuality that *Crash* describes once Ballard and Catherine become absorbed into the cult is indeterminate. The majority of sexual encounters that happen after Ballard's rebirth, in fantasy or diegesis, describe a variety of combinations of Ballard, Catherine or Vaughan in sexual unions that revolve around mixtures of semen, engine-coolant or anal mucus.

In a feminist reading of *Crash* (novel and film) Karen Beckman complicates the ubiquity of semen and other bodily fluids in the novel (semen most often appears in the novel on interior car dials, upholstery, etc.) suggesting they are not straightforward examples of phallocentrism: "The question of what a feminist reader should make of the ubiquity of semen is as complicated as the challenges offered by the novel's mutating members. As numerous feminist theorists have argued, fluids and tacky bodily substances are traditionally aligned with femininity, marking women as the baser sex. Vaughan however … is by far the novel's most viscous character" (Beckman 97). The endless mixture of fluids in *Crash* evinces a future sexuality that is reformulated not around traditional sexual differences but around a ubiquitous mechanical sexuality. Individuals do not partake in this neo-sexuality, in the novel, they are presented more like components of the mechanical sexuality. This neo-sexuality emanates from the death-bearing phallus that presides over all technology, producing "the extraordinary sexual acts celebrating the possibilities of unimagined technologies" (Ballard, 148)[24] The technologically diffused sexuality that emerges postnatally appears to be neither feminine nor masculine, homosexual or heterosexual. Descriptions of penetrative sex with crash wounds are suggestive rather than explicitly rendered—the implication is that both sexes may acquire these feminized wounds—yet only the males are anatomically equipped to penetrate the neo-sex organs. Thus there is an effective re-edit of the phallic law that accommodates its transference from the old order, that of the Christian God, to the new, that of technology and its miraculous power.[25]

The re-cut and re-edited Ballard is born unto technology's bosom; transformed in such a way as to have internalized a new kind of technological spirituality. The crash for Ballard and Remington is an epiphany. For Gabrielle, Seagrave and the high priest Vaughan, the inherent violence in the logic of postnuclear technology and pornography has become a mode for transcendence. The former paternal order, and the Oedipal drive it engenders have been subsumed into technology's totalization of subconscious desires. In this new Oedipal order, the formation of new orifices, and the ultimate transcendent ejaculation of energy takes place via the subconscious desire to return to the womb, thus technology's womb is the site of the new sexuality.

II. End Zone *and* Crash

Technology's totemic phallus is the ultimate projector of latent violence. The power of the Bomb's logic is irrefutable but the only promise of love and communion it contains is a vestigial one, the erotic communal death of the apocalypse. Thus the actors of *Crash* follow the logic of the new order by performing erotic feats of automotive violence—apocalypses that are miniaturized and technologically diffused—in pursuance of perfection, love and communion. In a reading of *Empire of the Sun*, Caserio points out the pre-dead aspects of life in the post-nuclear age (discussed above in relation to meaning and narrative), to which Ballard's fiction in general is attuned. Under the sign of the Bomb, life's only possible trajectory is towards an apocalypse:

> *Empire of the Sun* disambiguates the aftermath of World War II by imagining it as a universal death already effectively accomplished, because to remain within the uncertainty of freedom of choice not to disarm is to have already lost the war—and life itself. Ballard's novel suggests that we have not survived the war, but have survived our collective death. Individual life seems to go on, in all its immediate vitality; but the collective commitment to nuclear war nullifies this life [Caserio 306].

In *Crash*'s case they are individuated and miniaturized apocalypses, as the logic of the Bomb is terminal, so the only way out from under its imperative towards efficiency is by enacting erotic miniaturizations of the apocalypse via technology in order to subvert its prescribed use. "I looked out at the drivers of the cars alongside us, visualizing their lives in the terms Vaughan had defined for them. For Vaughan they were already dead" (111).

The paternal law of the new phallic order, as previously discussed, is one that demands efficiency and productivity. Abstract values such as love and morality are unquantifiable according to the mechanical rationalism that the Bomb requires, thus are irrelevant to it. The utopian cell in *Crash* challenges the paternal law by seeking love through irrational means. Ballard seems to abandon his profession as a director of television commercials for the real, physical acts of transformation that technology's womb can bring about. The camera's angle, the studio re-cut and re-edit effectively transform physical elements into the consumable semiotics of the hyperreal model. Ballard forsakes this mediation, and the law of productivity, for the real experience of transformation.

The flouting of the paternal law in favor of an Oedipal eroticization of the inherent phallic violence is a rebellion, undertaken by Ballard's utopian cell in *Crash*, that naturalizes a psychopathology in postmodern life: "Vaughan represents the nth point or terminal destination in the process. It's very important to realize that there is a normalization of psychopathology taking place. Elements of psychopathic behavior are tolerated and are annexed into normal life in a way that we are scarcely aware of" (Ballard, Lewis, 32). Psychopathology is defined in general terms as the inability to feel empathy towards others. The hope of the crash cell is to find spiritual communion *through* technology, as its ubiquity precludes any other mode. Thus the love that Vaughan seeks is necessarily a technological *liebestod*. The only means of communion available is through a violent diffusion of energy via the all-pervasive instrument of technology. In the narrative void that instrumentalism has created, human life, in *Crash* is deconstructed and distilled down to its elemental state: its energy. The miniature apocalypse of each crash is the only means by which humans can commune, by mingling their energy in its release, just as all human energy may be released simultaneously in a nuclear holocaust.

On the Psychopathology of the System

Ballard's answer to the puzzle of our committed participation in daily automotive slaughter, as he characterizes it, lies in subconscious, stifled or sublimated sexual desire. The sumptuous expenditure of energy in the recreational sex act, or the *petit mort* that it implies, is linked by the pornographic/mechanical logic of the camera image. (Borrowing from Bataille's conception of energy expenditure in *The Accursed Share*). The logic of the cut and edit in advertising, television, in all forms of media imagery implies the more literal and brutal cut and re-edit of the body in the car crash. The car is a kind of physical manifestation of the camera, a vehicle for libidinal desires and myths of transcendence: "I like to think of *Crash* as the first pornographic novel based on technology," Ballard has claimed, "By technology one means science in its practical applications to everyday life. In the case of *Crash* that has to do with the technology of, literally, the vehicle, for the pornographic imagination" (Ballard, Lewis, 29). Ballard's crash group, then, makes manifest the latent libidinal desires, as he sees them, that are inherent in driving and in the spectacular logic of late capitalism. For Vaughan, the camera was essential to the capturing of the sumptuous expenditure of energy in his planned crash with Elizabeth Taylor; to capture the physical re-edit, in order that the real event is translatable into the semiology of the model, as happened with the Kennedy assassination. Only then can the full erotic transcendence be realized. True communion must involve the perpetual recapitulation of the image of their violent union; it must become

II. End Zone *and* Crash

spectacular iconography to be ogled into the future by unborn eyes, it must be fetishized and eroticized in order for its full potential to be realized. Thus, the car and camera have a symbiotic relationship in *Crash*. They assume the order of primary and secondary technologies in the semiotics of the pornographic/mechanical imagination in postmodernity. Chapter ten of the novel sees Ballard and Helen Remington led to Seagrave's house by Vaughan. Ballard meets Seagrave's wife and the crippled young woman, Gabrielle at Seagrave's house, and Vaughan shows him a photo-journal he has been surreptitiously keeping of Ballard's auto-centric affair with Remington and with his secretary Renata: "The leitmotiv of this photographic record emerged as I recovered from my injuries: my relationships, mediated by the automobile and its technological landscape, with my wife, Renata and Dr. Remington" (80). Throughout the novel, the car acts as the primary technological translator of mortal flesh into sublime new expressions, and the camera as the secondary technology, the key to the virtual world, where the translated energy can be consumed and eroticized without limit.

Crash, in keeping with Ballard's style, does not offer much insight into the inner life of its characters. The characters are very much extensions of the world they inhabit, including the narrator whom he has titled James Ballard. Ballard, a disaffected middle-class TV advert director does not elucidate his feelings or internal life. He seems to exist primarily in the world of surfaces and appearances until his near-fatal car crash, which he admits, "was the only real experience I had been through in years" (28). No obvious moral judgment is cast upon the crash cult. Ballard has imagined new rituals and new moralities that may arise from the logic of the modern world, which, he posits may well be psychopathological if judged by current standards.[26] The group's method of experimentation, as described in *Crash*'s repetitive series of surrealist and highly cinematic auto-vignettes, may be disturbing or abhorrent; it certainly was to those early reviewers upon the novel's release.[27] The morality of the novel, however, does not reside in characteristic psychological didacticism, but serves to stand in juxtaposition to current prescribed moral standards and sensibilities, of what an extreme social externalization of the logic of nuclear "technarchy" may manifest (144): "Nearly all the characters in his utopian cells are experimentalists, eager to travel wherever their obsessions lead them, at no matter what cost. In this respect, Ballard belongs to the tradition of immoral moralists that begins in Western literature with Machiavelli and de Sade, and continues through Céline, Genet, Camus (in *The Killer*), and Burgess (in *A Clockwork Orange*), to William Burroughs" (Wagar 61).[28]

Ballard does not focus on the individual morality of his protagonists because their actions are more revelatory of a psychopathological system. Much has been written about the psychological effects of capitalism on society and the individual in recent years but few, understandably, will connect late capitalism's atomization and dehumanization to techno-capitalism's machine deity, the Bomb. Ballard's novel speaks to this broader implication, the social and psychological effects of a system charged with such incredible violence. The question is one that concerns many, in a variety of disciplines: what are the effects of the placing of selfishness as the prime motivation within our institutions? What effects will the placing of quantification over qualified reasoning have on our broader society? What are the psychological, cultural and evolutionary effects on human beings of an adaptive requirement to be mechanically and ruthlessly rational according to such narrow systemic requirements? What Ballard imagines is a deviancy from normative prescribed morality and, crucially, from the dictates of technical efficiency. The Bomb, as the totemic representation of all postnuclear technology, is accepted psychically as the all-powerful signifier of technical and logical perfection as well as the conduit for ancient and deep-seated mythologies and unconscious desires. In its religious and utopian acceptance, it is also the bringer of a new and perfect world through its purifying violence. The deviancy of the protagonists in *Crash* embodies and ritualizes the ancient, the violent and the sexual elements of our relationship with technology. Crucially, however, neither can technocracy make humans more machine-like in terms of efficiency or behavior, according to *Crash,* nor can it facilitate a circumvention of these perceived flaws. What emerges, Ballard suggests, from historical attempts to narrowly corral human behavior are dark, unintended consequences. Ballard has come to a similar philosophical position to that taken by Kubrick, as is evident in Kubrick's *ouvre* of the dehumanization and totalitarianism of trying to mold and psychically altar people to be more mechanistic or to fit imposed institutional dictates and systemic confines.

The extremity of the crash cultists functions for Ballard in a number of ways. The brutality underscores the logical terminus of a life lived under the sign of the Bomb, as a forewarning of where this logic leads. It may also act, for Ballard and reader as a cathartic satire of the increasingly dehumanized world we have created. Thirdly, it acts, in literary terms, as an imaginative rendering of "the collapsing moral world of late capitalism," and thus opens up a critical space between the reader and the totalized nuclear logic of late capitalism (Wagar 67). In the introduction, he wrote to *Crash* in 1995, partially quoted in the epigraph to this chapter, Ballard clarifies the moral motivations for *Crash*:

> The Marriage of reason and nightmare that has dominated the 20th century has given birth to an ever more ambiguous world. Across the communications landscape move the spectres of sinister technologies and the dreams that money can buy. Thermo-nuclear weapons systems and soft-drinks commercials coexist in an overlit realm ruled by advertising and pseudo-events, science and pornography. Over our lives preside the great twin leitmotifs of the 20th century—sex and paranoia [*Crash*, Introduction].[29]

The admixture of nuclear weapons, advertising, science, pornography, sex and paranoia that Ballard posits as the cultural materials of the 20th century (and the 21st undoubtedly) are filtered in the novel through the prism of the cutting, melding, re-editing of the human subject in the everyday car crash.

The Fate of Narratives Under the Sign of the Bomb

Ballard, as stated, depicts an imagined way in which the human need for a common story and shared goal if thwarted or debased may manifest in twisted ways. *Crash* portrays this twisted expression of a need to commune without casting judgment, yet rendering it in a way that is shocking to normative Western morality. Human irrationality means that humans cannot be corralled towards a mechanistic productivity, and so Ballard avoids that didactic and deterministic trap. Ballard's tale is, therefore, very far removed from the supposed rationalism of Ayn Rand's vehicle of objectivism, *Atlas Shrugged*, for example (1957). Rand's novel tells of heroic individuals who, by being rational (self-interested) and productive, save the world from weak philosophies based upon collectivism and empathy.[30] Ballard does not set out a new philosophy in *Crash*, as Rand does in *Atlas Shrugged*. *Crash* on the contrary proposes that any attempts to reshape behavior according to external criteria will almost certainly lead society to a dark place. There is no doubting, therefore, that his vision of a utopian cell seeking communion and transcendence in a world devoid of empathy and real connection is not intended to be a pleasant one:

> There is a sense in which a "new morality" (if you would like to call it that) has already started to emerge. People accept moral discontinuities in their lives in a way that older generations would not have done ... but I can see the same sort of moral discontinuities coming in peoples' lives more and more in the future, producing a rather unsettling world where one will need educated feet to be able to make the crossovers from one moral plane to the next [Ballard. Lewis 33–34].

The moral discontinuities of which Ballard speaks are brought about by the prescribed dictates of the system, the amalgamation and dissemination of enormous masses of commercial information, disinformation, public relations spin and pseudo-events, the presumed need for social control, obedience and productivity for its own sake. The systemic psychopathology is that which Baudrillard identifies in *Consumer Society*, wherein collective human considerations of quality of life, mental and physical health, and the question of what kind of society is desired, are secondary to those of growth and productivity. Baudrillard too, as has been mentioned, held up the quantified masses of road deaths, suicides, unemployment, homelessness and poverty, and other dehumanizing aspects of modern life as emblematic of the systemic psychopathology. Everything is accounted for in a balance sheet-style but it is a system that is utterly devoid of care or empathy, ultimately, as the statistics that enumerate the downsides of capitalism are really deemed externalities to the pursuit of profit, or as is the case with contemporary neoliberalism, are openly harnessed for that very purpose. Like a clinical psychopath, thereby, the system could similarly be described as lacking in empathy and fundamentally amoral.

The moral discontinuities in American life, as mentioned by Ballard (and detailed in the following chapter on *The Wire*), come about when the narratives of American mythology are disintegrated in the brutal reality of a dehumanizing instrumentalism. It can be legitimately argued that the Judeo-Christian morality, by which America and most of the Western world has ostensibly abided, is now a vestigial morality. The ostensibly secular religion of scientism appears to lack narratives about inner human life; the ancient need in humans to feel we have a story and that our story is a shared one. There are, of course, very pragmatic reasons for being moral, particularly surrounding a social contract embodied by community living but this message is perpetually under attack by the atomizing project of neoliberalism and does not have a narrative strong enough, as yet, to overcome this effect. When vestigial religious moral messages, as well as core American mythologies of freedom and transcendence come up against the imperatives of control and mechanical rationalization that capitalist technique (The Bomb) requires, we see what Ballard calls moral discontinuities.

The American Fever Dream Globalized

The American Dream has always implied transcendence—from the more naive mainstream idea of liberation through technology, to frontierism

II. End Zone *and* Crash

in all its recapitulations throughout the mythology and from the microwave oven to the Martian rover, technology has always been central to its modern expressions. The car has long been a key technological vehicle for American expressions of transcendence—speed, mobility, and freedom—in America's exceptionalist mythology, with Dean Moriarty and Raoul Duke using the dream machine (among other things) to explore the outer edges. *Crash* is nominally set in Shepperton, London, but it has a distinctly American feel to it.

Vaughan, as mentioned, seeks to consummate his desire for *liebestod* with "the actress" Elizabeth Taylor, a product of the Hollywood star-making machine. He had "woven elaborate fantasies" around the automobile deaths of Jayne Mansfield and James Dean, and Vaughan's vehicle of choice, the Lincoln convertible, is the car in which John F. Kennedy was killed (8). Kennedy's death has the implicit attraction, for Vaughan, of occurring in an automobile, and being captured on film. His death is, thereby, available to the technologic of the moving image, the image of his death and its recapitulation ad infinitum via the screen, Kennedy's exploding head one moment, a sexy advert for deodorant two moments later ensuring the autoeroticic death is available as pornography in hyperreality for all time. America's twentieth-century fever-dream, its nightmare and its beauty captured within the ephemera of moving celluloid, overcomes all in its wake.

Ballard has stated that the novel's setting is intended to be nondescript or to be blankly reminiscent of post-industrial urban landscapes anywhere. "*Crash* is set not in Shepperton but in the area around London airport which I see as a paradigmatic landscape of the late twentieth century. Wherever you go in the world, the road from the airport is always the same, and that's very peculiar" (Ballard, Lewis 38). It is the pursuance of *automobilic* autoerotic transcendence in *Crash* that is particularly attuned to American (technological) mythology, perhaps more so than to any other nation. Britain, of course, experienced nuclear terror as the United States did. Accepting Gannon's frontierist thesis of the Bomb, however, and Slotkin's powerful argument in *Regeneration*, America's mythology was much more attuned to the technological apocalyptic. The totalizing logic of the Bomb, which secularized the *means* of apocalypse, did not destroy the mythologies of regenerative violence but absorbed them and reconstituted them into new narratives about U.S. technical supremacy. God's apocalyptic power had been handed over to his ordained people when American science and technology mastered nature's most destructive force, allowing the United States to defeat evil, as was always its destiny. For Kubrick, DeLillo and Ballard, however, the technique (mechanical rationalization/technocracy) cannot contain the latent or sublimated violence of the technical (nuclear weapons); and so in *Strangelove* mechanical logic leads to the supremely logical conclusion of total annihilation, in *End Zone* the individual subject almost ceases to exist in the fog of nuclear gobbledygook and imperatives towards mechanical efficiency, and in *Crash* the car becomes a symbolic vehicle for the latent and manifest violence in a technologically dehumanizing system, ruled as it is by the Bomb and its representation, neoliberal capitalism.

The realization of the Enlightenment project to secularize the means of rule truly occurred in post–World War II United States with the advent of social sciences that were developed on the basis of Game Theoretical nuclear strategies. These new models for social organization were imbued with paranoia and radical individualism. The removal of God from the primary position of apocalyptic dictator to a mediatory position has arguably changed the form of the apocalypse in American mythology from a collective and all-encompassing event to one made up of infinitesimal atomized individual actions. In *Crash* the car and camera have thusly atomized the apocalypse according to the logic of late capitalism.[31] Under the dictates of the Bomb's technological apocalypse, the deeply instantiated American myth of the regenerative power of violence has reconstituted into miniature fragmentary apocalypses, which coalesce in *Crash* into autogeddon, occurring when individuals or small groups of individuals co-mingle their energies in an explosion of transformative violence. In *Crash*'s conception, the apocalyptic mythology of regeneration is enacted via technology's latent violence in a sublimated and diversified form, fragmented, yet for the crash group, still containing the old promise of rebirth and communion. The upshot of our religious affair with our technology (which is, of course, naturally imbued with all of our mythologies, hopes and nightmares at the point of its inception) is not a more rational world, but one in which our deepest fears and desires are enacted via this reciprocal communion.

The search for transcendence and freedom in American mythology, in essence, contradicts the technocratic imperative towards control. Control is the antithesis of spontaneity and freedom presupposes chaos (unpredictability) to some degree, thus this inherent contradiction causes moral discontinuities in American life and among the rest of its cultural and corporate colonies. The American mythology of individual freedom, which is continuously recapitulated through the media apparatus, is internalized into the

II. End Zone *and* Crash

culture to the extent that it is tantamount to a religion in its own right. The problem with freedom from a political point of view is that it is an abstract concept, one that can be interpreted endlessly by citizens of free countries, and by those in power. God's demotion to the position of intermediary of apocalypses and miracles via man's control of technology, means, in effect, that Christian morality is now superimposed onto the culture, after the fact. Christian morality no longer emanates from the center, it is an afterthought to the smooth running of an efficiently productive society—a palliative to the mass of human suffering in an inherently psychopathological culture, as Ballard sees it. The utopianists in *Crash* embody the most fundamental aspects of American mythology, religious transcendence, regenerative violence, freedom from control, and they do so, not by retreating from technology but by transmuting its latent libidinal and regenerative elements into religious rituals for the twentieth century—the car and camera as technological Eucharist for the new rites of transcendence and freedom.

Technology, Mythology and Transcendence

Ballard's vision of transcendence for the utopian cell in *Crash* is necessarily ambivalent, as our cultural relationship with technology in general seems to be inherently ambivalent. To this end, *Crash* evokes both what is alien to us in technology and how this may be translated into expressions of essential humanity. In this way, Ballard attempts to straddle a middle ground between pragmatic humanism and naive technophilia. The novel can be classified as speculative fiction, according to Margaret Atwood's summation of that genre, in that the technology around which it is based is contemporary and real, and as Beckman observes, its attachments to material history are anachronistically dated. It is the reverse, in some sense, of an author like Dick, who put man in the midst of a future technology that wields unimaginable power, in order to interrogate the morality (or lack) of contemporary man. Ballard sees an objectification and dehumanization of human beings under the auspices of techno-capitalism, imagines where this might lead the evolution of morality, and locates the exaggerated pathology he has imagined not in the future but in the present.

Beckman develops the metaphorical correlation in *Crash* between the cars and roads upon which they travel and frames and film upon which images travel into the collective consciousness. She does so in an effort to posit the novel in terms of its pop art influences—Warhol's infatuation with film and the blurred boundaries of artistic media—in order to illuminate its transformative aspects. *Crash* is a highly visual novel, stylized and cinematic, as if it is a translation of a hallucinogenic episode that is somehow filmed by Ballard's mind, into a novel: "*Crash* might be classified as a Pop novel primarily because it engages the question of what it means to translate the visual landscapes of Pop—its paintings, its photographs, and particularly its films—into the form of a novel" (Beckman100).

Vaughan's car signals that his obsessions lie in the decade when the car and camera became the transformers of ontological experience. The novel remains neutral in tone and representation of its neo-sex acts as, to judge the acts of his protagonists would be to undermine the thrust of the novel's force, and would also, ironically, imbue the novel with an inbuilt obsolescence in a world that was already at the time of its writing tending towards posthuman.[32] The clock cannot be turned back, at least not by human will. In interviews, Ballard has also been adamant that he is not in any way anti-technology.[33] Yet the novel is undoubtedly a warning about where our current system may lead. Ballard takes what he sees as the pathology of contemporary late-capitalism that is latent in our relationship with technology, the need for purifying violence and total objectification of nature and total control of our world—"manslaughter on a gigantic scale"—and projects it into the present or near future where its logic, literally, terminates (Lewis, 29). The car and camera in *Crash* are thus quasi-allegorical, they signal for Ballard, the psychological places that "the ever-more complex technologies of the future," technologies that necessarily remain as yet unimagined, will lead us (148).

American Heat and Reagan's Potlatch

In his comparison of the respective merits of Ballard's *Crash* and the subsequent David Cronenberg film adaptation, Chris Rodley describes the novel as "overheated" (*Cronenberg on Cronenberg* 189).[34] It is difficult to take on this criticism for a number of reasons, not least that the heat of the novel is undoubtedly deliberate on Ballard's part, as it is representative of the heat of postmodern life. As such, the dynamic and destructive energy wielded through technology is symbolized by the automobile and more importantly the automobile crash in the novel. What the novel achieves, in this regard, is the explication of an Oedipal post-nuclear techno-human landscape, a cold psychopathological mechanism, that nevertheless retains the dirt and heat of corporeal and psychological humanity. In Ballard's *Crash*, the postnuclear industrial world is an empire of energy, under the sign of the Bomb. This empire of energy manifested in America in the 1980s in Reagan's Star Wars program.

The novel *Crash* adopts Burroughs's depictions of energy or lifeforce vis-a-vis autoerotic death. *The Soft Machine* for example, features auto-erotic deaths by asphyxiation in Burroughs's cut-up style. This event in the *Soft Machine*, whereby the energy released by a violent death and in particular a violent sexual death, is quasi-holy. The thermodynamic aspect of Burroughs and Ballard's writing—where energy, death, sex, heat co-mingle—is the friction of essential human desire. In this sense the United States of America—in all its movement, endeavor, restless optimism, violence, in the dynamics of a nation of approximately 324 million people who believe it is their divine right to be free together in all their differences, (and what that means in terms of energy-consumption)—is a veritable sun of endothermic heat. Ballard's *Crash*, in its transgression and brutality, captures this sense of American heat.

In the 1990s North America had probably just begun to absorb the consequences of Ronald Reagan's two terms as president. The wholesale dismantling of industry, the asset stripping liquidation of hundreds of thousands of unionized working class jobs in the course of the decade had a huge effect on the country.[35] Many regulatory government bodies such as those of competition, consumer rights and standards were dismantled and the tenets of their operations were left to the mechanics of the free market, according to the doctrine of the Chicago School of Economics and its guru Milton Friedman. Friedman was a close advisor to the Reagan administration, which implemented the radical neoliberal economic policies that he proposed.[36] The fall of the Berlin Wall was instantaneously mythologized as the final and total victory of capitalist democracy in Francis Fukuyama's "The End of History?" (1989) and *The End of History and the Last Man* (1992). The fall of communism left no ideological barriers in the way of capitalism, its rationality could be reified, and according to the myth, the utopian project ordained by God had triumphed over the evil other once more. When it became clearer, to informed and balanced analysts, that the Soviet Union collapsed as a result of a complex of political and socio-economic reasons, there were some among Reagan's followers who claimed that his multi-trillion dollar Star Wars plan was deliberately put in place in order to bankrupt the Soviet Union.[37]

The Star Wars debacle is indicative of Reagan's presidency in that it is a sumptuary expenditure of enormous quantities of currency (that had undoubtedly, in part at least, been unlocked by the asset stripping of industry in the country) on what had become in every conceivable way a virtual war.[38] This huge expenditure takes on the aspect of a kind of Potlatch. According to Bataille's concept of the general economy, this huge expenditure of energy (once the currency has been changed from money to resources and effort in this case) is sumptuary, and displays the power of the United States, as judged by what it can afford to waste. Star Wars was a Potlatch, then, not in its ancient gift-giving sense, but in its virtual violence. Ballard, in typically prescient form, brought the Oedipal, the violent and the hyperreal in Reagan together in the non-narrative section of *The Atrocity Exhibition* called "Why I Want to Fuck Ronald Reagan." Nick Davis extrapolates these Reagan-related aspects of Ballard's fiction in his essay "'An Unrehearsed Theatre of Technology': Oedipalization and Vision in Ballard's Crash": "In this account the propagation of Reaganite politics involves, like infantile passage through the Oedipus complex, the installation of a set of directing wishes, felt to empower, as the subject's own; the conversion of trauma into empowerment is, once again, attended by strong effects of lawlike-ness and binding necessity—successful oedipalization is an epiphany of Law" (*Imagining Apocalypse* 139). In other words, in his paternal role, Reagan is both enforcer and transgressor of the law: "The imaginary prohibitor and definer of law-like desires is thus, latently, the one who escapes the Law's operation (Lacan writes "*perversion*" as "*pére-version*," or turning towards the imaginary Father). Evocations of sexual obscenity and lawless brutality in Reagan's media self-presentation can thus be strangely complicit with the establishment of Reagan as a paternally reassuring, benevolent political leader" (*Imagining Apocalypse* 140).

In this section of *The Atrocity Exhibition*, Ballard conceives of a variety of virtual, imagined, or real instances in which (in the late 1960s) Reagan is involved in auto accidents: "Powerful erotic fantasies of an anal-sadistic character surrounded the image of the Presidential contender" (165). Ballard thus elides the psychopathological, and the technological (both media and auto-apocalyptic) that were embodied in Reagan, and Ballard's insight foreshadows the characteristics of the decade in which Reagan would assume the Presidency. The liquidation of assets into currency that characterize Reagan's economic policies effectively concentrated American wealth—took currency, buying power, freedom from many citizens and pooled it in institutions, in

II. End Zone *and* Crash

investment banks and large corporations, to which only an already wealthy and privileged class had access.

American wars—the Cold War and its terminal logic in Star Wars as exemplary—became the twisted Potlatches of an empire of energy. In other words, the technological apocalypse was fully virtualized, yet, in Reagan's outward persona, and in his fundamentalist Christian faith, the apocalypse remained.[39] The vestigial element of the Christian apocalypse was still powerful in the American psyche as an ultimate Potlatch, a sacrificial release of endothermic energy, a transformation into the essence of the universe. The Reagan Administration's sacrifice to God was the labor, the suffering and the poverty of millions; what had been taken from them by a cruel chief was given over to a virtual technological apocalypse—the new theology. Ballard's "Crash" and "Why I Want to Fuck Ronald Reagan," presage this psychopathological Potlatch, and his criticism was indeed prescient of the Reagan Administration politics that were to emerge in the 1980s.[40]

Bret Easton Ellis's *American Psycho* (1991) and Oliver Stone's film *Wall Street* (1987) engender an American 1980s both psychopathological and rapacious in keeping with this view of Reagan's era (Thatcher in Britain; Haughey in Ireland). Gordon Gekko's dictum "greed is good" worked its way into the lexicon of popular American culture, a quintessentially naked 1980s statement, and an affirmation of the rational/mechanical logic of radical capitalism that traces its roots back to *The Wealth of Nations* or Mandeville's enigmatic *The Fable of the Bees*. Ellis's novel, however, externalizes the psychopathology in a most explicit way, with dark humor. Ellis's narrator, the Wall Street investment banker Patrick Bateman, is a paragon of empty vanity, greed and hypocrisy. Bateman describes for the reader at length, his daily health and beauty routine, listing the brand-name products he uses on himself with the fastidiousness of an actuary. The narrative takes the reader with Bateman as he travels from restaurant to restaurant, having heartless conversations with heartless acquaintances, having meaningless, heartless trysts with one-dimensional (from his own point of view) women, and treating his well-meaning secretary at his work office like a servant. Without missing a beat, the narrative intermittently describes sadistic and brutal murders that Bateman carries out, in detail as foul and explicit as has possibly ever been published, and his appreciation of the products and pop music of the day. One such random murder that Bateman carries out is on a homeless man and his dog near an ATM Bateman is using. Bateman pretends to be sympathetic to the man before he kicks the dog to death and stabs the old man. This episode, in a vicious irony typical of the novel, is juxtaposed with a non-narrative vignette, of which there are a number throughout, whereby Bateman ruminates on the merits of Phil Collins' poignant songs about the plight of the homeless. For Ellis, the emptiness, hypocrisy and psychopathology of 1980s Reaganism had insinuated itself into the heart of the culture.

Ellis's novel and Stone's film are good examples of critical fictional responses to the brutality of the Reagan years; however, the effects of the processes of unbridled capitalist rationalization post–Soviet break up are not as fully captured in any one work of film or fiction throughout the 1980s and 1990s as the seminal television program *The Wire*, which first aired in 2002. *The Wire* takes up its story where Reagan's industrial liquidation has eviscerated Baltimore's working middle class with consequent enormous rises in poverty and all its attendant ills, crime in particular. This crime is policed according to capitalist-rational models that have their origins in the social science models of the early American nuclear age.

Chapter III

The Wire and Game Theory
"All in the Game"

> Habitually, people treat the realities of personality and association and city as abstractions, while they treat confused pragmatic abstractions such as money, credit, political sovereignty, as if they are concrete realities that had an existence independent of human conventions.
> —Lewis Mumford, *The Culture of Cities*, 25

> At best, our metropolises are the ultimate aspiration of community, the repository for every myth and hope of people clinging to the sides of the pyramid that is capitalism. At worst, our cities—or those places in our cities where most of us fear to tread—are vessels for the darkest contradictions and most brutal competitions that underlie the way we actually live together, or fail to live together.
> —David Simon (Creator of *The Wire*), *The Wire: Truth Be Told*, 4

> The individual's self-preservation presupposes his adjustment to the requirements for the preservation of the system.
> —Max Horkheimer, *Eclipse of Reason*, 143

Introduction

The chapters of this book are presented in a chronological order. At its core is an inquiry into American postnuclear technique via those texts that engage with it most expressly and insightfully. In terms of chronology, the three previous texts analyzed are relatively close together and in consecutive decades, while this chapter's analysis of *The Wire* bypasses the 1980s and '90s to focus on a more contemporary moment. *The Wire* is here analyzed because it offers an accurate depiction of the effects of social science modeling systems (developed during the Cold War) on individuals and the city they populate. In this sense, this chapter moves away from the specifically nuclear element—while continuing to engage the specter of apocalypticism, as this is an ever-present in American culture—to focus on the dehumanizing systemic effects prevalent in the postnuclear society *The Wire* so comprehensively and uniquely depicts.

The Wire is an extremely dense text that in its five seasons and sixty hour-long episodes weaves one of the most complex television narratives yet produced. *The Wire* is often referred to as a visual novel, and its creator David Simon admits to its literary aspirations: "I really regard the structure of the show to be novelistic. That sounds pretentious, but frankly, the show has literary pretensions" (Ducker 4).[1] This chapter therefore focuses on *The Wire*'s interrogation of what it posits as a capitalism-as-game paradigm more than on discussing the tropes of the medium.[2]

Demonstrating how free-market capitalism in the mode of the Game paradigm can cause social dysfunction is an extraordinarily difficult task for a work of fiction. For instance, the implications of the use of performance targets in institutional life are manifold and infinitesimal across the spectrum of even one typical city. *The Wire* achieves this with the breadth of its scope and the accuracy of its detailing, what Linda Williams refers to as its ethnographic approach.[3] There is no doubt it is more effective, in this regard, in the television medium, than would be possible to achieve in the standard runtime of a commercial film. Its detailing from micro to macro of the political system is tuned precisely by the subtlety and pathos of its characters and how they operate within it. Adapting and getting by is essentially human. In an amoral and brutally competitive system, codes of ethics and morality are secondary to survival (or advancement) and this is the case for both the political elite and for those involved in the drugs trade, even though the blood on one's hands may be more immediate in the former instance. *The Wire*, then, while deeply critical of postnuclear institutional life and somewhat bleak in its portrayal of our collective social failure to see the wood for the trees, nevertheless locates the failures of our societies not in innate human selfishness or hardwired violence but in our failure to organize our institutions around the considerations of living well together.

From season one through five, different urban bureaucratic institutions are examined. Season one focuses primarily on the police department, in

III. The Wire *and Game Theory*

particular a special crimes unit that pursues a sophisticated drug gang. Season two examines the operation of a stevedore union and the smuggling that takes place on Baltimore's docks, including human trafficking and heroin importation. Season three focuses on the political system, in particular how grinding friction between the mayoral office and police brass causes suffering on the streets. Season three also has a fascinating take on the War on Drugs and their prohibition, which is discussed later in this chapter in the context of the illusion of social and institutional functionality. Season four focuses on the failure of the education system and the tragic irony of George W. Bush's No Child Left Behind policy. The fifth and final season, widening the scope of its critical purview yet further, takes in the inner machinations of a local Baltimore newspaper called the *Baltimore Sun* (a real Baltimore newspaper). Over its seasons, the series manages to incorporate the new plotlines into the overall narrative framework, dropping few of the old narrative strands, to depict the interconnectivity of the system, the people, and the events from micro to macro level.

The Wire is, unsurprisingly, the work of a duo of writers with knowledge of the inside workings of American bureaucratic institutions. Unsurprisingly also, perhaps, given the show's iconoclastic tendencies towards the conventions of the medium, the pair came from outside of the television industry's power base in Hollywood.[4] The show's creator and executive producer, David Simon, is a former journalist, police reporter, and novelist. His text, *Homicide: A Year on the Killing Streets*, was the basis for the television series *Homicide: Life on the Street*. He also co-authored a book with Ed Burns, the other producer and chief writer of *The Wire*, called *The Corner: A Year in the Life of an Inner City Neighborhood*, upon which an award winning *HBO* mini-series *The Corner* was based. Burns has had previous career incarnations as both a Baltimore Police detective, working on high-end wire-tapped drug cases, and following that, he worked as a teacher in an inner-city Baltimore school for seven years.

From the Cold War to Here

In its scope *The Wire* focuses upon the institutional systems of the municipal body, which are run according to the models and ideology of Game Theory as detailed in the introduction. Fred Kaplan's *The Wizards of Armageddon* and Adam Curtis's *The Trap* illuminate the means by which

Game Theoretical deterrence strategies, as are so accurately portrayed in *Strangelove*, became reified in the form of American social science models. Curtis's *The Trap* features interviews with former RAND employees who are advocates of quantitative social science and who designed the institutional models that were implemented in the 1980s. One such interviewee is Alain Enthoven. As discussed in the introductory chapter, the method of Systems Analysis, along with James Buchanan's Public Choice Theory, is founded upon the assumption that all individuals in any given system are driven by self-interest. In the interest of efficiency, thereby, all voters, employees, clients or indeed any members of an institutional body must be motivated thusly.[5]

Enthoven implemented the Performance Target method of individual motivation in the NHS system in Britain at Margaret Thatcher's behest, despite its disastrous use in the Vietnam War. In Vietnam, the performance target for the United States troops was known as the body count.[6] The Performance Target sets a nominal statistical target for the individual to reach in their given role. If the person reaches their target they will be rewarded in some way. On the other hand, if they fail to reach their numerical target they will be punished in some way. It is understood that individuals must be incentivized to do their utmost in any given role. The word incentivize is a readily familiar jargon term that is now part of everyday speech among commentators and talking heads spanning Western media. Its usage is a conscious or otherwise acceptance by the user that humans are inherently and primarily motivated by greed and it is at the core of neoliberal philosophy. The punishment or reward attached to these incentivized targets in most cases is monetary. Its first practical application in the Vietnam War as the body count involved the incentivization of U.S. troops to surpass a nominal target of enemies killed. The method, however, saw soldiers lie about their own targets or much worse, shoot innocent civilians and count them as enemy. This was a nightmare manifestation of the "juking of stats" which foreshadows *The Wire*'s portrayal of institutional corruption across Baltimore's police, education and political systems. By discarding the abstract linguistic and conceptual motivations that had underpinned pre–Cold War bureaucracy, such as common good, patriotism and so forth, and replacing them with the fundamental motivation of self-advancement, these models, it was thought, would herald a new era of institutional efficiency. What *The Wire* details so carefully in its depiction of these institutions, however, is not bureaucratic efficiency but a quagmire of corruption involving quantified judgments that have little bearing on or relation to reality.

III. The Wire *and Game Theory*

This chapter proposes that in the parallax view created by Cold War free-market instrumentalism, it is not efficiency that modern institutions require but the appearance of such. According to the neoclassical economics upon which these Cold War Game models are based, the individual is an instrument of the economy. The financial virtualization of the global economy, however, has disconnected wealth from the means of its production. In other words, Baudrillard's assessment in *The Consumer Society*, that the free-market logic of growth takes primacy above all other considerations within this system, is correct. Quality of life for those who are disconnected from the wealth their work generates is inconsequential to the requirements of growth. In *The Wire*'s narrative those who are disconnected and disenfranchised from officially sanctioned institutions are the underclass of urban America, whose drugs trade generates untold amounts of wealth that nevertheless feeds into the greater economy. Neither the illegality of the mode of wealth generation nor the suffering caused by it bears any relevance to the fully virtualized economy.

The War on Drugs thus becomes part of the framework of the Game paradigm: those at the bottom of the social hierarchy operate the drugs trade on the ground and the police partake in the illusion of policing by generating minor drug-arrest statistics. Many of those who have served their usage in bolstering the statistics generated by the War on Drugs end up as fodder for the prison-industrial complex too, where they can be further mined for profit. Where once the working class sold their labor in the manufacturing and production industries, so many who are now surplus to the requirements of labor with automation, de-industrialization and financialization are corporally exploited in a new way, through incarceration. The profits come on the double as tax payers fund privately owned prison facilities, while the inmates are often put to work manufacturing goods as close to free labor. The huge racial disparity of the United States prison population tells its own story too. The exploitation of the bodies of African Americans for profit continues into the twenty-first century, slavery in a new form. For all the deprivation, disenfranchisement, suffering and human energy that is poured into the War on Drugs, the only real outcome, according to *The Wire*, is alienated institutional factions within America's institutional Game paradigm and the unraveling of American exceptionalist myths.

What the statistical models produce, are illusory fallacies of functionality and efficiency based upon quantitative judgments, the real purpose of which is to adhere at all times to the logic of the bottom line. The weaving of this logic into the core of institutional life, in turn, has a powerful effect on the behavior of the individuals who populate the institutions. Horkheimer's observation that: "[t]he individual's self-preservation presupposes his adjustment to the requirements for the preservation of the system," is precisely the case as far as *The Wire*'s depiction goes (99–100).

In this sense, in their extremely narrow and limiting concepts Buchanan, Nash, Enthoven and other Cold War technocrats have built a social framework, in conjunction with the tenets of the global financial free market, in which internecine competition and paranoia are inbuilt. In the process of adaptation many individuals will adhere to their environmental requirements, and so the behavior of those who are locked into a system of internecine competition will naturally reflect the selfishness and paranoia that the system is based upon. The characters of *The Wire* are often shown to be motivated by selfish desires, occasionally by empathy and by senses of social responsibility, but their motivations are never characterized as simply rational and predictable according to the narrow neoclassical definition of self-advancement. Detective McNulty (Dominic West), for example, is undoubtedly driven by vanity in his relentless pursuit of the leaders of the Barksdale and Stanfield gangs but his endeavors jeopardize the institution to which he belongs and this effectively destroys his career. McNulty is often aware that his actions will have a destructive effect on his career, yet persists in his actions regardless. In other words, human desires, motivations and actions are infinitely more complex than that which the concept of rationality underpinning neoliberal economics allows.

The Wire is realistic in its characterization of human behavior, thereby acknowledging its complexity, while demonstrating the influence that institutions have over peoples' behavior. The current of human agency on a day-to-day and moment-by-moment basis is channeled by the need for survival, which is institutionally dictated. In this regard Gray writes: "The mass of mankind is ruled not by its intermittent moral sensations, less still by self-interest, but by the needs of the moment" (*Straw Dogs* 17). The needs of the moment, as depicted in *The Wire*, are very often dictated by the institution to which the character belongs: subjects of the often physically brutal street narcotics trade are driven by the needs of their survival as are those subjected to the numbers games of the political, police or school systems in their way. The series creator David Simon is clear on the matter of institutional influence over behavior:

III. The Wire *and Game Theory*

> One of the things we were very conscious of was that our heavies not to be completely venal. They can have that tendency, they can do what they need to do to survive at the top of an institution but Burrell [Police Commissioner] is not an effectively corrupt character, he is self-preserving. He cares about preserving himself and ultimately the department more than he cares about the department's ultimate purpose of police work ["The Target," audio commentary].

Having said this, there are certainly characters in *The Wire* with highly developed senses of empathy and there are those who seem to completely lack empathy for others. The latter are more prevalent at the tops of their respective institutional hierarchies. The character of Marlo Stanfield (Jamie Hector) is of particular interest in this regard. Stanfield becomes the drug lord of West Baltimore for the last two of *The Wire*'s five seasons but unlike his predecessors, Stringer Bell (Idris Elba) and Avon Barksdale (Wood Harris), he is particularly dehumanized. Unlike Bell and Barksdale, he does not seem to believe in any narrative, personal or collective, beyond the cultivation of his ruthless reputation in West Baltimore and to a much lesser extent the acquisition of wealth. As is discussed in detail later, Stanfield's psychopathic lack of empathy for others is in step with the destruction of binding narratives that radical capitalism appears to self-fulfillingly give rise to.

Fated by Institutions

The quantified judgments and targets that the Game Theoretical models are based upon adhere fundamentally to economic requirements. In *The Wire*, for example, the mayor's office constantly pressurizes the police management to reduce the overall crime rates, as the murder rate, in particular, is bad for appearances, which in turn is bad for business. The judgment of functional policing, thereby, is prescribed by financial economics and not by qualitative judgments such as quality of life.

In our contemporary Western democracies, this arrangement is tweaked and advanced by the Game models, which apply the logic of the market to bureaucratic institutions. The health services, police forces, school systems and other cornerstone institutions of modern Western states, if not yet completely given over to private interests, are nevertheless run like private entities where the quantified judgments adhere not to the nominal functions of the respective institutions but ultimately to the cost-effective logic of the bottom line. Thus, our institutions are plugged in to the implacable dictates of the global free-market economy. In turn, individuals within these institutions direct their energy towards sustaining themselves, which in turn sustains the institution and the system, according to the presiding framework of competitive struggle.

The Wire's literary and philosophical approach to portraying the implacable institutions of municipal Baltimore and the individuals that populate them, thereby, is not Shakespearean or Dickensian, instead it is reminiscent of the narrative tropes of ancient Greek tragedy. In *The Wire*'s depiction the institutions assume the roles of the implacable Greek gods of the pantheon. The institutions are beholden to the logic of unfettered capitalism and it is the violation of this logic that invariably sees these vengeful gods throwing lightning bolts and "hitting people on the ass." Simon explains the choice of Greek tragedy as the most pertinent reference for the fated nature of life as a subject of postindustrial institutions:

> We're stealing instead from an earlier, less-traveled construct—the Greeks—lifting our thematic stance wholesale from Aeschylus, Sophocles, Euripides to create doomed and fated protagonists who confront a *rigged game* and their own mortality. The modern mind—particularly those of us in the West—finds such fatalism ancient and discomfiting, I think. We are a pretty self-actualized, self-worshipping crowd of postmoderns and the idea that for all our wherewithal and discretionary income and leisure, we're still fated by indifferent gods, feels to us antiquated and superstitious. We don't accept our gods on such terms anymore; by and large, with the exception of the fundamentalists among us, we don't even grant Yaweh himself that kind of unbridled interventionist authority.... But instead of the old gods, *The Wire* is a Greek tragedy in which the postmodern institutions are the Olympian forces. It's the police department, or the drug economy, or the political structures, or the school administration, or the macroeconomic forces that are throwing the lightning bolts and hitting people in the ass for no good reason [Alvarez 384].

Those police in *The Wire* who try to do the work that their institution is nominally required to do, more often than not are halted in their tracks for economic reasons (if their investigations are too costly) or, more critically, if their investigations are in danger of exposing the wider systemic corruption they are invariably stripped of their power and silenced. Those who are ruthless and savvy enough, on the other hand, spend their energy eliminating their competition and sustaining the illusions of systemic efficacy so as to maintain and advance their positions within the institutions. Thus, in *The Wire*'s analysis, under the all-pervasive and powerful logic of the bottom line, society's energy serves the maintenance and preservation of the institutions, not the other way around.

III. The Wire and Game Theory

The Destruction of Social Narratives

The crucible for Game Theory was, of course, Cold War American technocracy and in this regard its basis in radical individualism is pro forma. What began with von Neumann and Nash during the height of the Cold War was a mathematical concept that claimed objectivity but was in reality steeped in ideological opposition to communism and all that it entailed. To copper fasten the theory's intrinsic bias, both men happened to vehemently loath communism, and so Game Theory was naturally antithetical to collectivism of any kind. According to the reasoning of the power elite, the advent of the Bomb required a scientific and completely objective framework for rational decision making. Game Theory, assuming capitalist doctrine at its most maximal, or anti-communist according to the polarized ideology of the time, provided the solution. The Game Theoretical solution, it was deemed, had much more vast applications than to just the Cold War but to all competitive interactions, the essence of capitalist society itself, and so, over a short space of time became the sovereign and incontrovertible model for social science in America. The theory assumes self-interest as the fundamental social force and sees cooperation only as a function of self-advancement. The radically individualist (and radically anti-communist) foundations of Game Theory's fundamental assumptions, stemming from the ideology of unfettered free-marketeerism, were completely aligned with those of the radical neoliberal economics that arose in the 1980s under the advisement of Milton Friedman. Simon writes: "Our economic and political leaders are dismissive of the horror, at points even flippant in their derision. Margaret Thatcher's suggestion that there is no society to consider beyond the individual and his family speaks volumes in the clarity of its late-20th-century contempt for the ideal of nation states offering anything approximating a sense of communal purpose or meaning" (Alvarez 6).

The updated Game Theoretical social models, such as those emerging from Alain Enthoven's Systems Analysis and James Buchanan's Public Choice Theory, have substituted social narratives like common good, racial pride and community for the non-narrative of individualism.[7] What *Crash* and *End Zone*, in particular, astutely grapple with is the destruction of binding narratives by the dictates of capitalist instrumentalism. *The Wire* looks more directly at the consequences and ramifications of the positioning of this non-narrative individualism at the heart of peoples' struggle to survive and get by. In *The Wire*'s extensive detailing of an empire in decline, binding narratives and core American myths of equality and justice are unraveled by the institutional requirements of unencumbered capitalism. Nowhere are these factors more prevalent than in the disenfranchised neighborhoods of urban America, upon which *The Wire* bases much of its analysis. Sheehan and Sweeney correctly identify *The Wire*'s focus on the effects of the unraveling of binding narratives, for the urban poor in particular: "Unemployment, underemployment, the priorities of the stats game, the victory of rampant capitalism have destroyed not only this world that made sense, but the prescriptive narratives and solidarities that grew from it. The labor movement, the black power movement and the ideals of empowerment through education have all been debased and eviscerated" (12–13). Stringer Bell's narrative is discussed in relation to this argument later in this chapter. The drug lord's former belief in black pride and racial uplift is corrupted by his adherence to the primary function of capitalism: acquisition at all costs.

Capitalism as Game: Unraveled Narratives and Unsustainable Myths

Among those involved in selling illegal narcotics in *The Wire*'s Baltimore the street dictum "it's all in the game," is a daily creed, a reminder that any slip, or any display of weakness can result in losing the game. The narcotics trade is a mirror for legitimate capitalism, which is the greater, sanctioned Game that is largely exclusionary or biased along class and racial lines. In this version, however, the rules are different and the hierarchy more precarious. The capitalism-as-game motif is consistently restated throughout the program's five seasons and sixty episodes. Although the dictum "it's all in the game" is most often used to denote the illegal drugs trade, it is acknowledged by characters from all walks of life, from the barely post-pubescent drug touts on the street corners to their bosses the drug lords, through their institutional counterparts the police and on up the official chain through career police, lawyers, judges and politicians. The Game for those on the illegitimate side of the law's divide, is played by harsher rules, a rawer form of capitalism, whereby failure can mean death; those on the official side of the divide play by the rules of the statistics games. On the side of officialdom, the competition is no less fierce, the consequences of loss, however, are less stark.

The postnuclear capitalist Game paradigm has dictated to *The Wire*'s Baltimore, therefore, not efficiency but a primordial, paranoid competitiveness. On the illegitimate side of the law, this competition is enacted on the basis of brutality. On the legitimate side, on institutional corruption, that is, the juking of stats. What can be seen in *The Wire* therefore, in the context of the previous texts analyzed, is a realistic portrait of the manifestations of postnuclear technocracy and technology in a typical contemporary Western city. *Strangelove* makes fun of Cold War technocrats' attempts to apply an uber-rationality to a fundamentally insane situation. Much of this uber-rational methodology took the form of Game Theoretical deterrence strategies which assume that what is in an individual's (or group's) self-interest is rational and, vice versa, that rationality is self-interestedness.[8] This rationale is unraveled in *Strangelove* by the revelation that rationality is a notional construct that is culturally prescribed and that the substitution of machine-logic for what Dr. Strangelove derisively calls "human meddling" (in the form of the doomsday device) amounts to the terminal logic of death as the end of all irrationality and contradiction. What both *Strangelove* and *End Zone* argue is that the attempts to rationalize human interaction by replacing human emotional responses with the means of quantification are doomed to fail as they can never encapsulate or account for our irrationality.

Much of the primary focus of *The Wire*, as stated, is an interrogation of the fundamental aspects of America's exceptionalist mythology. In *The Wire* the promise that hard work and ingenuity are naturally rewarded in America is held up against the reality that the only means of acquisition for an ever-increasing number of Americans who find themselves redundant in its postindustrial landscape is through crime. The Game paradigm, according to *The Wire*, dictates that only the most ruthless and dehumanized players achieve success or wealth. This wealth, for those on the wrong side of the law's divide, however, is nevertheless both rarefied and invariably short-lived, while the majority of the underclass suffers in dire poverty. Essentially—and crucially, in regard to this book's investigation—*The Wire* responds in its own polemic to the narrative void that is left in the wake of the dictates of instrumental rationality and neoliberal economics. As Sennett astutely observes in *Culture of the New Capitalism*, "Most people are not like this; they need a sustaining life narrative, they take pride in being good at something specific, and they value the experiences they've lived through. The cultural ideal required in new institutions thus damages many of the people who inhabit them" (Sennett 5).

The Wire imparts this sense that the narratives and mythologies by which America (as an ideological nation) sustains itself are no longer tenable in the face of its overwhelmingly contradictory reality. The coming into being of the Bomb and its Cold War secular theology of individualistic quantified rationality has undermined the myth of America as a just and inclusive society. In *The Wire*'s portrayal of criminal enterprise simply as a matter of self-preservation, wealth-acquisition for its own sake, career advancement for its own sake and so forth, there is the sense of the death of collective narrative and the mortal wound to the basics of the American Dream. The psychopathology that Ballard predicted is manifested, not in the dramatic acts of radical extremists operating outside of society, but is intrinsic to the system of competition itself and a conduit for the more ruthless and baser human traits.

American Institutional Fiction in *The Wire*

The Wire's portrait is undoubtedly one of an empire in decline due to the unsustainable contradiction between America's core myths and the reality of life in America for a growing number of disenfranchised citizens. When *The Wire* was first aired on *HBO* in 2002 the global economy was in the midst of a boom and when the fifth and final season finished in 2008 the global economy was on the precipice of its huge and sustained recession. The numbers of disenfranchised Americans have vastly increased since *The Wire* has ended. Its main thematic concerns, therefore, regarding the death of work in postindustrial America, which has swept a large swathe of the population of former working and middle class into poverty, has never been more relevant. *The Wire* illustrates the irrefutable pull of the urban narcotics trade for those who in real terms have no other means by which to earn a living. It is also attractive to those more ambitious and ruthless characters that ascribe to the American myth that anyone can make it and who regard it as an opportunity to display the signs of success in the semiotics of conspicuous consumption. The policing of prohibition—its labeling as the War on Drugs (echoing Slotkin's thesis of regenerative violence)—is revealed in *The Wire*'s narrative to be a chimera and a fallacy that actually thwarts real policing and is instead a war on those surplus people who make up America's underclass.

The first season of *The Wire* focuses on the dysfunction of the drug war and, as David Simon puts it, self-sustaining "postmodern institutions devouring the individuals they are supposed to serve or who serve them" (Alvarez 387). In this regard, *The Wire* sets up a narrative trope that runs throughout

III. The Wire and Game Theory

its five seasons, whereby the policing and criminal institutions are held up to mirror each other. They are seen to be co-dependent institutions within an autotelic system, the Game paradigm of virtualized neoliberal economics. In other words, the game according to the street dictum is cops versus criminals, but as part of the overall Game, the neoliberal economy, the dividing line of the law is irrelevant to the processes of capital acquisition and more generally economic growth. The quantitative models by which *The Wire*'s Baltimore Police Department is run do not reduce or thwart the drugs trade in any significant way; instead, they create the illusion of effective policing. Similarly, the statistical models of the schools and political systems create not efficacy and functionality but the appearances of such. What the illusion masks, in *The Wire*'s depiction, is entrenched and rapidly increasing social decay and human suffering, on one hand, and entrenched systemic corruption within the official institutions, on the other.

The second season switches its focus dramatically to examine the consequences of, as Simon puts it, the "death of work and the destruction of the American working class in the postindustrial era" (Alvarez, 387). It does so by examining Baltimore's dockland, whereby union leader Frank Sobotka (Chris Bauer) does business with a ruthless criminal known as "The Greek," (Bill Raymond) and his right-hand man Spiros Vondas (Paul Ben-Victor), in order to keep his beloved dockers' union, Local 295, afloat amidst dwindling contributions from members of a dying occupation. The narrative of the second season makes some cogent points in advancing the text's overall criticism of contemporary America and its neoliberal politics. In *The Wire*'s cinematography urban space is inextricably bound up in peoples' narratives and the city itself is given enough visual impetus that it feels like a character in the greater narrative. Throughout season two there are wide-angle vistas of ruined factories and rusted hulking cranes on the docks. This visual signifier gives depth to Sobotka's desperate attempts to hold on to the traditional livelihood and solidarity of the dockers and, in turn, goes towards explaining the growing numbers of the urban underclass that are surplus to the requirements of labor. In the first episode of the second season McNulty ruefully acknowledges this trend while looking at a ruined factory on the docks from the police boat to which he has been banished by his nemesis Major Bill Rawls (John Doman). It was formerly Bethlehem Steel, he tells the boat's skipper, where his father used to work until he was let go in the 1980s and now it's going to be torn down to make way for luxury apartments. Here the docks serve as a double-edged sword in *The Wire*'s criticism. The 1971 Bretton

Woods agreement, which saw the U.S. dollar become a widespread reserve currency, foreshadows the neoliberal economic policies adopted with such gusto by the later Reagan administration.[9] The ensuing financialization of the economy saw the dismantling of much industry in the 1980s, enthusiastic asset-stripping that made investment banks, corporations and elite investors fortunes, while concurrently, unions and many working class were cut out of the social currency of economic involvement and left powerless.[10] Added to this, is the threat to labor by technological advances in automation and robotics, which increasingly renders human labor obsolete. This is emphasized in a narrative vignette whereby Sobotka watches a presentation on the future of dockland, one where it was made clear that robotics will further diminish the role of the laborer. The presentation both enrages and chills Sobotka to the bone; the old science fiction nightmare of the rise of the machines made real and personal to him. As Sennett writes: "In heavy industry, from 1982 to 2002 steel production in the United States rose from 75 million tons to 102 million tons even as the number of steelworkers dropped from 289,000 to 74,000. Their jobs were not exported; for the most part, sophisticated machines took over" (92). The role of technology in the devaluation of human life in the postindustrial world is vital to *The Wire*'s core and is discussed in detail further in this chapter in relation to the use of surveillance technology in policing strategies and the political and social consequences of this trend.

In their desperation to retain the social currency and value of their work, Sobotka and his nephew Nicky (Pablo Schreiber) get involved with The Greek in international smuggling of obscure chemicals, luxury cars and inadvertently, for Sobotka, of prostitutes, as is seen when the container with dead eastern European women is found. In essence, The Greek and his enterprise highlight the global nature of capitalism as it is now, detached from labor and detached from production. As Sheehan and Sweeney write:

> What becomes clear through viewing *The Wire* is that the triumph of capital over labor is accentuated by the triumph of finance over manufacturing capital.... The political structure, as portrayed in *The Wire*, is one that has adopted the priorities of finance capitalism. Commodity value is consistently prioritised over use value. The public sector is increasingly impoverished to the point where it cannot meet basic needs, while money accumulates in other sectors, particularly in the drug trade, beyond any possible need or use [11].

For many disenfranchised working and middle class Americans the triumph of finance over manufacturing capital has effectively destroyed the core American myth that those middle and lower class who are willing to

III. The Wire and Game Theory

work hard will be rewarded. The detachment of capital from labor and production is also destroying the narratives with which working people traditionally engage, as can be seen in *The Wire*'s tragic portrayal of Sobotka, his son Ziggy (James Ransone) and nephew Nicky's outcomes. The Sobotkas are a family of Polish immigrants who had worked on Baltimore's docks for generations. It is their place in the grand American narrative of which Frank is enormously proud, so much so, that in his effort to save stevedore jobs in Baltimore he is willing to become embroiled in a smuggling operation with dangerous criminals and partake in the kind of global capitalism that has destroyed his way of life in the first place, in an inevitably tragic irony.

In its focus on the Sobotkas and the docks in general *The Wire* puts a human face on the consequences of the death of work in postindustrial America and the direct consequences of macroeconomic forces. In the implacable free-flow of wealth in a fully digitized and globalized financial capitalism, the realm of wealth creation becomes radically detached from the realm of the social. Social matters such as unemployment and crime are irrelevant to the detached and autotelic global capital system. Capital had been inextricably bound up in the social, of course, in that its production was reliant on a willing workforce, who primarily through the advancements of labor movements had gained many favorable rights and conditions. This no longer appears to be the case in *The Wire*'s ruined Baltimore docks, however, a microcosm of greater postindustrial America and a portent of the future of the Western world. The essential point is that deregulated and unimpeded financial capital has only a virtual connection with the social realm, thus, as is seen in *The Wire*'s portrayal, what does not affect the system's primary function is external to it. Collective labor and the power it provided has disintegrated; the social decay that has arisen from this has no more bearing on the all-prescriptive dictates of growth and the free-flow of digital wealth and is thus irrelevant to the needs of the system.

The third season introduces the politics of City Hall into the narrative. This inclusion gives the viewer a view from the top down of the municipal system as run according to statistical models. For example, the incumbent mayor Clarence Royce (Glynn Turman) insists that the yearly murder rate stay below three hundred on the year of the mayoral elections. Royce puts pressure on the police chief, Commissioner Burrell (Frankie Faison), who in turn puts pressure on the commanders and so on down the line, to what is seen on the streets as a police enforcement that usually amounts to cracking heads. These quantitative statistical values are the source of political currency throughout the police and political systems of *The Wire*. Certain prescribed numerical values in *The Wire*'s Baltimore Police Force (such as a desired yearly murder rate) describe success or failure for both the police and the political administration. Thus, the numbers become the all-prescriptive currency of political success and those within the political apparatus pressurize the police brass to come back with the numerical indicators of success in the battle against crime, which, in turn, leads to the wholesale massaging of the statistics within the police force. The process of juking the stats is a function of self-preservation for individuals within these institutions and ensures the preservation of the institutions above and beyond their nominal functions. The preservation of the institutions and the appearance of their functionality serves the needs of the market better than if they attended to their primary function as this would require long-term strategy and ultimately, large investments of money into an institution that is not designed to directly create profit.

The illusion of effective policing that the statistical models engender is reinforced by the focus of the police force on drug prohibition. The third season of *The Wire* includes a narrative strand that sees frustrated and disgruntled police major "Bunny" Colvin (Robert Wisdom) create a free zone in an unpopulated sector of West Baltimore, whereby drugs can be bought and sold without fear of arrest, so long as the dealers stay within the designated area and no violence is perpetrated. The development of the free zone storyline in *The Wire* allows the text to further criticize and deconstruct drug prohibition in America by portraying a flawed but nevertheless viable experiment in decriminalization. Colvin's experiment in policing strategy, which becomes known among the street touts as "Hamsterdam," comes about not through a liberal or moral crusade on his part, but out of a veteran police officer's frustration at the waste of resources, time and energy that has gone into the vain attempt to police the drug trade in the poor inner city. In the span of his career, despite the energy given over by so many police to the war on drugs, Colvin has seen his district slide into further decay, further poverty, further ghettoization and crime.[11]

Colvin's experiment demonstrates the seeming impossibility of reform against the tide of self-preserving institutionalism and the enormous weight of the competitive logic prescribed by the economic system. His experiment in prohibition is short-lived despite signs that it is beginning to have positive effects on the West Baltimore community and is providing the opportunity to at least address the health issues of addicts. The experiment is crushed by

III. The Wire and Game Theory

the political and police apparatuses because it bears no political currency. Decriminalization would in fact undermine the police system and political system as they are currently structured. In other words, it is within the vested interests of those who bear power in these institutions to keep the status quo, as reform will undermine their power. The police brass in *The Wire*, especially Burrell and Rawls, are the most enraged by the revelation of Colvin's experiment and Rawls in particular takes an ugly glee in tearing down the Hamsterdam experiment. In episode twelve of the third season, we see Rawls uniformed like a soldier all in navy blues blowing his whistle and shouting "over the top gentlemen" at the officers charged with breaking up Hamsterdam. Rawls reaches into his patrol car and Wagner's *Ride of the Valkyries* begins to blare from the car's bull horn. The episode is sardonically titled "Mission Accomplished" and the ironic use of this piece of music intertextually references the famous helicopter scene from *Apocalypse Now*. The triumphalism of the music as the Viet Cong in the village below are crushed by the huge military might of the 9th Airborne contradicts the absolute futility and slaughter of the Vietnam conflict, and the fact that America was defeated by the Vietnamese in the conflict itself. The use of *Ride of the Valkyries* in this scene thereby intonates the point that the War on Drugs, like the Vietnam War, is futile and destructive, as are all American attempts to cleanse the world through regenerative violence. Rawls and Burrell have come to power in the police system through adherence to the political power of the numbers and stats. It is within their best interests to maintain the system as is, and they duly do their parts regardless of either the patent benefits of reform or the absolute amorality of the system, as it currently exists. Russell "Stringer" Bell does his best on the other side of law's dividing line to reform Baltimore's drugs trade but meets an even more ignominious fate than Colvin (who is disgraced and forced to retire on a reduced pension).

The final two episodes of the third season also draw attention to the role that the currency of numerical fiction plays not just in creating an illusion of social efficacy within America's institutional life but also in its foreign policy. The season has begun with the demolition of the Barksdale gang's primary drug retailing real estate, the Franklin Terraces, in a visual analogy to the falling of the Twin Towers. What follows is the virtualization of the West Baltimore drugs trade in its subsequent detachment from a specific location. The drugs trade becomes mobile and detached, more in tune with the globalized free-market economy. This is summed up in Bell's attempts to reform it under the creed of his new business approach; the Game isn't about territory anymore, it's about product. Bell's attempts at reform fail and he ends up being assassinated. What follows is *The Wire*'s analogy of the War in Iraq and the War on Terror, whereby Barksdale and his lieutenant "Slim" Charles (Anwen Glover) have committed to retaliation against their rival Marlo Stanfield, even though Barksdale knows very well that Stanfield is not responsible for Bell's execution. Barksdale has betrayed Bell to his eventual executioners, Omar (Michael Kenneth Williams) and "Brother" Mouzone (Michael Potts) out on a revenge mission against Bell for an earlier move that has backfired. Barksdale's guilt over causing the death of his childhood friend, it seems, has finally brought him around to Bell's business oriented way of seeing things. "Fuck Marlo," he tells Charles, "[a]nd fuck this fucking war. All this beefin' over a couple of fuckin' corners" (Alvares 269). Charles's retort echoes through *The Wire*'s criticism of all of America's futile and tragic wars, both internal and external, but most specifically through the Iraq War: "Fact is, we went to war, an' now ain't no goin' back.... If it's a lie, then we fight on the lie" (269). This is one of many examples in *The Wire* whereby official political fictions are mirrored in the actions of both legitimate and illegitimate institutions. *The Wire* uses these analogies to criticize American political and cultural life. The politics of an illicit drug organization in this case not only critically encapsulates American foreign policy in microcosm but also proposes that these pernicious fictions permeate American institutions from the top down. The dictates of power, how to seize it or control it, are prescribed from the highest echelons of America's power structures and are recapitulated throughout the culture in ways that conform to those dictates and their specific adaptation of myths of American exceptionalism. In other words, America's foreign policy often involves force in its acquisition and maintenance of global dominance, while simultaneously using propaganda to maintain the image, for its own citizens, that it is a torchbearer for democracy in the world.

The fourth season draws again on Burns's first hand experience, this time in his role as a middle-school teacher in Baltimore. In an interview with Nick Hornby, Simon explains that the fourth season interrogates the American myth of equal opportunity (Alvarez 387). Specifically, it examines the education system from the point of view of the disadvantaged inner city Baltimore, and rails against the Bush Administration's No Child Left Behind educational policy with its own take on the reality for these geographical and economic ghettoes in the season's subtitle: "No Corner Left Behind." The fourth season continues with *The Wire*'s fly-on-the-wall view of the machinations of Baltimore's (American) political and policing systems, while intro-

III. The Wire and Game Theory

ducing four new characters into its focus. The narratives of the four children of inner city West Baltimore is *The Wire*'s most cogent and powerful demonstration of the real prospects of those born into America's underclass. The pull of the game for the four kids in their early teens—Michael, (Tristan Wilds), "Dukie" (Jermaine Crawford), Namond (Julito McCullum) and Randy (Maestro Harrell)—is made very clear and the outcome is often tragic. Furthermore, in this season, there is a continuation of the examination of the possibility of reform, or lack thereof, under the auspices of neoliberal institutionalism with its storyline about the mayoral race. The slick outsider making all the right noises about reform, Tommy Carcetti (Aiden Gillen), is challenging the incumbent Royce on the basis of his administration's failure to fight crime and improve the city. Carcetti scores a shock victory—for a white man in a majority black city—on the back of many promises of reform. What transpires in the following season is a devastating critique of the modern American political system, and the impossibility of reform in the face of institutional primacy. Season four also examines the transference of political currency away from the War on Drugs and towards a new endless autotelic and unwinnable war, the War on Terror.

More With Less: The Presiding Fiction of *The Wire*'s Fifth Season

The fifth and final season focuses on the newspaper *The Baltimore Sun*, by which Simon was previously employed as a crime reporter.[12] It is yet another institution under which *The Wire*'s motif of juking the stats is critically examined. Not only do so-called serious newspapers and the media in general fail to report wide-scale systemic corruption, according to *The Wire*'s analysis, but they are often complicit in the fiction of a functional society. To this end the final season introduces the fake serial killer plot line, whereby McNulty has lapsed back into alcoholism and is more angry and frustrated than ever with the lack of resources available to the police. Carcetti has come to the mayoral seat in the knowledge and understanding—having paid close attention to the words of the overseer of the successful Barksdale case, Lieutenant Daniels (Lance Reddick)—that the numbers game was anathema to meaningful policing. He has promised the police pay raises, all the resources they need to do good police work, and has committed to supporting long-term policing strategies like McNulty and Daniels' wiretap cases. The budget deficit that Carcetti inherits, however, sees him divert resources away from the police and towards the school, as this arena ultimately holds more political currency in terms of his ambition to become Governor of the State. The police, as well as those remaining employees of *The Baltimore Sun* who have not been made redundant, are met with the constant and all too familiar everyday austerity mantra: "more with less."[13]

On the other side of the law's divide, Marlo Stanfield's rise to king of the drugs trade in West Baltimore in the wake of the Barksdale gang sees a player that is much more attuned to the ruthless and amoral dictates of the system than his predecessors, having none of Bell's racial uplift ambitions or Barksdale's (albeit dubious) concession to the bonds of family. Stanfield's short reign as drug lord of the West inner city has seen his two enforcers and executioners in chief Felicia "Snoop" Pearson (Felicia Pearson) and Chris Partlow (Gbenga Akinnagbe) kill at his behest upwards of twenty-two people for matters of enforcement, reputation and in the case of one unlucky security guard, on a seeming whim.[14] Snoop and Partlow walk their live victims to a pre-chosen abandoned row house, as is seen in "The Boys of Summer," the first episode of season four, in order to carry out their grisly executions. In the opening scene of the season Snoop is in a hardware store buying a nail gun, the purpose of which later becomes apparent. The scene sees the two kneel their unknown victim on clear plastic in a dark room of the row house. As they discuss their diminishing supply of quicklime, the victim pleads to Partlow for his life, responding to which, Partlow tells him, almost soothingly: "Don't fret boss, I got you covered. Quick and clean, I promise."

Lester Freamon (Clark Peters), one of the detectives from the first wiretap case on the Barksdales in season one, through exceptional investigative prowess discovers one of the grisly mausoleums and realizes that any abandoned row house with a new nail gun nail in its chip board will entomb a Stanfield murder victim. Despite the fierce resistance of the Homicide Division's Lieutenant, Jay Landsman (Delaney Williams), all the row houses in West Baltimore and some in the East (with these new nails in their boards) are torn open, after which twenty-two bodies are found in ad hoc mausoleums. Landsman, as a disciple of the numbers, bemoans the statistical slump this will cause to his department's yearly clearance rate, and describes Freamon as a "vandal." The decision to open the row houses comes ultimately from the new mayor Carcetti, but only after it is made clear to him that the statistical abomination the bodies will quantify can be officially attributed to the previous administration's watch.

III. The Wire *and Game Theory*

Daniels, who Carcetti is nominally grooming for the role of commissioner, is charged with solving the case. Daniels, McNulty, Freamon and the other clued-in police, as well as the careful viewer, are aware that a wiretap that had been set up by the Special Investigations Unit on the Stanfield gang earlier had been gutted by Bill Rawls for internal political reasons. Again, as has been discussed above in relation to Rawls' gleeful destruction of Hamsterdam, the preservation of the institution and the preservation of the individual within the institution take precedence over the institution's nominal function. Season five sees the investigation into the Stanfield organization and the bodies in the row houses again hobbled by the cessation of the original wiretap and all but forgotten in the passage of the year or so since their discovery. The outrage of the murders has dissipated, the national and local media have long since turned their attention elsewhere, the matter no longer has any political currency, and so Carcetti diverts his budget supply away from the investigation, away from the Baltimore Police Department, and towards the political boon that is Baltimore's school system.

In episode two of season five, "Unconfirmed Reports," one of *The Wire*'s many bar scenes sees McNulty and Freamon rage to their Homicide Unit colleague and drinking buddy "Bunk" Moreland (Wendell Pierce) over the gutting of the row house investigation. Here they acknowledge the huge racial issue that is mostly implicit in *The Wire*'s analysis of a typical American city. The murders took place in the wrong zip code; they acerbically refer to the murder of young black males as "misdemeanor homicides," pointing out that it if the victims had been white and middle-class the story would be very different. This implicit race and class issue runs to the core of *The Wire*'s criticism of postmodern America. In majority black inner city urban America, where ghettoization and deprivation are already entrenched, the drugs trade is the only means by which many can partake in the American Dream, the pliable myth that is constantly recapitulated and sold to Americans throughout its media apparatus. Thus, even in urban ghettoes the population of forgotten and effectively discarded people nevertheless engages with the mythology of their culture. These areas, as is portrayed with convincing realism in *The Wire*'s detailing of inherent corruption, are only virtually policed. In other words, amongst the police, barring the exceptions that *The Wire* exonerates to a certain extent, such as McNulty, Freamon, Moreland, Colvin, Kima Greggs (Sonja Sohn), there is no real understanding of the people and the community they are policing beyond cracking the heads of barely post-pubescent street touts for the sake of the statistics by which the system sustains itself. The realities of American life among these disenfranchised urban populations can no longer be obscured by the quantitative models or the blatant falsehood of equal opportunity. The perceptive police officers who are on the ground in these areas discern the modes of postmodern policing as creating a fiction that may be impossible to circumvent.

The injustice of the termination of the row house murder investigation, its scandalous race and class prejudice enrages McNulty and deeply offends his intellectual and professional pride. His alcoholism and injured vanity sees him fabricate a murder investigation into a serial killer of the homeless. McNulty concocts a fiction about a sexually deviant serial killer who "preys on the weakest among us" in an attempt to get the funding the department needs for him to surreptitiously continue the Stanfield investigation ("Unconfirmed Reports"). "Fuelled by Jamesons and genius," McNulty manipulates the death scene of a homeless man and applies post-mortem marks and injuries to the body in order to make it look like murder (Alvarez 427). He continues on in this vein, later with Freamon's help adding little flourishes that will titillate the media. In one darkly humorous scene, McNulty and Freamon manipulate a corpse in a way that could be glibly described as a biting satire of the media, whereby they introduce a biting fetish into the serial killer's repertoire. McNulty does the honors with a pair of dentures he has procured, and later feeds this tidbit to the *Sun*'s crime reporter Alma Gutierrez (Michelle Paress), and Scott Templeton (Thomas McCarthy), who has tagged along with her, clearly has his interests piqued by this detail.

In fabricating the serial killer story, McNulty thereby concedes to the requirement of manufactured falsehood in order to gain traction within the system. In this way, Season Five interrogates the role of illusory fallacy, in both reflexive terms and in terms of American institutional life. Kinder argues in "Re-Wiring Baltimore" that "The plot of the fake serial killer violates the commitment to truth and realism that *The Wire* demands throughout the series" (55–56). In so doing, however, *The Wire* may be making its most pointed criticism of institutional life, and at the same time taking aim specifically at the institution that is most culpable in its acquiescence to fictions. The season's critical focus on *The Baltimore Sun* is fascinating in light of Simon's former employment at the paper. In "Ethnographic Imaginary" Williams reveals that Simon was let go from the paper for editorializing his stories of West Baltimore drug players and street folk more than was warranted.[15]

What is seen in the newspaper narrative of the fifth season is that news-

III. The Wire *and Game Theory*

papers and media in general are necessarily invested in propagating fictions for the sake of their own survival, just like all *The Wire*'s other institutions. This point is encapsulated, most specifically, in ambitious reporter Templeton's pretense that the so-called serial killer has phoned him to tell him why he does what he does. Templeton's "City Desk" editor Gus Haynes (Clark Johnson) has extreme reservations about the veracity of Templeton's claims, but the paper's management persist with the supposed scoop regardless, as the story brings them into Pulitzer Prize territory. *The Wire*'s (and David Simon's to some extent) complex relationship with narrative, the media and the telling of the truth come to the fore in this aspect of its analysis. *The Wire*'s, and by extension Simon's telling of the truth, thereby, is predicated on the artist's belief that a fictional story can get closer to the truth of something than supposed objective facts can. There is an element of poststructuralism in the competing narratives aspect of this conundrum, whereby interrogating the origins and structures of a jargon or narrative is essential to decoding its real meaning. In this sense, *The Wire*'s (and Simon's) criticism of newspapers and news media becomes clearer. In this narrative strand of the program, Simon is, in effect, criticizing *The Baltimore Sun* for dismissing him because he dared to challenge the *status quo*, to which the newspaper, as a subsidiary of a large profit-making media corporation, is invested in maintaining. *The Wire*, then, is his uncensored editorializing, closer to the truth than a newspaper can be. The previous chapter analyses how DeLillo appropriated the logic of nuclear jargon in order to show that its meaning was, at its core, related to mechanization and instrumental control of society, the upshot of which was the hollowing out of spiritual narratives. *The Wire*, as Simon himself would no doubt claim, has been much more effective and wide reaching in its fictional rendering of real social problems in America and beyond than any factual localized work of journalism could have been. As Williams writes: "The vivid and concrete interlocking stories are what fiction affords, what ethnography aspires to, and what newspaper journalism can only rarely achieve" (209).

Broadsheet newspapers, according to their own mythology, were once the watchdogs against corruption and institutional failure in America and beyond. Their perceived job was to expose corruption and injustice and hold to task those responsible through its exposition and the prompting of public debates about these problems. *The Wire*, however, depicts a newspaper business that has been hollowed out and made acquiescent to the dictates of radical capitalism. The constant upper management refrain of the non-sequitur "more with less," and the persistent cut backs and redundancies shown in *The Wire*'s fictional version of *The Baltimore Sun*, underpin the all-powerful law of the bottom line to which newspapers and most other American institutions are beholden. As Simon has stated: "*The Wire* is about capital and labor and when capitalism triumphs, labor is diminished. Season five is the same as what happens to labor and middle management in every other [depicted] institution" (Alvarez 404). The concentrated ownership of newspapers by fewer behemoth corporations is yet another example of the triumph of virtualized capital over labor. Detached from the grounding of its nominal basis in Baltimore, the *Sun*'s interests are no longer attached to the abstractions of an older world, such as those of journalistic integrity or social responsibility, as it is no longer invested in them. Instead, it is invested fundamentally in shareholder profit and every aspect of the paper must be tailored to its profitability, thus always doing "more with less." The *Baltimore Sun* and newspaper media in general, are not simply complicit in the institutional fictions but are propagators and integral parts of sustaining these fictions. The fallacy of doing more with less precipitates the fallacy of Templeton's concoction, and in broader terms the virtualization and concentration of wealth precipitates the fallacy of a functional American society.[16]

McNulty's fabrication of the serial killer fiction, therefore, signals his tacit concession to the fictional currency of pseudo-events and stage managed reality by which the now hybrid public relations/mainstream media upholds a fallacious and interminably unjust system. In broader terms, this plot line proposes that in late capitalism the illusions of functionality that American mythology demands have much more currency than the truth does within the stage-mangaed neoliberal system. *The Wire* is taking aim at what it sees as an American unwillingness or inability to look objectively and truthfully at its own reality. McNulty, who is joined in the weaving of the fiction by Freamon (an unlikely participant given his characterization up to this point), is successful in procuring the money and resources he needs. McNulty and Freamon engineer a wiretap out of the serial killer investigation with which they surreptitiously set up on the players of Stanfield's organization once more. Their efforts lead to the organization eventually being brought down. Stanfield himself, however, is set free on the condition he leaves the Game forever. His pernicious lawyer Maurice Levy (Michael Kostroff) has noticed a discrepancy in the wiretap documents that lead him to be able to obtain Stanfield's freedom.

McNulty and Freamon's lie has brought down a monstrously violent organization, but the price of the lie is that the perpetrator in chief walks away with his freedom. The exposition of the lie ultimately ends their careers, but the size of the lie prevents them from being punished further. Carcetti's mayoral office has gotten much too embroiled in the lie and too much political traction from its newfound focus on the plight of the homeless for it to reveal the lie by publicly punishing the errant cops. The media too, as embodied in the *Sun*'s super-ambitious fabricator of fictions, Templeton, have derived much too much currency from the lie to rescind. What is noticeable in the institutions on either side of the divide is that those at the top of the hierarchies go unpunished or, as in Carcetti's case, actually gain from the lie and their actions preceding it, while those lower down take the brunt. *The Wire* highlights a double-edged injustice brought about by the system's steep hierarchy. Radical competition is instilled on both sides of the law's divide and usually precipitates the rise to the top of its hierarchies of the most ruthless and amoral individuals. Once at the top, the currency of their power (gained through systemic fictions) ensures their safety and well-being at the expense of those below them. In other words, in its institutional Game paradigm, neoliberal economics creates a zero-sum, or a winner-takes-all social scenario that is deeply unjust.

McNulty and Freamon's crossing of the line, their succumbing to the currency of institutional fiction, is a tragic acquiescence to the lies that facilitate corruption and injustice. Their actions can be contrasted directly with Colvin's reaction to the terminal fiction of the War on Drugs and the career-advancing numbers-game when he tells a Westside community meeting prior to his free-zone experiment that he doesn't know what do about the crime problem, but "whatever it is, it can't be a lie" ("Hamsterdam," S3, E4). This narrative of *The Wire*, therefore, is much more damning of the intrinsic corruption engendered by the system than it is of the specific immorality of McNulty and Freamon's actions. While McNulty and Freamon may be inoculated, to a certain extent, the same can hardly be said of Templeton. At the early stages of McNulty and Freamon's lie, Templeton weaves his own fabrication into what he is unaware is someone else's lie by pretending he has received a telephone call from the killer. This gives the obsequious Templeton an inside track on the story with the paper's managing editor Thomas Kelbenow (David Costabile) and executive editor James Whiting (Sam Freed). Templeton's lie becomes a boon for McNulty and Freamon, who see it as a way for them to set up a wiretap. There are a number of instances in the fifth season in which Templeton makes up sources and quotations prior to taking his leap into fully fledged fabrication. Haynes's reservations about the ethical standing of Templeton's reportage is seen in these instances, and in his serial killer claims, but Haynes's judgment is overruled by the senior management of the paper, Klebenow and Whiting, for whom the *scandale du jour* and the titillation of a serial killer are too alluring to resist. Thus, as a result of its structure and the dictates of shareholder profitability, *The Wire*'s *Baltimore Sun* refuses to acknowledge the everyday scandal of institutional corruption, injustice and media manipulation and, in doing less with less, chases potential Pulitzer Prize-winning bullshit instead.

The Wire therein demonstrates the everyday institutional implementation of postmodern *virtuality* that Baudrillard first wrote about in *The Consumer Society* and later in "The Beaubourg Effect" and "The Gulf War Did Not Take Place" (1991). As argued throughout this book, the Cold War in America precipitated the application of postnuclear technique to the social sciences. *The Wire* vividly depicts how this occurs through the Game paradigm that underpins America's neoliberal institutional systems. As mentioned previously, the fictions that prop up the more pernicious interpretations of American mythology, those that justify the use of violence and maintain a starkly unjust society, tend to permeate the culture. It becomes apparent, that the fictions and virtualizations of the Vietnam and Iraq wars presage the fictions of the War on Drugs and the War on Terror. The majority of wars are fought nominally for ideological reasons but in actuality for maintenance of power and for profit. The economic system, which accounts for growth, only intersects with ideology insofar as it provides the coherence, in terms of nationalistic identity, reasons of morality and so forth to facilitate the agency towards further acquisition, be that through war or other avenues. The nominal moral reasons for America's invasion of Iraq, then, are the same kinds of fictions that underpin the illusion of a functional and coherent American society. The profits of all the wars, foreign and domestic, come at the expense of the suffering and death of the disenfranchised but this is irrelevant to the virtualized global finance system into which we are all plugged. The detachment of capital from labor, the virtualization of economic power, means that institutions are beholden to the managed illusion of functionality in order to survive.

The couching of what is essentially a social and public health issue—the social ills that cause and are caused by the illegal drug industry—in the term war reminds us again that apocalypticism is perhaps the only truly surviving American metanarrative. The use of *Ride of the Valkyries* reminds the

III. The Wire *and Game Theory*

viewer that the apocalypse is now and always will be so long as America makes its path to Eden, or more specifically, to profit, through violent purifications. The formative American purification of the natives to make way for trade, commerce and manifest destiny is recapitulated throughout American history and so American wars, both inward and outward, adhere to the apocalyptic myth. Since the coming into existence of the Bomb, however, most public expressions of the American experiment as a shared one, the source of narratives that stitch society together, have been replaced with the dictates of the radically individualistic capitalism that the Bomb prescribes. This criticism of postnuclear America runs through *The Wire*, whereby the viewer is presented with a view of the clear erosion of community and collective consciousness in these disenfranchised urban areas. The senses of race and group consciousness embodied by the various civil rights movements of the sixties have been replaced by the dictates of rapacious acquisition and the illusions of equality. The drugs trade, as *The Wire* makes abundantly clear, makes up a considerable portion of the Baltimore economy (as does the illegal drugs trade and black market in general in the overall American/global economy), yet it is those at the bottom of the capitalist hierarchy who suffer the most in the generation of these enormous profits. These are profits, in which Lester Freamon explains we are "all of us complicit" due to the interconnectivity of the economic system ("Unconfirmed Reports"). The War on Drugs and the statistics that prop up the illusion of legal veracity and justice effectively mask the reality of an inherently unjust system and a lopsided financial capitalism.

The Game paradigm only requires the illusion of a functional society, thus the corruption and human tragedy engendered by the numbers system bears no effect on the higher echelons of the capitalist system as it is fully virtualized and freed from any attachment to messy human abstractions. Thus, the fictions that the numbers provide are woven into the illusion of a functional society, which is addressed toward pre-existing American exceptionalist myths pertaining to equal opportunity, democracy and the rugged individualism of the self-made man. In this way, the Pulitzer Prize that the senior editors of *The Wire's Baltimore Sun* are chasing represents a simulacrum of journalistic integrity. They are chasing the currency of prestige through a fiction masquerading as news (that those individuals within their respective institutions who are seeking agency have fabricated) in a society that is fueled by fabrication and illusion.

Stringer Bell: Capitalism, Race and Class

The institutional fictions that the Game paradigm provides, in *The Wires* depiction, go towards maintaining the broader illusion that Americas is a fair and democratic society—the myths of exceptionalism and equal opportunity—while their effect on a local or individual level is to destroy binding and communal narratives. This is seen in the way it has depicted the erosion of the civil rights gains of the sixties and how the all-versus-all nature of radical individualism, most notably in the brutal form that the drugs trade takes, has destroyed collective narratives like community and other forms of collective agency. On this point Sheehan and Sweeney observe: "Unemployment, underemployment, the priorities of the stats game, the victory of rampant capitalism have destroyed not only this world that made sense, but the prescriptive narratives and solidarities that grew from it. The labor movement, the black power movement and the ideals of empowerment through education have all been debased and eviscerated" (12–13).

As well as being an exemplary capitalist whose misfortune was to be born in the wrong neighborhood, Stringer Bell's story also encapsulates the destruction of these narratives. The radically individualistic nature of the neoliberal capitalism that permeates the culture and has been thoroughly absorbed by Bell contains no binding narratives; in fact, it requires the opposite. As is discussed in this section, Bell is trapped by the inherent contradiction of his ambitions, as they grind against the monolithic reality of the institution he energizes. His desire for legitimacy stems from a desire for racial uplift but the nature of his incendiary ambitions and their consequences ultimately produces the opposite when two other African American men, on Barksdale's tip-off, execute him. The third season, which begins with the demolition of The Franklin Towers where the Barksdale gang had sold the bulk of their narcotics, also contains an analogy with the War on Terror. As discussed above, the virtualization of their drug trade in the aftermath of the towers' destruction leads to a war based on a lie.

Bell and Barksdale's long-standing friendship turns rapidly into internecine opposition when Bell's ambition to reform the drugs trade along the lines of a more legitimate business model bumps up against Barksdale's gangster ethos. This ambition sees Bell go behind Barksdale's back and orchestrate a move in which he hopes both to destroy Omar, who has robbed the organization of drugs and cash on a number of occasions and drive off Brother Mouzone, whom Barksdale has hired to protect the gang's territory

III. The Wire and Game Theory

that Bell feels is irrelevant to the new Game. Bell is attempting to change the rules of the Game by deemphasizing the territorialism of the urban drugs institution and instead emphasizing profit by means of wholesale purchasing of the product. A side effect of the territory-sharing is less violence among competing drug gangs. Bell and his East-side compatriot, Proposition Joe Stewart (Robert F Chew) are essentially trying to financialize the Baltimore drugs trade along the lines of a legitimate capitalist enterprise. In this move, however, Bell overextends himself and this one wrong move in the Game that he otherwise flawlessly plays is enough to unravel his strategy and eventually end his life. Omar only wounds Mouzone in his attack and both later learn of Bell's deception. When Mouzone returns to Baltimore from New York for revenge, it takes little coercion of Barksdale for him to give up the place that will be Bell's execution site. The game-within-the-Game, which those at the bottom of America's social and economic hierarchy play, is identical to the legitimate capitalism that is played throughout the wider social economy in almost all but one aspect: the consequences of a bad move for those born into and occupying the legitimate Game may amount to bankruptcy while the consequences within the drug trade are usually prison or death. Bell and Barksdale's mutual betrayal is one of a number of close correspondences in *The Wire* to the dictates of Game Theory.

This desire for respectability, expressed in Bell's attempt to reform the Baltimore drugs trade and to divert his drugs profits into (nominally) more legitimate enterprises, such as property development, is one not shared by Barksdale. In *The Wire*'s narrative, Bell uses his considerable intelligence and business acumen to generate ever-greater profits for the Barksdale gang while at the same time avoiding McNulty and Freamon's attempts to catch him. As is clear from his attitude and how he dresses, Bell dislikes the posturing, territorialism and disreputability of the drugs trade.[17] The distasteful ghetto mentality of playing gangster, for Bell, is limited and blinkered and he clearly desires to reform the Game around the dictates of legitimate global capitalism, particularly in the wake of the fallen towers, whereby the geographic location of the business is no longer very relevant. "Game ain't about territory no more," he states, "it's about product" (Alvarez 219). In Barksdale's absence a crew is organized with meetings, chaired by Bell, and set according to *Robert's Rules of Order*. He has even gone so far as to organize a co-op between Baltimore's main drug players. The co-op ensures less turf warfare between the dealers, thus less police attention, while at the same time the players pool their money and buy their product in bulk at wholesale prices. An ironic narrative strand sees McNulty tail Bell's car to a local community college, where he discovers Bell enrolled in a business studies course. Bell, peering studiously over his spectacles at his notes, learns the rules of good marketing and product positioning.

Bell's insistence on a cessation of territorial warfare may not be rooted in ethics but upon good business principles. His distaste for violence undoubtedly stems from his business ambitions, most specifically his desire for legitimacy and a movement away from the brutality and short-sightedness of the ghetto drug game. Despite Bell's distaste for the "gangster bullshit" of territorial warfare and posturing, however, he is still shown to be ruthless when it comes to protecting himself and his profits ("Middle Ground," Ep 36). He has Barksdale's nephew D'Angelo (Larry Gilliard, Jr.) murdered in prison when he fears D'Angelo is going to stand witness against the organization. In general, however, for Bell gun murders over drug real estate always attract unwanted police attention, which not only slows down their operation but also exposes him and Barksdale to deeper investigation. It is for this reason that Bell allows Stanfield to take over a few Barksdale corners: Bell avoids an all-out war by trying to bring Stanfield into the fold of the co-op. Barksdale, however, is furious when he discovers these events upon his release from prison. He does not share Bell's vision for their drug game, seeing it not as an opportunity for capitalist legitimacy or entry into a virtual and global realm of profit-making but as a localized affair. He wants to be the king of West Baltimore, the world he grew up in and that made him, and he wants to rule according to his fearsome reputation. The easy secession of part of his territory by Bell is a detriment to his reputation as a player with heart and the following exchange between the two encapsulates their divergent worldviews:

BELL: How many corners do we need?
BARKSDALE: More than a nigger can spend.

"And we ain't gonna be around to spend what we got," reasons Bell, telling Barksdale they can invest the cash they now have into the drug trade like an investment bank. In effect Bell seeks to disconnect their profits from the machinations of what generates the profit and to move up the food chain towards legitimate financial profiteering:

> We in a money game where nary a motherfucker goes to jail. We could finance the packages and never touch nothing but cash. No corners, no territory, nothing but making like a goddamn bank. We let the young'uns worry about how to wholesale, where

III. The Wire *and Game Theory*

to retail. I mean, who gives a fuck who's standing on what corner, when we pulling our cut off the top and putting that money to good use?

Barksdale's response suggests he is less enamored with money-making than Bell and more interested in protecting his reputation: "I ain't no shirt-wearin' suit like you. Just a gangster, I suppose. And I want my corners" (Alvarez 240).

Barksdale's worldview, although limited, is closer to the reality of their place in society. As discussed previously, the Game paradigm depicted by *The Wire* underpins a neoliberal economic system that is oblivious to the means of how growth (profit) is acquired, thereby rendering the division between legitimate and illegitimate ultimately irrelevant to the overall economy. As discussed above, the police bolster their statistics and feed the prison industrial complex with the arrests, in the vast majority of cases with meaningless drug arrests of the poor and marginalized. On the other hand, legitimate corporate business responsible for grievously harmful financial, social and environmental crimes almost always seem to go unpunished.[18] Morality is hardly factored into the bottom line of the vast majority of large shareholder-floated corporations, in fact, signs of morality in decision making are most often seen as a bad bet in the marketplace. The notion that the law is first and foremost an instrument of social justice and equality is part of the overall American mythology.[19] As such, under the aegis of the all-pervasive market requirements, the law is largely an instrument of the managed illusion of social functionality, underpinned as it is with the policing statistics of meaningless drug arrests. It is therefore, certainly not perceived as a source of protection or justice among the marginalized, but the exact opposite. For Stringer Bell, therefore, a man of great intelligence and talent, whose acquisition of wealth could only have come about initially via the illegal drugs trade, there is surely no quandary in the illegality or immorality of his general business dealings. Bell sees the narcotics trade as a stepping-stone to legitimacy where no other exists. This is a point that *The Wire* makes most cogently and powerfully in season four, in which the social forces by which poor, disenfranchised kids are both pushed towards and drawn into the narcotics trade are unfurled in the narratives of the four children. The ubiquitous American myth of equal opportunity, *The Wire* insists, is a pernicious falsehood for those who find themselves at the bottom of America's economic hierarchy. What's more, those who are continuously told that they live in the land of equal opportunity, of capitalist enterprise but who are in reality "excluded from the legitimate economy," as Simon puts it, "make their own world"; a neoliberal capitalist model that mirrors legitimate business in all but one aspect, its prohibition ("The Target," David Simon commentary).

While Bell's drugs co-op is shown to reduce the murder rate and civilize the drugs trade more than the law has managed, he is nevertheless undone by the naivety of his ambitions regarding two aspects of his understanding of the Game. His attempt to reform the Baltimore drugs trade is naïve because he thinks the only thing that motivates people is the acquisition of money, which his friend Barksdale proves wrong. Barksdale doesn't comprehend the enjoyment of making money for its own sake; he relishes the battle to maintain control of the ghetto drug trade. The game within the game, for all its destruction and violence, is nevertheless from Barksdale's viewpoint rooted in the real. There is a macho warrior masculinity of a more ancient kind in localized territorialism, for Barksdale, than can be found in Bell's delibidinized financial game. As is discussed in the previous chapters, in *End Zone* Major Staley laments the passing into history of a more visceral warrior masculinity and the SAC movies present the ruthless machine-man as the exemplary masculinity. The new masculinity is observed according to the dictates of capitalist rationality, and Bell is most certainly attuned to this kind of expression. Barksdale, however, holds on to a more primitive and visceral warrior narrative. For Barksdale and his ghetto ambition, the mere acquisition of money is not fulfilling without the narrative of battle that goes with it.

The other aspect of Bell's naivety is his ghetto understanding of the bigger Game, a naivety that the supremely corrupt shakedown artist, Senator Clay Davis (Isiah Whitlock, Jr.) is very quick to exploit. The business of "making like a goddamn bank" through the legitimate means of property development, Bell discovers, has its own headaches ("Middle Ground" Ep 36). The price of steel is constantly in flux and he is required to procure a plethora of zoning and building permits, a time-consuming process that Bell has had little experience of in his other business. He hands over two hundred and fifty thousand dollars to Davis, on the promise he will speed up the process: "Twenty gets you the permits. Five is to me for bribin' these downtown motherfuckers. I mean, I'm the one got to risk walkin' up to these thieving bitches with cash in hand right?" (Alvarez 238). Bell discovers that he has been played for a fool when his lawyer, Levy, tells him that he has been "rainmade" ("Middle Ground"). If it rains, the lawyer tells Bell, Davis tells you he made it happen. If it doesn't, he comes up with reasons for Bell to pay him more. This is a terrible insult to Bell's intelligence and ambition, forcing him to realize that he is still excluded from the bigger Game by his background, his poverty and

III. The Wire *and Game Theory*

his skin color. The realization prompts Bell to revert to gangster solutions to this problem. He turns up at Barksdale's hideout drunk and angry and demands that Slim Charles, Barksdale's lieutenant, kill Clay Davis. Bell and Barksdale argue, eventually culminating with Bell's revelation to Barksdale that he had Barksdale's nephew executed in prison to protect their drug business. The following extract encapsulates the divergence of their worldviews:

BELL: That nigger took our money, man.
BARKSDALE: I seen it coming.
BELL: Well, he got to go.
BARKSDALE: Nah you a fucking businessman. Handle it like that. You don't want to get all gangster wild with it and shit, right? What I tell you about playing them fucking away games? Yeah, they saw your ghetto ass coming from miles away, nigger. You got a fucking beef with them? That shit is on you ("Middle Ground").

What transpires between the two is their mutual betrayal, which is discussed in relation to the dictates of Game Theory below. Under pressure from the co-op to call off Barksdale's war, Bell betrays Barksdale's location along with an army's worth of weapons to Major Colvin. Bell tells Colvin, who is suspended for his experiment in decriminalization, that he came to him with the information for the very reason that Colvin was behind the free-zone, recognizing an attempt to reform the War on Drugs from the other side of the divide. This is typical of *The Wire*'s intricate plot detailing of unexpected causality and one among many significant pieces of commentary on the effects of different kinds of policing which is discussed in the following section.[20]

In the meantime, however, Barksdale has betrayed Bell's future whereabouts to the assassin Brother Mouzone and Omar Little, both of whom seek revenge against Bell. When the pair corners him he shouts: "Look man, I ain't involved in that gangster bullshit no more ("Middle Ground"). The desperate plea reveals his wishful thinking. He then tries to bribe them: "What y'all niggers want, man? Money? Is that it?" His answer comes from Omar, whose boyfriend Bell previously had tortured and killed. "You still don't get it, do you? Huh? This ain't about your money, bro" (*ibid*). Bell can't seem to comprehend that money won't fix the problem with Omar. His last words, "get on with it motherfuckers" echo those of Colvin's when he is made to fall on his sword by Rawls and Burrell for his particular attempts to reform the War on Drugs. These narratives run parallel with each other through the third season intertwining finally when Bell gives Colvin the tip-off as to Barksdale's whereabouts. Both have attempted to reform the institutions into which they have put their life's energy and both are chewed up by their respective institutions (albeit with Bell paying the street toll for his attempts to change the Game).

In episode five of the third season, "Straight and True," Bell welcomes the freshly released Barksdale back into the fold with gifts provided by Bell's legitimate dealings. Bell brings him to a luxury penthouse and tells him the title is in his name and that with all the "straight money" they're making, they can carry out these acquisitions in the open. They begin to reminisce about the good old times in a scene that foreshadows a later encounter between the two in the penthouse in the episode "Middle Ground," in which they speak fondly about their long friendship, even though at this point of the narrative they have betrayed each other. In this initial scene, there is a brief but significant exchange that reveals the difference in their motivations, which eventually, through circumstance and the destructive force of their institution, blossoms into the mutual betrayal. Bell asks him: "You remember when we used to sit on the top of 734 building, man, looking at the city, talking about what we gonna do?" Barksdale's response signals not only the exact locus of their philosophical divergence, but it is also very revealing of Bell's motivation for legitimacy and his distaste for gangster life: "And you was all into that black pride bullshit, talking like you gonna make motherfuckers proud." Barksdale's tone has a disdainful edge but Bell seems unperturbed and quickly retorts: "Sure was, man, an' you was out hunting on a AK-47, talkin' 'bout, 'I'm gonna get a-warrin'" ("Straight and True" S3, E5). The exchange is also revealing of the impotency of what were once meaningful narratives of solidarity, dissolved in Bell's *modus operandi* by greed and prevented from ever influencing Barksdale's actions by the cynicism of a ghetto-gangster attitude to his surroundings. Bell may have abandoned any notion of community but nevertheless his ambition for legitimacy is as potent as ever and it contradicts Barksdale's gangster ethos.

The scene also emphasizes the fact that Barksdale and Bell are products of entrenched poverty; they are from the bottom of the capitalist hierarchy, which *The Wire* makes clear is a growing pool of unwanted labor in postindustrial America. Yet prevailing American mythology constantly recapitulates, through the media apparatus, the fiction that anyone can make it. As rappers who make it have invariably rapped their way out of the 'hood, this happens as a function of rugged individualism and not out of community

III. The Wire and Game Theory

solidarity and racial uplift and the flip side of this pernicious neoliberal myth is that if you don't make it it is because you are unworthy of it, not because of the radically unjust system. In Barksdale's cynical and limited worldview there are no binding narratives of race and class, none beyond the bonds of immediate family: the myth of upward mobility for Barksdale is false. His ambition is limited to his ruling of the West Baltimore drugs trade with blood and guts. Bell's belief or former belief in black pride fuels his ambition for legitimization. His attempts to achieve this by reforming the drugs trade and investing in property come at the price of his life, however, as the contradiction between black pride and radical individualism poisons his actions. He orders the execution of his own in order to preserve his profits and freedom and, in turn, is executed by his own in vengeance for earlier actions.

Bell fails to realize what D'Angelo and Bodie (J.D. Williams) do, that the "game is rigged" ("Final Grades"). The fallacies of justice and equality, in *The Wire*'s depiction, mask the real efficacy of the Game paradigm, which is the upholding of a strict class and racial hierarchy. Upward mobility for certain American citizens, as is shown in Bell's narrative, is extremely difficult and rare. Thus, Barksdale, in his instinct to stay within the confined boundaries of small scale localized narcotics sales is proven correct, while Bell's ambitions to break out of the ghetto and into the larger game end with his death. The upshot of this wisdom is the tragic fact that the underclass, even those at the tops of their respective hierarchies, stays in the underclass and a Game that mirrors legitimate business in its advocacy of competition usually concludes in either death or prison for its players.

The game-outside-the-game is insulated from the messy ghetto crime of the drug trade but it is no less corrupt. Bell, seeing that legitimate business, while corrupt, is removed from the gristle and direct exploitation of the drugs trade, believed that he could insulate his profits by moving up the food chain. By virtualizing his profits, making them more attuned to free market and the global financial economy, he could detach himself from the often brutal, exploitative and unjust consequences of their generation. The institution into which he was born, the class, and his racial heritage, however prevented this from occurring.

Bell's narrative in *The Wire* is given a final blackly humorous barb in a scene in which McNulty and Bunk examine his apartment following his death. They walk around, agape at its tasteful decoration, its clean lines with expensive modernist furniture, deep pile rug and neatly stacked library. McNulty walks to the library, eyeing the book spines, and reaches for a volume, Smith's

The Wealth of Nations. McNulty raises his brow, peers around once more and mutters to himself: "Who the fuck was I chasing?" ("Middle Ground"). It is as if McNulty realizes he was pursuing the spirit of neoliberalism made flesh in his capacity as an officer of law and order. The arch irony of the presence of the capitalist bible in Bell's library points to the fact that Bell was indeed a great captain of industry who just happened to be born the wrong skin color and in the wrong neighborhood. The self-interest that Smith posited as regrettably inherent in man, in *The Wealth of Nations*, is now accepted as the core virtue and driving force of modern neoliberal economics. It is the very thing that the Game Theoretical models, with which *The Wire* is concerned, seek to harness for the sake of productivity. It is this assumed inherent greed, however, that causes Bell's eventual downfall.

Bell and Barksdale's replacement at the top of the food chain, Marlo Stanfield, clearly has no interest in reforming the drugs trade and in contrast to Bell has a discernable appetite for the gangster elements of the business, in particular a cold fondness for murder. Ironically, however, at the end of *The Wire*'s narrative, Stanfield is offered the legitimacy that Bell so desperately craved but finds no thrill in being a suited shark among many; he is clearly uncomfortable outside his own world and his own game.

Marlo Stanfield: The De-human Capitalist

Without ascribing to human behavior or motivation an essential humanity, it is safe to say that we have evolved as a collective animal. It is indisputable that cooperation has facilitated our evolutionary success and, in turn, it is safe to assume that our capacity for empathy undoubtedly stems from this fact.[21] Empathy or the lack thereof in a society is a crucial factor in determining what kind of society it is or will be. Neoliberal economics is based upon a framework that assumes individual atomization and essentially serf-serving acquisition. Cooperation, as it exists in neoliberal economics and in the Nash Equilibrium of Game theoretical models, exists as a strategic function of individual advancement. In other words, empathy, a potent force in our evolutionary constitution, is systemically devalued in the neoliberal institutions of the West. The absence of empathy leaves more room in our societies for our capacity for tribal violence, which is also surely a factor of our evolution.[22] It is the systemic denial of the cohesive force of empathy in a society that is encapsulated in *The Wire* on micro and macro levels of examination.

III. The Wire and Game Theory

The condition of psychopathology is generally defined as the inability for a person to feel empathy towards others and this is examined on an individual basis in the Marlo Stanfield character. Much more difficult to encapsulate in screen media fiction or any other kind is a broader social drift towards psychopathology. The effects on society of the devaluation of empathy are insidious and abstract but *The Wire* is successful in its depiction of a psychopathological and amoral system, while remaining mostly objective about the actions and behaviors of individuals within the system. While characters like Burrell and Rawls in the upper echelons of the police force, and their counterparts in the drug trade institution such as Barksdale, Bell and Omar Little, are shown to be capable of extreme ruthlessness and brutality, all of these characters are also shown to have the capacity for empathy. As discussed earlier in the chapter, while ruthlessness and venality have contributed to their respective hierarchical rises none of them is devoid of empathy.

The tendency in a framework founded upon atomized competitiveness and self-advancement is for psychopathological behavior, for which Rawls, on the official side, seems to have a particular capacity. Regarding Simon's assertion that the writers consciously wished to give even their most ruthless characters empathetic traits, the viewer is reminded of an episode in the first season in which a sting operation goes wrong and Greggs, working undercover, is shot and seriously wounded. McNulty, who has pushed and maneuvered within the department to make the wiretap investigation into the Barksdale gang happen, realizes that for reasons of his own intellectual vanity, one of his close colleagues has been shot and may die. His departmental nemesis Rawls, upon meeting a distraught McNulty in the hospital waiting room, tells him that despite his hatred for McNulty and his wish to see his career destroyed, Greggs' shooting is not his fault. Rawls sees the bigger ethical and moral picture in this instance, when the stakes are so serious, and uses his contempt for McNulty as leverage with which he can ease McNulty's guilt. "Rawls cares about preserving himself and the clearance rate more than the ultimate mission of police work," Simon says, "but there are moments where they [Rawls, Burrell] become essentially human, in all facets, and we were very conscious of doing that; giving them moments where they show that aside from their priorities they are perfectly capable of striking a deal or being reasonable" ("The Target," audio commentary). Here Simon is stressing the psychopathological tendency induced by the system of Hobbesian competition, where outside of the prescribed priorities of competition empathy still exists. Barksdale too is shown to be capable of something approaching generosity and kindness when acting outside the dictates of competitive brutality that his institution demands. When reformed ex-con Dennis "Cutty" Wise (Chad Coleman), a former employee of Barksdale who has subsequently walked away from the organization, comes to him looking for a donation towards a community gym Barksdale is forthcoming with a large sum. Although, as mentioned, Barksdale's emphasis on family bonds and his friendship with Bell are questionable for obvious reasons, they make up a code that is based upon solidarity and empathy. This code is unraveled, not by Barksdale's immorality, but by the contradictions and impossibilities of his position within an illegal and cut-throat capitalist operation.

The Wire's representation of human nature is relativist, ascribing the capacities for extreme or antisocial behavior not just to assumed intrinsic factors but to a great extent also to environmental conditions. The denial or destruction of binding narratives that the radical competitiveness of the free-market system calls for has created a hostile environment in which paranoia and strategizing against those with whom you share the environment is part of the Game of survival. This is rendered extensively and in detail both in the sanctioned and unsanctioned social institutions of *The Wire*. While the violence of the sanctioned Game is sublimated and de-libidinized through the statistical dictates of competitive efficiency, in the running of the police force, the schools and the media, the violence at the production end of wealth generation in the unsanctioned sector of enterprise remains raw and unmediated. The environmental necessity for violence in the drugs trade presupposes an unsophisticated concept of psychopathology, which is encapsulated most clearly in Marlo Stanfield.

Stanfield is *The Wire*'s only major character that appears to be devoid of empathy and that does not acknowledge any code or narrative beyond his own acquisition of power. It is perhaps for this reason that we see him succeed where Bell failed, in being initiated into the world of legitimate businessmen towards the end of the final series. There is no secession to racial pride, to the bonds of friendship or family and certainly not to the more abstract bonds of community or solidarity. Stanfield is a predator who is perfectly adapted to his environment and the manner of his brutality is cold and calculated. Hector's portrayal of the psychopathic drug lord is understated and effective; most of the expression on Stanfield's otherwise blank visage is only detectable in his eyes.

What is most chilling about the character is his willingness to kill for the most innocuous and spurious of reasons, beyond those of passion or self-

III. The Wire *and Game Theory*

preservation. Bell and Barksdale murdered frequently during their reign but always for reasons of self-preservation. Stanfield, however, as is encapsulated in a narrative involving his ordered execution of a security guard, kills simply because he has the power to do so, displaying a complete lack of empathy for his fellow man. The fourth season sees Stanfield take complete control of the West Baltimore drug trade in the wake of Bell and Barksdale's fall and he exercises his power with absolute ruthlessness. The fourth episode, "Refugees" begins with Stanfield stepping out of an all-night poker game. At a corner shop he goes to the counter to purchase a bottle of water, and while a security guard watches, Stanfield glances derisively back at him while deliberately putting two lollipops into his pocket. The guard follows him out to the street trying to appeal to Stanfield's reason: "What the fuck? You think I dream about coming to work in this shit hole on a Sunday morning? I'm working to support a family, man." Stanfield's response is to turn away dismissively and slug from the bottle. The security guard tells Stanfield that he knows what he is and he's not threatening him, he just appeals to Stanfield's empathy, pointing out that he has to live in this world too: "Now you just clip that shit and act like I'm not even there," the security guard says. "I don't," Stanfield answers, before taking off in a black truck chauffeured by Partlow ("Refugees" S4,E4).

Later Partlow and Pearson are seen outside the corner shop. Pearson asks what the offender has done, to which the response is: "Talked back." The final trace of the security guard is seen when Partlow throws his badge into one of their ad hoc dumping grounds and they proceed to board up the mausoleum, which clearly contains the recently murdered victim. The guard's reasoned appeal to Stanfield's supposed empathy has a terrible outcome for him. In telling Stanfield that he has a family to support and is trying to do so legally with hard work, he has aggravated Stanfield's ego, insulting his self-appointed position as king of West Baltimore. "You want it to be one way," he tells the guard icily before jumping into the truck, "but it's the other way." Stanfield wants the guard to pay for his slight against the order of the world and such things as family and the everyday human struggle to get by are completely beyond his disaffected purview. These appeals may have had traction with Stanfield's predecessors, whose codes, while distorted by their own greed and the machinations of the institution to which they belonged, nevertheless were predicated on the acknowledgment that some sort of value must be put on solidarity. It seems Bell's black pride and Barksdale's emphases on family bonds during their reign of West Baltimore were moribund encumbrances in such a fierce arena of capitalism, encumbrances from which Stanfield is obviously free.

The author of the teleplay for "Refugees," Dennis Lehane (author of novels including *Mystic River* and *Gone, Baby, Gone*) sheds some light on Stanfield's character and his adaptation to his environment:

> Marlo is very *de*-human. That's different than sub-human which suggests an evolutionary disconnect or an insult in regard to intelligence. Marlo is exceptionally intelligent and in an evolutionary sense he's Machiavelli's ideal ... he's been dehumanized to the point where he's incapable of understanding why he should care about anyone or anything that doesn't enrich his bottom line [Alvarez 323].

Stanfield is a product of his environment to the extent that when he is given the keys to legitimacy upon his release from captivity at the end of the fifth season (due to McNulty and Freamon's fictionalized wire evidence), he is unable to adapt. A suited Stanfield is introduced to a high-powered set of Baltimore's captains of industry (finance) by his lawyer, Levy, in a penthouse suite overlooking Baltimore's harbor. It is made clear that Stanfield is a multimillionaire beyond reckoning, who will want for nothing for the rest of his life. For the first time the viewer sees a frightened, uncomfortable Stanfield, who ducks out of the building and heads back to the street, where he reaffirms his gangster machismo by taking a gun from an unnamed street hoodlum and running him off. Stanfield can no more become a legitimate businessman than Barksdale or Bell, as he is a product of a Game with harsher rules, a Game more visceral in its primitive machismo and mostly sealed off from the bigger Game in social and racial terms if not in terms of the wealth it generates and its presiding logic.

The Game Is Rigged

The transition of power in the West Baltimore drug trade from Bell and Barksdale to Stanfield is indicative of an overall trend in *The Wire*'s narrative. It plots a decline in social cohesion and quality of life, particularly for those at the bottom of the capitalist pyramid, where once there was at least a semblance of community spirit and legitimate work available. The macroeconomic forces of the Game paradigm have had the twin-pronged effect of increasing the numbers of surplus Americans, many of whom are inevitably drawn into the narcotics trade, while tending to the numerical fiction of a functional society that the market requires. The market requires this fiction,

III. The Wire *and Game Theory*

which imbues the numbers with a political currency that supersedes any other political requirements, thus ensuring that the fiction is tended to, rather than the reality of a drastically dysfunctional society. The Game paradigm is a self-sustaining system that adheres to the needs of the financial capital of the free market, which has now very little connection with or investment in labor (the drugs trade) and thereby no requirement for a functional society. While nominally there is a political will and need to address crime and other social problems, the War on Drugs in *The Wire* is shown to be a futile game. The nuisance is crime and the corrective is the law, but this is the circular logic of the Game paradigm. The money generated by both crime and its corrective nevertheless accumulates at the top of the hierarchy where those who benefit are insulated by the virtuality of financial capital. In effect, industrial labor has been replaced by the drugs trade in *The Wire*'s West Baltimore, and where once collective narratives such as the labor movement empowered the working class there is now criminality and complete disenfranchisement. The drugs trade, the law that feeds large numbers of petty non-violent criminals into the prison-industrial complex and the black market in general more than suffice in terms of wealth production as far as the market and those who benefit from it are concerned. The system is thus amoral, or psychopathological. In making competition and radical individualism the primary mode of institutional life, binding narratives are undercut. Binding narratives are undoubtedly ancient in humans and have facilitated our evolution as a cooperative species. These narratives are often the vehicles for our empathy. In relating to and identifying with others violence it can be said is, at the very least curbed.

In *The Wire*, therefore, there is a less dramatic but more starkly realistic representation of the social trend towards psychopathology than is represented by the actions of the crash-cell in *Crash*. Whereas the protagonists of *Crash* formulate their own narratives and quasi-religious rites, the characters of *The Wire* seem to obey their own personal and disparate codes, fraught as they may be, from the machismo of tribal violence and acquisition in the drugs trade to the preservation of family bonds. The refraction of all older narratives through the prism of scientism is broached in *End Zone*'s interrogation of the technical jargon of nuclear war. The precision and certainty that science and technology promise—as well as the quintessentially American myth of progress—are denied by the terminal logic of the Bomb and the language it created. The myth of progress is indirectly undercut by the picture that *The Wire*'s narrative paints of disenfranchisement, alienation and increasing social dysfunction. The problem with the numerical fiction of social efficacy and progress that the Game paradigm provides is that it contains no coherent narrative beyond the utopian myth of progress through science. In the essay "The Concept of Enlightenment," Adorno and Horkheimer write, "On their way toward modern science human beings have discarded meaning. The concept is discarded by the formula, the cause by rules and probability" (Horhheimer, Adorno 3). The purpose of the fiction is to preserve American exceptionalist ideology but this is no longer sustainable in the face of the presiding economic aegis of atomized individualism, according to *The Wire*. Where multitudes of disenfranchised citizens are no longer bound by any narrative the threads of nationhood begin to unravel. This is in evidence, perhaps, with the wide scale political disenfranchisement and civil unrest in the United States now, and can go some way to explaining the popularity of a white xenophobic proto-fascist strong man in Donald Trump.

American mythology and ideology, however, has always been based upon spurious fictions. The formative one—that the passage for God's chosen people to heaven comes via the cleansing violence of apocalypse—is reconstituted throughout American history/mythology, and the so-called War on Drugs and War on Terror are couched in these terms. Perhaps the formative ideology and mythology has thus contained the seeds of its own destruction. *The Wire* seems to suggest, nonetheless, that the effects of radical individualism and cyber-capitalism on postindustrial American society is speeding up this process, in that the disparity between instrumentally derived fiction and patent reality is quickly proving the ideology to be untenable. As Simon puts it: "Mythology is important, essential even, to a national psyche. And Americans in particular are desperate in their pursuit of national myth. This is understandable, to a point: coating an elemental truth with the bright gloss of heroism and national sacrifice is the prerogative of the nation-state" (Alvarez 4).

The myth that anyone can make it, that there is a level playing field for all and, perhaps the most pernicious of all, that those who work hard and remain committed to their families, their communities and other institutions, will earn a good standard of living, for Simon serves "as ballast against the unencumbered capitalism that has emerged unchallenged.... In Baltimore, as in so many cities, it is no longer possible to describe this as a myth. It is no longer possible even to remain polite on the subject. It is, in a word, a lie" (Alvarez 6).

While the Game paradigm is part of what allows the unencumbered passage of money throughout the system to accumulate ultimately in greatest

III. The Wire *and Game Theory*

concentration in the disconnected and virtualized world of financial capital, the same is not true regarding (American myths of) social mobility. As Bell's narrative shows, for people born into certain racial or socio-economic backgrounds upward mobility is a chimera. In *The Wire*, there are a number of significant references to the exclusionary logic of the Game paradigm, some of which address the logic of Game Theory itself. In the introduction, there are examples of the Game Theoretical thought-exercise called the Prisoner's Dilemma, in which values are given to certain strategies within the parameters of a game. The logic of the quantitatively assigned strategies of the Cold War, specifically the strategy of Mutually Assured Destruction, is played out throughout *The Wire*'s narrative by Rawls, Burrell and Carcetti, as well as those on the other side of the law. Many of the competitive situations in *The Wire*'s narrative adhere to this competitive strategic logic and the rationality of distrust and betrayal that the Prisoner's Dilemma exercise reveals.

According to Nash and von Neumann's theory, distrust and competitive strategizing are the only rational courses of action. Following the example of the Prisoner's Dilemma, Bell and Barksdale's mutual betrayal can be summarized in the following four permutations:

Bell betrays Barksdale; Barksdale does nothing (in other words cooperates).
Bell does nothing; Barksdale does nothing.
Bell does nothing; Barksdale betrays Bell.
Bell betrays Barksdale; Barksdale betrays Bell.

In keeping with the logic of Game Theory as is exemplified in the Arms Race of the Cold War, trust is an irrational strategy and so, for a mass of complicated reasons, Bell's attempt to move up the hierarchical ladder and attain legitimacy fails. The narcotics trade is sealed off from the larger Game by the law and is thus played according to more brutal stakes; the rules of the Game into which he is initiated as a capitalist competitor do not allow for his transition into the sanctioned Game. Both Bell and Barksdale's strategies of betrayal were rational according to the logic of Game Theory but the outcome was one of mutual destruction with Bell being killed and Barksdale going to jail, presumably for a very long time.

Another direct reference to the Game paradigm as an institutional trap comes in the first series, whereby D'Angelo Barksdale displays his insight into this tragedy. D'Angelo comes upon the touts Bodie and Wallace (Michael B. Jordan) playing checkers on a board in the open area of their low-rise tenement block. He chides them for playing checkers and proceeds to explain the rules of chess by using a closely observed analogy of the chess hierarchy with that of his uncle's drug organization to teach them.

D'ANGELO: Now look man, it's simple. See this? This the kingpin," he says holding the piece aloft and kissing it. "A'ight? Now he the man. You get the other dudes king, you got the game. But he tryin to get your king too, so you gotta protect it. Now the king, he move one space in any damn direction he chose, cos he the king, like this, this, right? But he ain't got no hussle, right? But the rest of these motherfuckers on the team, they got his back and they run so deep, he ain't really gotta do shit.

BODIE: Like your uncle.

D'ANGELO: Yeah, like my uncle. Now you see this? This the queen. She smart, she fierce, she move any way she want, as far as she want. And she, is the go-get-shit-done-piece."

WALLACE: Remind me of Stringer.

D'ANGELO: And this over here is the castle. It's like the stash. It move like this, and like this.

WALLACE: No, the stash don't move man.

D'ANGELO: Yo, c'mon man, think. How many times we move the stash house this week? Right? And any time we move the stash, we gotta move a little muscle with it, right? To protect it.

BODIE: True, true, you right. A'ight, what about them little bald-headed bitches right there?

D'ANGELO: These right here, these are the pawns. They're like the soldiers. They move like this, one space at a time, unless they fightin. Then they move like this. The like the front line, they be out in the field.

BODIE: So how they get to be the king?

D'ANGELO: It ain't like that. See the king stay the king. Everybody stay who they is. Except the pawn. If they get all the way down to the other side, they get to be queen. Like I said, the queen ain't no bitch, she got all the moves.

BODIE: A'ight, so, if I make it to the other end, I win?

D'ANGELO: If you catch the other dude's king and trap it, then you win.

BODIE: But if I make it to the end, I'm top dog? Bodie, is here internalizing his own position as a pawn in the game.

D'ANGELO: Naw yo, it ain't like that. Look, the pawns man, in the game, they get capped quick, they be out the game early.

BODIE: Unless they some smart ass pawns.

III. The Wire and Game Theory

This deftly realized analogy is given grim weight by the subsequent knowledge that all three are dead before the story's end. Bodie, who is obviously possessed of the most street-smarts of the three, is the last to go. In the fourth season he is killed by Marlo Stanfield's men, but not before realizing that the Game is indeed rigged against the pawns. Stanfield's killing spree came to include Bodie's friend "Little Kevin" (Tyrell Baker). Having been forced to sell for Stanfield for a much-reduced percentage after the fall of the Barksdale gang, the killing of his friend, again for innocuous reasons, sees him pushed to become an informant. Bodie realizes that his jail-time, his loyalty and his earning power have garnered him absolutely no loyalty from the top of the hierarchy. He realizes the futility of the last number of years he has spent in the game and decides to meet McNulty and give up Stanfield's crew. "This game is rigged, man," he tells McNulty, recalling the scene from forty-seven episodes previously, "we like them little bitches on the chess board." Unfortunately, he is spotted getting into McNulty's car by one of Stanfield's men and the execution is ordered.

The Wire acknowledges the capitalism-as-Game paradigm in this chess analogy. D'Angelo tries to leave the Game he has been born into, turning his back on his uncle and the drugs organization he leads but is murdered in prison, on Bell's orders, on the chance he may turn informant on the organization. Bodie's attempts to get out from under the oppression of his institution sees his execution by Stanfield's men. Thus *The Wire*'s narrative undercuts the American myth of social mobility, particularly for those of a certain class and race.

The power structures of sanctioned institutions in *The Wire* are also shown to maintain steep inequality. As discussed previously, the Baltimore municipal system is shown to adhere to the market-derived numerical fiction of social efficacy. The individuals who are most competitive and ruthless, according to the underlying logic of the institutions, are invariably the ones who also adhere to this fiction. In other words, the police brass, such as Rawls and Burrell, gain advancement by adhering to the statistical fiction of effective policing, which in turn sustains the institution. Rawls and Burrell are shown to maintain their power thusly, often at the expense of those beneath them in the power structure, as is seen most pertinently in the "COMSTAT" meetings of the third series. In one such meeting of the police brass and middle management, in which Colvin is being berated by Rawls for a jump in the crime statistics in his sector, Burrell interjects and tells him "if the felony rate doesn't fall, you most certainly will" ("Dead Soldiers," S3, E3). In keeping with *The Wire*'s basis on Greek Tragedy—whereby the institutions are the Gods and individuals are fated by the machinations of the institutional priority of self-preservation and the bottom line—Burrell tells Colvin that the God that is the Baltimore Police Department can only be appeased with juked stats. "If the gods are fucking you, you find a way to fuck them back. It's Baltimore, gentlemen, the gods will not save you."

The Wire's criticism of the Game paradigm encapsulates a very contemporary and very relevant socio-historical phenomenon. Its argument against the de-emphasis of social cohesion caused by the desire for calculable rationality, however, has a long precedent in history. It was a manifest goal beginning around the later Enlightenment to make the social affairs of people subject to the calculability and predictability of science. While the viability and desirability of this project has been resisted and denied and criticized by many since, the idea and the urge are as strong as they've ever been. Under the guise of statistical models inherited from the Cold War, whereby technocrats believed they could remove the fallibility of human judgment from the nuclear stand-off, the postindustrial world is subject to this instrumental attempt at rationality more than any time in previous history. *The Wire* may be fiction but its depiction of the framework of institutionalism, not just in the United States but in all the postindustrial world, is very accurate. The science upon which the statistical models of the framework are based, assumes that free markets are the natural state and that atomized competition is a faux–Darwinian function of evolution. In their adherence to the market logic of the bottom line, these institutional models deny any abstract thinking based upon the indeterminacy of language by which people can understand irrational humanity. They deny narratives that point to our cooperative evolutionary process. Instead, as *The Wire* extensively argues, there are statistical fictions that sustain a terribly unjust class, race and economic system in the face of an unraveling ideology.

Police, People, Technology and Wars in *The Wire*

There are quite a few literary references in *The Wire* apart from the stated bases in Greek Tragedy of the all-powerful postmodern institution. Kinder is observant in her essay "Re-Wiring Baltimore":

> Through its network of intertextual allusions (to TV, cinema, literature, theatre, and journalism), which continues growing through the final episode (with its pointed ref-

III. The Wire *and Game Theory*

erences to Shakespeare, Kafka, and H.L. Mencken), *The Wire* explicitly mentions both precursors and foils, with which it should be compared, training us how to remix or resist what we previously have been encouraged to admire [50].

When it comes to the dehumanizing effects of industrialization, or in this case, postindustrialization, Dickens stands out as an obvious influence. He is less frequently mentioned by critics than the Greek influence but is referenced in the text itself in a couple of rather irreverent ways. When Bodie wishes to tell a narcotics colleague that he has been left high and dry without product for his trade he tells his colleague that he has been left holding his Charles Dickens, while demonstrably grabbing his crotch. Even more pointed is an editorial meeting at the fictionalized *Baltimore Sun*, when executive editor Whiting tells his reporters to explore the "Dickensian aspect" of the homeless plight, while completely missing the Dickensian aspect of bottom-line utilitarianism that is dehumanizing the entire society. While the great concern of Dickens' novels was the dehumanization of the proletariat, the grinding up of the poor in the gears of industrialization, *The Wire* is concerned with the devaluation of a forgotten underclass and the dehumanization of all in the postnuclear neoliberal west. Dickens' great tract against utilitarianism, *Hard Times* (1854), criticizes the idea that the world can be fully rationalized according to the dictates of capitalist utility.[23]

Dickens and the Greeks may have been the literary forbears of *The Wire*'s critique of postindustrial America but in terms of filmic touchstones for institutional dehumanization, it is unsurprising that Simon turned to Kubrick. As Kinder puts it: "Significantly, Simon cites Stanley Kubrick's *Paths of Glory* (1957) as his primary cinematic model and 'the most important political film in history,' a war film that succeeds in combining systemic analysis with more traditional forms of realism and emotional identification" (Kinder, 51). If there is a common thread in Kubrick's life's work, from *Paths of Glory*, through *Strangelove*, *A Clockwork Orange* and *2001*, it is his concern with institutional primacy over human life (not dissimilar to Dickens), often in the form of the orthodoxy and rationality of science and technology. Kubrick wasn't a naïve humanist, of course, and he often played with the notion of essential humanity by making his heroes brutally violent, as in *A Clockwork Orange*'s Alex, or by ascribing irrationality and emotion to a machine and cold robotic rationality to men, as in *2001*. The writers of *The Wire* have taken this lesson on board, making sure the characters are motivated by irrational forces as much as the institutional dictates. Speaking about *Paths of Glory*, Simon says, "Well, it really is about what happens when institutionalism becomes paramount. And the paradigm becomes, what can you do for the institution? Not what is the purpose of the institution, or how can the institution serve you or serve society as a whole. Now, if you look at everything, from what's going on Wall Street right now to how we got into Iraq, it's the same echo" (Inskeep 2).[24]

Institutionalism in postindustrial America (the West) adheres to statistical calculations of efficiency that are dictated by the bottom line of financial capitalism. The dehumanizing effects of this instrumentalism are less dramatic than Alex's brainwashing in *A Clockwork Orange* and more akin to the banality of evil. The drift in society is an insidious one; however, if Baudrillard's theories regarding the totalitarianism of calculable rationality and technological alienation in postmodernity are captured in *The Wire* most clearly, it is in policing strategies and how they fit with moribund American ideology.

In "The Political Technology of the Individual," Foucault discusses the historical relationship of the individual to the state and how a certain concept of policing has arisen in the postindustrial world. "Political arithmetic was the knowledge implied by political competence," he writes, "and you know very well that the other name of this political arithmetic was statistics, a statistics related not at all to probability but to the knowledge of state" (Foucault, 408). *The Wire*'s depiction of the War on Drugs, as discussed, demonstrates that the couching of what is a policing or public health issue in the terms of war has a destructive and alienating effect on society. This alienation is underscored in *The Wire* by the increasing distance and disconnection between the two factions, the police and the dealers. Technology is used instead of older methods of policing that rely on face-to-face interaction and communication, in mostly vain attempts to breach this distance. The wire to which the wiretaps on criminals' phones refers, is also a figurative wire that runs through the system, the schemata of postindustrial life connecting us all, but connecting us virtually through the digital routing of money and through the closed circuit camera that always watches, much like in Foucault's great metaphor of the panopticon in *Discipline and Punish*. The enmity between the factions cannot be bridged, mediated or interrogated with either the technology of spying or the strategy of statistical reflexivity. In "The Concept of Enlightenment," Adorno and Horkheimer write about the general disconnection that comes as the price of rational control that humans have pursued since the Enlightenment: "Human beings purchase the increase in their power with estrangement from that over which it is exerted" (7). Certainly in *The Wire*'s depiction the technological distance between the factions prefigures

III. The Wire and Game Theory

the lack of understanding. The police routinely underestimate or misunderstand their nominal foes and the cracking of heads, racking up of statistics and the feeding of the prisons with those made surplus to the requirements of hyper-capitalism keeps the circular logic of the Game paradigm and the War on Drugs intact.

The War on Drugs adheres to the formative American myths of apocalyptic cleansing that have run through the heart of American political life since its inception. The War on Terror follows the same patterns of policing as the War on Drugs, in that it is virtual, autotelic and carried out via technology, from a distance.[25] American wars from Vietnam until the present have tended towards the same fundamental misunderstandings of the enemy. In the Vietnam War, the rationalization of the conflict with the statistics of performance targets illuminates the alienation and misunderstanding that proved disastrous for the Americans and their foe. Indiscriminate killing undertaken by American soldiers convinced more and more Vietnamese to join the Viet Cong in fighting off the invaders, while the vast and incredible technological arsenal at the disposal of the United States did not obliterate the will of the enemy, but rather strengthened it. In the book *The Fog of War*, McNamara records attending "Critical Oral History," in which he met with the past leaders of the Viet Cong to discuss, among other matters, why the conflict escalated in 1960. In these meetings, McNamara was shocked by the revelation of the level of profound misunderstanding and misreading of the then enemy, to what were disastrous effects. McNamara lamented the lack of communication between the enemies and speculated that had there been communication between them, there would have been empathy and the conflict may not have become as bloody and prolonged as it did.

The War on Drugs as is depicted in *The Wire* reveals the same kind of misunderstanding, predicated on the same kinds of narrow assumptions of the so-called foe's motivations and quantified rationalizations of the war. There can be no empathy and no understanding to bridge the gap between the instrument of the state and the ever growing underclass who participate in the American Dream, either through their own capitalist Game model or through the transcendence and escapism of a drug high. In a scene from the episode "Reformation" from the third season, Colvin berates Sergeant Carver (Seth Gilliam) for not having any informants, for not policing the community with humanity and laments the implied internecine enmity of the term war, in a futile police directive:

> This drug thing, it ain't police work. It ain't. I mean I can send any fool with a badge and a gun up on them corners and jack a crew and grab vials. But policing? I mean, you call something a war, and pretty soon everyone gonna be running around acting like warriors. They're gonna be running around on a damn crusade, storming corners, slappin on cuffs, *racking up body counts*. And when you're at war, you need a fucking enemy. And pretty soon, damn near everybody on every corner is your fucking enemy. And soon the neighborhood that you're supposed to be policing, that's just occupied territory.… Soldiering and policing, they ain't the same thing. And before we went and took the wrong turn and started up with these war *games*, the cop walked a beat, and he learned that post. And if things happened on that post, whether they be a rape or robbery or shooting, he had people out there helping him, feeding him information. But every time I've come to you, my DEU Sergeant, for information, to find out what's going on out there in them streets, all that came back was some bullshit. You had your stats, you had your arrests, you had your seizures. But none of that amounts to shit when you talking about protecting the neighborhood, now do it? [S3, E10].

Policing that is dictated by the interests of the free market has no investment in interactive community-based policing. The War on Drugs, like the War on Terror, is a virtual war, fought at arm's length through technological means. Both are chimeras: the former, a war on the growing American underclass, excluding them from the higher sanctioned Games.

Good policing is generally achieved in *The Wire* by those cops who are swimming against the tide of statistics-generation that is pursued as par for the course by the Baltimore Police Force. These examples of good policing invariably involve a level of human interaction with both the law abiding and law breaking population that is actively discouraged by the numbers game. In broader thematic terms, as mentioned, *The Wire* concerns itself with the devaluation of people in the postindustrial world and the dehumanizing effects of quantitative models on people within official institutions. There are numerous vignettes within the narrative complex where the loss of human interaction and the binding narrative of community is lamented. Most notable for its powerful acting and pathos is a scene in which Bunk admonishes Omar for his part in the destruction of the community spirit they had in their shared neighborhood upbringing. The use of human interaction, communication and reason as police strategies is repeatedly shown to be superior to technological and technocratic means in *The Wire*. Human informants, in the form of Reginald "Bubbles" Cousins (Andre Royo) and Bell, invariably prove to be more integral to the police operations than the surveillance technology employed, in much the same way as the messy human silliness of Muffley and Kissoff's interaction in *Strangelove*, for example, is closer, and thus infinitely preferable, to the inflexible modulations of technology. All of the texts

III. The Wire and Game Theory

analyzed, of course, emphasize human considerations, in particular the inscrutable and vital subtleties of communication, and the importance of narrative, over mechanized logic.

The proliferation of technology in the world means the proliferation of information or white noise, the majority of which is inconsequential. Simon articulates the program's approach to policing technology in his commentary accompanying the first episode:

> We tried to layer in these sort of innocuous shots of surveillance throughout the first season, to give you a sense of a world that is increasingly watched, even watched with a certain indifference. And we are trying to create a world not where there was little nuggets of information that were precious, and that's all there was, which is often the way of so many police procedurals on tv; we were trying to create a world where there was almost *too much information* being put in front of the detectives and it was their job to sift ["Middle Ground," Simon commentary].

The detachment of policing from its need for human interaction recalls Baudrillard's theory about the Gulf War, and the policing philosophy that *The Wire* expounds opens out to encompass the broader context of both internal and foreign American political policy. The War on Terror as it was expounded by the Bush administration, insofar as it was a war against the uncivilized and savage believers in Islam, was actually predicated on a lack of understanding of America's antagonists. The technological means of surveillance and destruction became central means of fighting the War on Terror, while intractable enmity and binary ideological opposition were par for the course, at least in the media and public political response to the anomalous but all-purpose bogeyman: Al Qaeda. The lack of understanding the quantification models and the surveillance technology prescribes comes to some extent from the distances these modes engineer between institutions, between groups and between individuals. Again, in this instance, *The Wire*'s criticism of postmodern American politics and culture encompasses both the macro and the micro. The institutional fictions of neoliberal economic modeling permeate the culture, and the same fictions that the cracking of heads enumerates on a local level are reflected in the macro fictions that underpin American aggression in foreign lands.

Conclusion
Imagination Is Irrationality

The postnuclear imperative towards rationality was given the credence of scientific objectivity and the infallibility of mathematics but this instrumentalism was received through the prism of the Cold War's apocalyptic battle. As with the making of America, the problem of the other, the battle between civilization and savage, was fought with the apodictically correct numerals of capitalism and its gift of liberty.

The postnuclear Game models that facilitated, and brought the civilized world through the looking glass of the end of history, are pregnant with the psychological proclivities of those who formulated them, as well as the pre-existing belief system in which they were immersed. The Bomb marks the birth of neoliberal economic orthodoxy, and many of the traits of the contemporary era of postmodernity. This is most notable in the acceptance of the means of technology as ideology and secular theology, where its objectivity and calculable rationality are in danger of snuffing out all non-instrumental narratives. The placing of purposive instrumentalism, the primary function of which is acquisition and growth, at the heart of human endeavor and interaction leaves nothing to guard against the endless vacuum of meaninglessness except scientism's own false promise of certitude. Apocalyticism is still alive, of course, the sense of a nameless dread remains, most commonly that of the lethal toxicity of the environment we have created.[1] Ironically, however, the Bomb is no longer the (specific) purveyor of literal destruction. This, it seems, will most likely come about through unfettered capitalism's insatiable requirement for growth, when the environment is no longer able to sustain the population. We cling to vague notions of techno-utopianism, the sense of the cycle of birth-death-rebirth that is ancient in humans is diminished by our belief in perfectibility, yet the knowledge of our ending remains present behind the ceaseless throb of information technology.

Conclusion

The Bomb saw a transference of the power of Christian apocalypticism from mythology and theology to the secular means of science. This transference allows the continuation of some of the formative strains of American exceptionalist mythology into secular modernity, as is revealed in *End Zone*'s delving into the theology of the bomb. The narrative of apocalypticism has, of course, remained an ever-present, but God has been replaced by science as a conduit of American exceptionalism. The civilizing mission, as the pilgrims saw it, was to order society according to a godly decree of commercial and scientific rationality—the path to utopia, to the promised Eden, is reached through the progress of order and efficiency. The civilizing mission became the secular and rational domain of man's instrument, when technology became the means of a real apocalypse. In other words, the civilizing mission of the Cold War, for the United States, was to remove the unnatural collectivist ideology from America's path to Utopia. This war was fought in the virtual realm; technological and industrial capabilities were the weapons, backed up by the ultra-rational, allegedly infallible scientific means of capitalist technocracy. The technology and technocracy was ideological, which precipitated the ideology becoming technological.

The collapse of the Soviet Union was mythologized as a year zero for capitalism and global democracy, as such it was seen by neoliberal ideologues like Francis Fukuyama as proof that American ideology and the attached technological methods of social organization were natural and unequivocally correct.[2] The sense of mission that the Puritans and Pilgrims brought with them on the boats, to harmonize the lives of humankind under the aegis of godly progress, is still prominently visible in this Cold War triumphalism. As Gray writes, "The Puritans who colonized the country in the seventeenth century viewed themselves as creating a society that would lack the evils of the Old World. Established on universal principles it would serve as a model to all of humankind. For these English colonists, America marked a new beginning in history" (*Black Mass* 150). The defeat of Soviet communism has been perceived as a *carte blanche* for the doctrinal spread of capitalism across the international spectrum by United States power elites in the intervening years. It is the unfettered neoliberal market capitalism that was shaped to a large extent by the peculiar circumstances of the Cold War, under the guidance of anti-communist and anti-collectivist zealots such as von Hayek, Friedman, von Neumann and Nash. It is the binary opposite of communism, thus the apodictically correct form of capitalism, and its assumptions have been accepted and implemented across the postindustrial world, from the macro

Conclusion

(markets) down to the micro (institutions) levels. The events of 9/11, Gray argues, have accelerated the spread of this kind of liberal democracy. Further to this effect, the global recession that began in the early twenty-first century late two thousands has locked the democracies of the Western world into the vagaries of free-market capitalism, with no apparent way out.

The processes of the market have been implemented across the institutional system of the developed world, as is seen in the analysis of *The Wire*, ensuring that each individual within is also subject to the vagaries of a financial market that has no investment in their lives whatsoever. Gray is unequivocal on this matter, stating that as far as elite power is concerned "Democracy may be desirable but it must be limited to protect market freedoms" (*Black Mass* 120). Within the hierarchy of the Game paradigm, democracy is enacted only as a function of the financial market, and in *The Wire*'s depiction, an individual's place in the hierarchy is very much contingent upon their class and race. The ideals of America's nationhood, such as justice, equality and equal opportunity are exposed as fallacies by the death of work and the fact that so many Americans are now surplus to the requirements of the financial marketplace. These noble abstractions that are continuously recapitulated as the core values of American life and politics, are in reality, secondary considerations, nuisances to be attended to after the absolute, unfettered autonomy of the market has been secured. *The Wire* debunks the fallacy of the odious non sequitur, the now all too familiar austerity mantra, more with less, with particular precision in its fifth season.

The Bomb's destructive power in the Cold War found its true expression not in physical terms but in its destruction of the ancient narrative of rebirth. Ironically this includes the Christian apocalyptic version of this myth, which held that a violent cleansing of the world would lead to the dawning of heaven. The secular apocalypse, however, does not contain this notion of rebirth in its destruction, and as such the Bomb is a destroyer of meaning, the individual meaning that is inextricably bound up with collective and shared meaning. The atomic effect of the Bomb is figurative, it atomizes shared narrative bonds. The effect of the loss of meaning—where the Bomb (technology) has killed God and is now the source of terrible awe and power—is that the search for meaning, or certitude, at the very least, is now prescribed by the techno-ideology that surrounded the weapon's deployment by the U.S. in the Cold War.

As is seen in *Strangelove*'s acute satire, there was little that was rational about the elite who rose to power as thermonuclear priests, those who spoke

Conclusion

to the Bomb and understood the power of its rationality, nor was the situation that facilitated their rise a sane or rational situation. Without overstating a point that should now be abundantly clear, the Game paradigm of statistically derived marketplace ordinances is not an objective, scientific method of social organization. It is not so-called human irrationality that is the problem; it is the dangerous fallacy that technology can circumvent our perceived fallibilities. The greatest danger comes, as is so effectively demonstrated in *Strangelove*, when human beings forgo communication and empathy, and abdicate moral judgment for machine logic. In this regard, *Strangelove* prefigures *The Wire*'s criticism of the neoliberal Game paradigm. Where President Muffley may be effete and silly, his empathy and communicative ability almost prevents nuclear annihilation. Decision making has been given over to the inexorable certitude of mechanical processes, however, and mutual destruction is the true end point of logical certitude. In *Dr. Strangelove* communication, empathy and moral judgment are denigrated in favor of mechanical processes. Precisely the same thing occurs in *The Wire*'s depiction of the War on Drugs, where the requirements of market-dictated institutional efficiency always trump empathy or individual moral agency. This takes place within the prescribed enmity of the Game paradigm—between these nominally opposed factions of American society, the civilized versus the uncivilized other—in which surveillance technology is now used in the attempt to bridge the gap that once required communication and interaction. The result, according to *The Wire*, is a clearly declining civilization. The free market only requires the appearance of social functionality, however, and those within its institutions are beholden to its power, as seen in the ubiquitous practice of juking the stats. We are beholden to the instrumental processes to the detriment of society, according to *The Wire*, which is a forewarning that *Strangelove* and Kubrick's other films from the period impart. In general terms the human abdication of morality to the requirements of growth dictated by the market is leading to the destruction of the environment that sustains us.

Uncertainty is what humans fear more than any other factor. This state is apparently intolerable to us a species: the truth of our frailty, our subjection to the perpetual flux of the universe and our contingency on the conditions of inscrutable nature are obscured by the systems we create. This fear is the source of a faith in science and technology as much as it is the source of spiritual faith. The advent of the Bomb and its scriptural decree towards efficiency facilitated the rise of the extreme beliefs of a narrow cult, from the corridors of power in Washington and at RAND in Santa Monica, to virtual global dominance. Christian faith is no longer powerful enough to shield the masses of the West from the terror of uncertainty, yet the civilizing mission against the economic enemy has been victorious, and thus, radical, unfettered capitalism (and its techno-ideology) has become a secular religion, one that is devoid of any binding narrative beyond a vague and atomized techno-utopianism.[3] Neoliberal economics and its institutional Game system effectively seek to corral human behavior according to some neat mathematics based upon extremely narrow, ideologically preconceived notions about human nature. The unthinking assumption that our logic and our mathematics are unbound by human limitations is inherently contradictory, and is part of *Strangelove*'s deeply ironic satire of the abdication of moral responsibility for infallible machine-logic. "Given the fact of human fallibility," Gray writes, "the model is sure to contain flaws, some of which may be fatal. The result of persisting in the attempt to realize it is bound to be a society very different from the one that was envisaged" (*Black Mass* 74).

This leads to the essence of Ballard's novel. Our lived existence within technology and as technology, the novel posits, has reconstituted our Oedipal desires, given them over to post–Cold War technology's destructive and psychosexual properties. The attempt to corral human nature according to technology's assumed flawless logic does not precipitate the rise of a more logical or rational society of people in the novel, but creates a cell of people whose passions and subconscious desires see them construct a new binding narrative that revolves around a fusion of energy in violent automotive death, and in the filming of this event, its endless reproducibility for consumption.

There is a lack of empathy for the pain and suffering of others in the crash cell's neo-narrative. From Ballard's perspective, their actions are undoubtedly intended to shock, in order to convey the point that this newly conceived techno-world is abhorrent to our sensibilities. Ballard's story is highly stylized, the actions of the crash cell are science fictional, yet its engagement with the social and cultural factor of an emerging psychopathology is hugely relevant. The abdication of morality for machine certainty in *Strangelove*, underscored a psychopathology that was personified at the time in ultra-rational technocrats like von Neumann, Nash and Kahn. The tenets of their Game models deny empathy, communication and binding narratives, relying instead on the efficiency of (radical capitalist) logic. Technology and its means are used more and more, it seems, to bridge the gaps between people, so to speak. In *Crash*, technology is used to bridge the gap in a shocking and unexpected way, yet it is still done in a way that narrativizes and binds those involved.

Conclusion

In *The Wire*, we see this psychopathology too, in the erosion of binding narratives and an imperative towards ruthless acquisition, albeit following a vastly different approach to that of *Crash* or the other works. Marlo Stanfield is a product of his environment, the nadir of a brutal capitalist institutionalism, where the law only extends if the status quo of growth and profit is somehow upset. Stanfield represents the extreme, however, in a system that is organized around the tenets of selfish acquisition. As such, in *The Wire*'s depiction, the psychopathology does not reside with the majority of people, but resides in the system itself, in its denial of empathy, of communication and of any collective narrative. The Game paradigm implements amoral market values on a micro level, leading to a self-fulfilling dysfunction of institutions and the greater society. The market, however, only requires the appearance of a functioning society.

Technology is used in the attempt to bridge the gap between people, particularly in the institutional factionalism between the police and those involved in the drugs trade. In *The Wire*, the police officers that try to bridge the gap between the police force and their nominal enemy are often the ones who are effective at their job. Understanding, or at least respect for the intelligence and humanity of the enemy, is shown in *The Wire* to work against the interminable slide into further dysfunction that is the general state of atomized capitalist society. Like Muffley and Kissoff in *Strangelove* and even Alex in *A Clockwork Orange*, so-called human irrationality is vastly preferable to the amorality of machine logic.

Lesson number one, empathize with your enemy, from the eleven lessons laid out by Robert McNamara in *The Fog of War*, is particularly significant in this regard. Just as the technical imperative that underpinned the United States' fight in Vietnam precipitated the catastrophic entrenchment of enmity between the two sides, so too are the deepening enmity and factionalism of the War on Drugs and War on Terror precipitated by techno-economic imperatives. The body count engendered the same kinds of corruption and the same lack of understanding in the Vietnam conflict as is depicted in *The Wire*'s performance target-run Baltimore. McNamara should understand this lesson very well, as it was under his tenure as Secretary of Defense that these methods were brought to bear on the war.

The Bomb and its techno-economic imperative destroy meaning, and hollow out narratives, apart from a weak techno-utopian one. Stories and narratives in general are the vehicles for empathy and a sense of a shared purpose. In *The Wire*, only fractured narratives are evident, such as Stringer

Conclusion

Bell's corrupted ambition towards racial uplift, or Stanfield's brutal interpretation of American free enterprise: any binding narratives of solidarity are difficult to sustain in the postindustrial world. This is most clearly and poignantly depicted in the story of the Sobotkas in season two. Under the aegis of radical financial capitalism and its all-pervasive decree of instrumental efficiency there is very little room for binding narratives, nor is there room any more, according to *The Wire*, for citizens to engage with American myths of equality, democracy and justice. The rank and file police display solidarity but generally what is seen in *The Wire* is the attempt of many individuals who are frail, funny, silly, weak, brave and irrational, to simply get by in a system that enforces their separation.

Harkness's vain attempt to find comfort or meaning in the technical certitude promised by the Bomb and its jargon in *End Zone* seems at first rather bleak, yet it is in the telling of the tale that the seemingly insurmountable systemic gap is bridged. DeLillo's narrator survives, leaving Logos on a stretcher, being force fed by plastic tubes, and so, in the telling of the story, DeLillo's Harkness bridges the gap between author and reader and between readers. The Bomb and its techno-imperative atomizes binding narratives, the vehicles of empathy and understanding, but DeLillo subverts this affect, harnessing, as he puts it, "the tendency of language to work in opposition to the enormous technology of war" (*New York Times*, September 7, 1997). Where the indeterminacy of language has meant its denigration as a means of social organization, DeLillo, Ballard, Kubrick and the creators and writers of *The Wire* know that the attempt to modulate or control human behavior instead of understand it, is dangerously naïve and doomed to failure. It is the flexibility of language that can facilitate deeper understanding, meaning and empathy; this is the magic and numinousness of language for DeLillo and the others. The role of the storyteller in postmodern society is therefore vital. The saturation of information in the postmodern era takes the usual form of commercial or power-serving narratives, the subjection of humans to the prescriptive fictions of nationhood and (economic) ideology. The storytellers that decode and debunk these prescriptions and humanize its characters are the ones who create vital narratives for our time.

In *Dangerous Knowledge*, David Malone presents the stories of four scientists whose discoveries so challenged scientific and mathematical orthodoxy that they have been all but forgotten by history. The reason for this, Malone points out, is that their discoveries destabilized the assumed basis of science and mathematics in unequivocal, objective certitude. German mathematician Georg Cantor's study of infinities inadvertently proved that once numbers became extremely large, they were no longer rational any more, and most interestingly he proved that in order to work with these numbers one had to think irrationally oneself. The Austrian physicist, Ludwig Boltzmann, tried to prove the existence of atomic particles, while his countryman Kurt Godel, a logician trying to prove the veracity of logical thinking, inadvertently proved that there were things that logic could never prove and, moreover, that figuring out what cannot be proved is an impossibility. This is Gödel's uncertainty theory, which illuminated some of the limitations of logic, a discovery that was rejected by his scientific peers.[4]

Finally, Alan Turing tried to prove that humans were, at their core, logically computational machines that acted in terms of stimulus and response and that a machine could be made to replicate the decision-making of a human if enough information was fed into its programming, but again, Turing inadvertently proved that no such thing was possible. What is most notable, and deeply ironic in these discoveries is that they all prove, whether intentionally or not, that the faculty of human imagination is essentially irrational. The concept of rationality as it is understood today has been hijacked by an ideology and as a result is dangerously prescriptive. As the above examples demonstrate, rationality is vastly reductive, and the fear and loathing that greeted the above discoveries is more evidence that what humans fear most of all is uncertainty, and that we will go to great lengths to construct ameliorative fictions against it. Scientism is the dominant fiction of the contemporary moment.

We cannot revert back to pre-scientific faith, much as fundamentalists refuse to accept this, but neither will narratives cease to be the central element of collective human life. To narrate our own lives, usually as part of a greater collective (tribal, national, creed, etc.) narrative, is something that will exist as long as people do. The denigration and unraveling of mainly religious narratives cannot spell the end of narratives, or religion, but it is difficult to see what will emerge in the coming times. The best stories, as those of the works analyzed herein, as long as they are told, written or shown, will always see to it that binding narratives will provide meaning beyond hollow instrumentalism or desperate fundamentalism.

Chapter Notes

Introduction

1. This case has been strongly made by Gray in *Straw Dogs* and *Black Mass*.
2. Steven Belletto's *No Accident, Comrade: Chance and Design in Cold War American Narratives*, as well as his essay, "The Game Theory Narrative and the Myth of the National Security State," discuss the fate of "stalled narrative(s)" in Game Theory's autotelic parallel universe (343). In the above essay, Belletto also astutely observes the connection between religion and Game Theoretical formulations as faithful beliefs (or hopes) in the power of either to inoculate against the terrifying chaos and uncertainty of the universe.
3. Friedrich von Hayek, the Austrian economist, formulated the concept of the "self-directing automatic system," a theoretical counterpart to Nash's "Equilibrium." It is essentially radical, unfettered capitalism, and Hayek was a huge influence on Friedman, the chief architect of contemporary neoliberal capitalism.
4. For clear examples of Prisoners' Dilemmas as applied to the Cold War stand-off see László Méró's *Moral Calculations: Game Theory, Logic and Human Frailty*, pp. 32–34.
5. *The Trap* contains interviews with Nash, Buchanan and other significant figures in Game Theory's application to social sciences after the Cold War. See also the chapter in Kaplan's *Wizards*, "The New Generation," pp. 356–385.
6. Steven Belletto has written insightfully on the connection between Game Theory and the ludic in postmodern fiction.
7. As is discussed below in the detailed discussion of Game Theory, the two mathematicians most influential to its development and emergence during the Cold War period, John von Neumann and John Nash, were both rabidly anti-communist. There is no doubt this had a bearing on the theory's formulation. There is no doubt also, that the psychological problems and foibles of both men had a bearing on the theory and its implementation, a point that *Strangelove* did not miss in its satirical characterizations.
8. See Sacvan Bercovitch's *The Puritan Origins of the American Self* for insight into formative American ideology, and for his argument for the American tendency towards a regenerative violence see Richard Slotkin's *Regeneration Through Violence* and *Gunfighter Nation*.

Chapter I

1. In *The Rites of Ascent* Bercovitch complicates the Puritan influence on America, but nevertheless posits a mixture of commercial, apocalyptic and progressively secular aspects as influences on their "mission," and in turn, the formative American ideology.
2. Fordism and Taylorism were ideologies, but they had not insinuated into the heart of politics of the time in the manner Game Theory, systems analysis and so forth have in the postnuclear age.
3. See Slotkin's *Gunfighter Nation: The Myth of the Frontier in Twentieth Century America*, pp. 345–486, for more on the Cold War's re-imagining as frontierism.
4. *End Zone*'s protagonist also gets a pornographic thrill from reading technical descriptions of nuclear fallout, but the emphasis is on the language element in DeLillo's

Chapter Notes

novel more so than the Freudian sexual elements.

5. For more on Ballard's Freudianism see Caserio, Wagar and Foster. For arguments as to Kubrick's adaptation of Freudian aspects see Feldman's "Kubrick and His Discontents."

6. This is discussed in detail in the final chapter of this book, which analyses *The Wire*.

7. The sexuality of African slaves came to be conceived in much the same way.

8. The fall of the Soviet Union in the late 1980s undoubtedly removed an important bulwark in America's mythopoeia, and America may have lacked definition until the next civilizing mission, a holy war, no less, came to define American freedom as non-"terrorism," non–Muslim, non–Arab.

9. Kissoff is intonated by Muffley's telephone conversation, his voice is not heard in the film.

10. See Thomas Byrne Edsall's *The Age of Austerity: How Scarcity Will Remake American Politics* (2012).

11. Credit to Feldman for this reading of Kubrick's other films.

12. Kubrick also drafted in a young German set designer, Ken Adam, to design the sets. It is undoubtedly no accident that the giant table at the center of the War Room looks very like a poker table, underlining the game aspect of the strategies.

13. Cohen was also known as the chief inventor of the neutron bomb.

14. See the various arguments of Seed, Linden, Strathern and Stillman in this regard.

15. For more insight into the conservatism and paranoia engendered by von Neumann's conception of Game Theory see Kaplan's *Wizards*, p. 66.

16. As mentioned, the other great mathematician of the twentieth century responsible, along with von Neumann, for elevating Game Theory to its elite position was John Nash, who had his own psychological issues. For more on Nash see Nasar, pp. 11–22.

17. She later reappears as the centerfold of Major King Kong's *Playboy*, Miss Foreign Affairs.

18. This stands as an ironic counterpoint to *Strangelove*'s insightfulness, which it achieved in spite of the Air Force's lack of co-operation.

19. See Jackie Byars, *All That Hollywood Allows: Re-reading Gender in 1950s Melodrama* (1991) and Steven Cohan's *Masculinity and the Movies in the Fifties* (1997) for more on gender ideologies of the time.

20. "Peter George detected so many parallels to *Two Hours to Doom*," Baxter writes, "that he sued for plagiarism, and won an out-of-court settlement" (175).

21. See Edward Said's essay "Democracy as Agonistic Pluralism" in *Rewriting Democracy: Cultural Politics in Postmodernity*.

22. Pat Frank's *Alas, Babylon* is an example of American fiction that emphasises the survivability of nuclear war.

23. From *Gulliver's Travels*, an island of scientists and philosophers who are too engrossed in their problems to sexually fulfill their wives.

24. See "Part IV, Democracy and Force: The Western and the Cold War, 1945–1966," pp. 345–486.

25. See Leo Marx's *The Machine in the Garden*.

26. Ripper's diatribe also recalls the rabid anti–Communist rants of Major Edwin "Teddy" Walker. Texas-born General Walker, infamous for instigating riots around the enrolling of African American student James Meredith to the University of Mississippi in 1962, was also known to say that Harry S. Truman and Eleanor Roosevelt were "pink" (Dale, 34, 50).

27. See David K. Johnson, *The Lavender Scare: Cold War Persecution of Gays and Lesbians in the Federal Government* (2004), Seed, *Imagining Apocalypse: Studies in Cultural Crisis* (2000) and *Masculinities in Politics and War: Gendering Modern History*, edited by Stefan Dudink, et al. (2004).

28. It is pertinent to note that John Nash was immediately dismissed from RAND when it became known that he occasionally partook in gay dalliances with men he met on the beach near the offices. His sexuality was perceived as a security threat. Alan Turing, the most famous British code-breaker at Bletchley Park during World War II, likewise, was chemically castrated when his sexuality

was perceived to be a "security threat." See Nasar, pp. 184–190, for Nash's arrest and see the BBC documentary *Dangerous Knowledge* for more on Turing.

29. Guano is Spanish for feces. "Batshit" is a colloquial term for an individual who is mentally unstable.

30. See Blight, Laing, pp. 28–60.

31. Incentivization is a ubiquitous Game Theoretical economic term, predicated on exploiting an individual or group's supposed self-interest.

32. See Morris's documentary *The Fog of War* or Laing and Blight's book version for Robert McNamara's assertion that the deterrence rationale failed and that luck is what prevented nuclear war during the Cuban Missile Crisis.

33. See John Gray's *Black Mass* for more on this idea.

Chapter II

1. This Harper Perennial version of the novel from 1998 has a very short introduction by Ballard. No page numbers are given, this quote is taken from the first of three.

2. Jacques Ellul uses the term *technique* in *The Technological Society* (1964) to embody technology and its rational processes.

3. Once again, these aspects correlate closely to Baudrillard's conception of the cultural era of postmodernity, particularly those set out in *Simulacra and Simulations*.

4. See Norman Cohn's "The Pursuit of the Millennium" for the connection between Christianity and Enlightenment Science, pp. 13–17.

5. To "Hark" is to return to a previous point in a narrative, which is relevant to the novel's overall sense that modern instrumentalism and the bomb has meant the loss of the narrative of meaning, which is discussed in detail further on in this chapter.

6. In his case, his creed is the mantra of order and masculine ruthlessness.

7. A college course in "Modes of Disaster Technology" is faux-postmodern and ironic within the context of the novel's narrative, and in wider satirical terms. It presages the kinds of courses taught at The College on the Hill in *White Noise*, like Jack Gladney's "Hitler Studies," that DeLillo clearly delights in devising.

8. This attribute is mentioned by Osteen in the context of *End Zone* (p. 39). For a more a comprehensive insight into deterrence strategies see "The Logic of Deterrence" by Ola Tunander.

9. This is not a homocentric presumption, as the sentience of animals would probably be doomed to the same fate.

10. See Chris Marker's 1962 science fiction masterpiece *La Jetée* for a haunting vision of the post-nuclear pre-deceased.

11. Jacques Derrida also engages the matter of pre-deceased meaning in his essay "No Apocalypse, Not Now (Full Speed Ahead, Seven Missiles, Seven Missives)" (1984).

12. Metaphysics has been linked historically with Christianity, the belief in the mystery of the Lord. Metaphysics is somewhat open-ended and open to all kinds of pie-in-the sky in a sense. Empiricism has been linked with the rigorous deduction of science, but this is drastically limited, and the greatest scientists were those who could imagine things beyond circumscribed prescriptions.

13. Roughly 25 million to 37 million dead.

14. Just as McNamara's "body count" sought to make America's Vietnam conflict more efficient, so too radically capitalist contemporary social science models evaluate only what is quantifiable as a factor of human self-interest.

15. See *Black Mass* by John Gray for more on postmodern teleology, Utopia and scientism and their historical precedents, pp. 104–150.

16. Recent history's most potent evidence of the continued power of the revolutionary violence/apocalyptic utopian current of thinking in the United States is the invasion of Iraq. Saddam Hussein, the source of tyranny would be removed, and after the cleansing effect of a holy bloodletting, Iraq would be reset to democracy, justice, secularization, rationalization, opened up to the free-market instrument—so the thinking presumed.

17. The myth of revolutionary violence is reconstituted not just in fiction but, Slotkin argues, also underpins the United States' approach to all its wars. He points out that the North Vietnamese were referred to by both U.S. command and infantry as "Indians" as par for the course, suggesting the desire to repeat the same root and branch destruction of the enemy and reset-to-zero.

18. In both *Simulacra* and *The Gulf War Did Not Take Place*. See also cult comedian Bill Hicks' view of the Persian Gulf War in *Revelations* as an American fetishization of destructive technology.

19. A university that sounds like a factory; denoting the instrumental aspects of education under the dictates of efficiency.

20. Staley has slightly changed the names of the opposing powers to "COMRUS" and "AMAC" to remove emotional responses.

21. Kaplan's *The Wizards of Armageddon* was published in 1983, eleven years after *End Zone*.

22. See section Patriarchal Priests—Empiricism vs. Metaphysics.

23. In Britain, the binding of radical individualism with the automobile fully took root in the 1980s during the time of Margaret Thatcher's government, in a period which also saw the privatisation of rail and other forms of public transport.

24. See Donna Haraway's *Simians, Cyborgs and Women: The Reinvention of Nature* for a feminist exploration of these ideas. Haraway's outlook is somewhat more utopian than what Ballard has conceived.

25. It is noteworthy that Hank Searls' novel *The Penetrators* (1965) is a SAC novel following the standard call for "de-libidinized" male rationality and female subservience as detailed in the previous chapter's examples.

26. For example, see "An Interview with J.G. Ballard," by Jeremy Lewis, p. 32.

27. Martin Amis wrote it was hard "not to see the book as just an exercise in vicious whimsy." Amis has subsequently revised his initial review. (*Crash*: "Ideas, Interviews & Features," postscript to HarperCollins edition, 13. Taken from a review in *Observer*, July 1973).

28. *Crash*'s connection to *A Clockwork Orange* and Burroughs are the most clearly defined of the above authors and works. The totalitarianism of the state's act of brainwashing Alex from *A Clockwork Orange* makes him into a very unlikely hero of sorts. His actions leading up to this eventuality are brutal and sadistic, but they are nevertheless the actions of a sovereign being and do not come close to the sadism and dehumanising actions of state totalitarianism. Burroughs was a very significant influence on Ballard's writing; the combination of black humour and an obsession with descriptions of surreal sex acts are the most readily apparent Burroughsian aspects of *Crash*.

29. There are no page numbers given to the short introduction by Ballard in this edition of the text.

30. Ayn Rand's novels now sell in large volumes in the United States achieving a cult status in the late 1980s (after Rand's death). For an insight into Rand's current influence in the United States, see Adam Curtis's BBC documentary series *All Watched Over by Machines of Loving Grace* Part 1: *Love and Power*.

31. The term "late-capitalism" is taken from Fredric Jameson's *Postmodernism or, The Logic of Late Capitalism* (1991). It is useful here as it denotes a time period, 1945 to the present, that crucially encapsulates the beginning of the atomic age.

32. This concept is borrowed from Scott Bukatman's "Postcards from the Posthuman Solar System." He defines it as: "The posthuman solar system is a comic book world of infinite possibilities and cyborg multiplicities, defined in and through the technologies that now construct our experience and therefore our *selves*" (355).

33. See the websites www.ballardian.com/ and www.jgballard.ca/ for extensive lists of academic interviews with Ballard over the years.

34. Cronenberg's film adaptation is not discussed in detail herein. For more detailed discussion, see, for example, Marq Smith's "Wound Envy: Touching Cronenberg's Crash."

35. See David Woodard's *The America that Reagan Built* (2006) for a factual political account. See Michael Moore's "documentary"

Roger and Me (1989) for a sense of the consequences of these changes.

36. See Naomi Klein's *The Shock Doctrine*.

37. See Adam Curtis's *The Power of Nightmares*, Episode 2, "The Phantom Victory," and *Pandora's Box*, Episode 2 "To the Brink of Eternity," for first hand interviews confirming that this assertion was indeed held.

38. A justification and literalisation, perhaps, of Baudrillard's conviction in "The Precession of Simulacra" (1981), that the Cold War became an exercise in technique given to the order of the models of simulation and simulacra.

39. See Diane Rubenstein's "The Mirror of Reproduction: Baudrillard and Reagan's America" for analysis of Reagan's presidency as synecdoche, from a Baudrillardian point of view.

40. Bukatman writes: "Perhaps the only other novel to appropriate Bataille's notion of sacrificial mutilation is Bernard Wolfe's *Limbo* [published in Britain as *Limbo 90*], first published in 1952—an extraordinary anomaly, deriving imagery from Bataille while anticipating the cybernetic paranoia of Pynchon" (345).

Chapter III

1. For more on its literary aspects see Linda Williams' "Ethnographic Imaginary," and Marsha Kinder, "Re-Wiring Baltimore."

2. See Kinder and Tyree's essays for more in-depth analysis of *The Wire*'s radical use of the medium.

3. See her essay "Ethnographic Imaginary: The Genesis and Genius of *The Wire*."

4. What was at the time iconoclastic in *The Wire*'s format, for example very little plot exposition and deep complexity, have since become common in its wake in programs such as AMC's *Breaking Bad*.

5. See Michael Hill's *The Public Policy Process* for a clear overview of Public Choice Theory as it is applied to economics, politics and the social sciences.

6. See Laing and Blight's *The Fog of War* and Curtis's *The Trap* for insight into the use of the "body count" method in Vietnam.

7. See Adam Curtis's three-part documentary series *The Trap*. It features interviews with Buchanan and Enthoven about their beliefs and practices.

8. The details and essence of which are depicted with absolute accuracy in *Strangelove*, as mentioned in the first chapter, which draws the surprising connection between *Strangelove* and *The Wire*; that both are accurate in their representations of Game Theoretical thinking.

9. See Sennett, pp. 37–38.

10. See Woodard's *The America that Reagan Built*.

11. Much of the force of *The Wire*'s criticism comes from its co-producer Ed Burns, who was not only a detective serving on the Baltimore Police Force for nearly twenty years in a previous career, and a middle school teacher after that, but had also served in the Vietnam War. Burns had first-hand personal experience of the economic models by which all three of these arenas were systematically dictated. All three were run according to the dictates of Game Theory-based performance target models, two of which Burns has criticised in *The Wire*'s narrative.

12. Williams' essay provides insight into Simon's previous role as a journalist, his eventual ignominious parting of ways with the paper and how these factors influenced his writing for *The Wire*.

13. "More With Less" is the title of the first episode of season five.

14. There is a further examination of the Marlo Stanfield character as a product of his environment and his culture later in this chapter, based upon his execution of the security guard in the episode titled "Refugees."

15. p. 218.

16. Neoliberal economics as they exist today originate in America, developed by Friedrich von Hayek, propagated by the Chicago School of Economics and implemented under the tutelage of Milton Friedman. The austerity measures under which most of the postindustrial world is subjected at the time of writing renders what is being discussed both familiar and relevant. See Klein's *The Shock Doctrine*.

17. Bell and Barksdale's respective senses of dress signal their divergent aspirations and ambitions quite clearly. Barksdale opts for sports jerseys, sun visors and expensive velour tracksuits, while Bell opts for slacks, polo necks and muted colors. In the semiotics of consumption, Bell's tastes, including the decoration of his penthouse apartment, as discussed below, signal his desire for legitimacy and acceptance.

18. See Achbar and Abbott's *The Corporation* (2005) and Gibney's *Enron: The Smartest Guys in the Room* (2005) for recent examples.

19. But not exclusively American, of course.

20. For a historical detailing of different concepts of "police," see Michel Foucault's "Technologies of the Self."

21. The term "success" is used advisedly, as the number of humans, normally the predicate of evolutionary success, is the largest contributing factor to the destruction of the environment that sustains us.

22. The importance of empathy in society is discussed in the introductory chapter to the thesis. See *Fog of War* (both text and documentary) for Robert McNamara's thoughts on the impact of empathy in war situations. McNamara argues that empathy, predicated on dialogue and communication, between enemies potentially prevents wars and countless needless deaths.

23. Mencken, a famous Baltimore son, is undoubtedly an influence on Simon too, particularly given Simon's previous career as a journalist and reporter.

24. This aspect is prevalent in Cobb's novel upon which Kubrick based his film, as is the techno-totalitarian aspect present in Burgess's *A Clockwork Orange* (1962).

25. As is exemplified by the use of unmanned drones by the United States in the Middle East and Africa.

Conclusion

1. An element that is captured in DeLillo's *White Noise* (1985).

2. The assumption that the free market obeys the laws of spontaneous organization that are assumed to occur in nature, in so-called ecosystems, is tied in with these exceptionalist beliefs.

3. The civilising mission has been redrawn around the East versus West, Christianity versus Islam binary since 9/11, the Bush administration in particular drawing out the biblical comparisons to the great apocalyptic battle in Revelations. As was seen in Iraq, however, the razing to the ground of Baghdad was step one in the process of implementing liberal democracy in this foreign land, and this was undertaken in what could be described as the world's first fully privatised war, a war that was stupendously profitable to a number of select American corporations.

4. The well-known Douglas Hofstadter text, *Godel, Escher, Bach: An Eternal Golden Braid,* also goes into the various logical paradoxes that we may meet in everyday life.

Bibliography

Above and Beyond. Dirs. Melvin Frank, Norman Panama. MGM, 1952.

Alvarez, Rafael. *The Wire: Truth Be Told.* New York: Canongate, 2009

Baker, Stephen. *The Numerati: How They'll Get My Number and Yours.* London: Johnathan Cape, 2008.

Balaban, John. *After Our War.* London: Feffer & Simons, 1974.

Ballard, J.G. *The Atrocity Exhibition.* London: Fourth Estate, 2006.

———. *Crash.* London: Harper Perennial, 2008.

———. *High Rise.* London: Fourth Estate, 2011.

Bataille, Georges. *The Accursed Share: An Essay on General Economy.* New York: Zone, 2003.

———. *Visions of Excess: Selected Writings, 1927-1939.* Trans. Allan Stoekl, Carl R. Lovitt and Donald M. Leslie, Jr. *Theory and History of Literature,* Vol. 14. Minneapolis: University of Minnesota Press, 1985.

Baudrillard, Jean. *The Consumer Society: Myths and Structures.* London: Sage, 1998.

———. *The Gulf War Did Not Take Place.* Sydney: Power, 1995.

———. *Simulacra and Simulation.* Ann Arbor: University of Michigan Press, 1994.

———. *Symbolic Exchange and Death.* London: Sage, 1993.

———. *The Transparency of Evil: Essays on Extreme Phenomena.* London: Verso, 1993.

Baxter, John. *Stanley Kubrick: A Biography.* London: HarperCollins, 1997.

Beckman, Karen. "Film Falls Apart: 'Crash,' Semen, and Pop." *Grey Room* 12 (Summer 2003): 94-115. Retrieved from *JSTOR* 22 September 2012.

Bellis, Mary. "Willhelm Reich and the Orgone Accumulator: The Device the U.S. Government Wanted Destroyed." 2012. Aboutwww. 15 September 2012. http://inventors.about.com/od/qrstartinventors/a/orgone.htm.

Belletto, Steven. "The Game Theory Narrative and the Myth of the National Security State." *American Quarterly* 61, no. 2 (June 2009): 333-357.

———. *No Accident, Comrade: Chance and Design in Cold War American Narratives.* New York: Oxford University Press, 2012.

Benjamin, Marina. *Living at the End of the World.* London: Picador, 1998.

Bercovitch, Sacvan. *The Puritan Origins of the American Self.* New Haven: Yale University Press, 1975.

———. *The Rites of Ascent: Transformations in the Symbolic Destruction of America.* New York: Routledge, 1993.

Blight, James G., and Janet M. Lang, eds. *The Fog of War: Lessons from the Life of Robert S. McNamara.* Lanham, MD: Rowman & Littlefield, 2005.

Boxall, Peter. *Don DeLillo: The Possibility of Fiction.* London: Routledge, 2006.

Brereton, Pat. *Hollywood Utopia: Ecology in Contemporary American Cinema.* Bristol: Intellect, 2005.

Brown, Dee. *Bury My Heart at Wounded Knee.* London: Vintage, 1991.

Bukatman, Scott. "Postcards from the Posthuman Solar System (Cartes du systéme solaire posthumain)." *Science Fiction Studies* 18, no. 3, Science Fiction and Postmodernism (November 1991): 343-357. Retrieved from *JSTOR* 22 September 2012.

Burgess, Jackson. "The 'Anti-Militarism' of Stanley Kubrick." *Film Quarterly* 18, no. 1 (Autumn 1964): 4-11. Retrieved from *JSTOR* 31 July 2013.

Bibliography

Burdick, Eugene, and William Lederer. *The Ugly American*. New York: W.W. Norton, 1958.

Burgess, Anthony. *A Clockwork Orange*. London: Penguin, 2000.

Burroughs, William. *The Adding Machine: Collected Essays*. London: Calder, 1985.

———. *Disposable Heroes of Hiphoprisy. Spare Ass Annie and Other Tales*. Island Red, 1993. CD.

Butler, Bill. "William S. Burroughs and J.G. Ballard." *Reality Studio: A William S. Burroughs Community*. March 2012. Retrieved 25 September 2012. http://realitystudio.org/scholarship/william-s-burroughs-and-j-g-ballard/.

Byars, Jackie. *All That Hollywood Allows: Re-Reading Gender in 1950s Melodrama*. London: Routledge, 1991.

Byrne Edsall, Thomas. *The Age of Austerity: How Scarctiy Will Remake American Politics*. New York: Anchor, 2012.

Callinicos, Alex. *The New Mandarins of American Power*. Cambridge: Polity, 2003.

Caserio, Robert L. "Mobility and Masochism: Christine Brooke-Rose and J.G. Ballard." *Novel: A Forum on Fiction* 21, no. 2/3, Why the Novel Matters: A Postmodern Perplex Conference Issue (Winter—Spring 1988): 292–310.

Chernus, Ira. *Nuclear Madness: Religion and the Psychology of the Nuclear Age*. New York: State University of New York Press, 1991.

Chomsky, Noam. *Rethinking Camelot: JFK, the Vietnam War, and U.S. Political Culture*. London: Verso, 1993.

Cioffi, Frank L. "Post-Millennial Postmodernism: On the Professing of Literature in the Centrifugal Age." *College Literature* 26, no. 3, The Profession of Literature at the End of the Millennium (Fall 1999): 88–94.

Cohan, Steven. *Masculinity and the Movies in the Fifties*. Bloomington: Indiana University Press, 1997.

———. *Screening the Male: Exploring Masculinities in Hollywood Cinema*, eds. Steven Cohan and Ina Rae Hark. London, New York: Routledge, 1993.

Cohn, Norman. *The Pursuit of the Millennium: Revolutionary Millenarians and Mystical Anarchists of the Middle Ages*. London: Paladin, 1970.

Cook, Pam, and Mieke Bernink, eds. *The Cinema Book, 2d ed.* London: British Film Institute, 1999.

The Corporation. Dir. Mark Achbar and Jennifer Abbott. DVD. Meterodome, 2005.

Countdown to Zero. Dir. Lucy Walker. Channel 4, 16 August 2011, 10pm.

Cowart, David. *Don DeLillo: The Physics of Language, rev. ed.* Athens: University of Georgia Press, 2003.

Crevecoeur, Hector J. "Letters from an American Farmer." 1782. *The Heath Anthology of American Literature*. Ed. Paul Lauter, et al. New York: Houghton, 2002. 898–934.

Curtis, Adam. *The Century of the Self*. Parts 1–4. BBC Four, 29 April–2 May 2002.

———. *Pandora's Box: A Fable From the Age of Science*. Episodes 1–6. BBC Two, 1992.

———. *The Power of Nightmares: The Rise of the Politics of Fear*. Parts 1–3. BBC Two, 20 April–3 November 2004.

———. *The Trap: What Happpened to Our Dream of Freedom*. Parts 1–3. BBC Two, 11 March–25 March 2007.

Dangerous Knowledge. BBC 2. 11 June 2008. Television.

Debord, Guy. *Society of the Spectacle*. Trans. Ken Knabb. London: Aldgate, 1967.

DeLillo, Don. *Cosmpolis*. New York: Picador, 2003.

———. *End Zone*. London: Picador, 2004.

———. Interview. *The Guardian*. 8 Aug. 2010. Web. 24 July 2012.

———. *Libra*. Harmondsworth: Penguin, 1989.

———. *Point Omega*. New York: Scribner, 2010.

———. "The Power of History." *New York Times*, Oct. 7, 1997. *NY Times*. Web. 13 July 2012.

———. *Underworld*. New York: Scribner, 1998.

———. *White Noise*. London: Picador, 1985.

Derrida, Jacques, Catherine Porter and Philip Lewis. "No Apocalypse, Not Now (Full Speed Ahead, Seven Missiles, Seven Missives)." *Diacritics* 14, no. 2, *Nuclear Criticism* (Summer 1984): 20–13. *JSTOR* 22 September 2012.

Dickens, Charles. *Hard Times*. London: Chapman and Hall, 2003.

"Donald Trump and the Plague of Atomization in the Neoliberal Age." *Truthdig Main News*. N.p., 2016. Web. 31 Aug. 2016.

Douglas, Mary. *Purity and Danger: An Analysis of the Concepts of Pollution and Taboo*. New York: Routledge, 1991.

Ducker, Eric. "Inside *The Wire*'s World Of Alienation and Asshole Gods." *The Fader* ("Listening in to *The Wire*: Part IV.") 12 Aug. 2006. Web. 7 Feb 2013.

Dudink, Stefan, Karen Hagemann and John Tosh, eds. *Masculinities in Politics and War: Gendering Modern History*. Manchester; New York: Manchester University Press, 2004.

Dusek, Val. *Philosophy of Technology: An Introduction*. Oxford: Blackwell, 2006.

Duvall, John N. *The Cambridge Companion to DeLillo*. Cambridge: Cambridge University Press, 2008.

Eatwell, John, et al., eds. *The New Palgrave Dictionary of Economics*. London: Macmillan, 1987.

Enron: The Smartest Guys in the Room. Dir. Alex Gibney. DVD. Magnolia Pictures, 2005.

Ermath, Elizabeth Deeds. *Rewriting Democracy: Cultural Politics in Postmodernity*. Burlington: Ashgate, 2007.

Fail-Safe. Dir. Sidney Lumet. 1964. DVD. Columbia Tristar Home Video, 2007.

Fekete, John. "The Post-Liberal Mind/Body, Postmodern Fiction, and the Case of Cyberpunk SF." Rev. of *Storming the Reality Studio: A Casebook of Cyberpunk and Postmodern Science Fiction* by Larry McCaffery. *Science Fiction Studies* 19, no. 3 (November 1992): 395–403.

Fiedler, Leslie A. *Love and Death in the American Novel*. Normal, IL: Dalkey, 2003.

_____. *The Return of the Vanishing American*. New York: Stein and Day, 1968.

Firsching, Lorenz J. "J.G. Ballard's Ambiguous Apocalypse." *Science Fiction Studies* 12, no. 3 (November 1985): 297–310.

The Fog of War: Eleven Lessons From the Life of Robert S. McNamara. Dir. Errol Morris. Sony Pictures, 2003.

Foster, Dennis A. "J.G. Ballard's Empire of the Senses: Perversion and the Failure of Authority." *PMLA* 108, no. 3 (May 1993): 519–532.

Foster Wallace, David. *Infinite Jest*. London: Little, Brown, 1996.

Foucault, Michel. *Discipline and Punish*. Trans. Alan Sheridan. London: Penguin, 1991.

_____. *Technologies of the Self: A Seminar with Michel Foucault*. Luther Martin, ed. London: Tavistock, 1988.

Freud, Sigmund. *Civilization and its Discontents*. London: Hogarth, 1951.

Frey, Bruno S. *Economics as a Science of Human Behaviour: Towards a New Social Science Paradigm*. Boston: Kluwer Academic, 1999.

A Gathering of Eagles. Dir. Delbert Mann. Universal International Pictures, 1963.

Ghamari-Tabrizi, Sharon. "Dr. Strangelove." *The Kubrick Site*. www.visual-memory.co.uk/amk/doc/0097.html. 6 March 2012.

Gold, Matea. "'Wire' Leaves a Legacy of Hope." *Los Angeles Times*, 9 March 2008. Web. 2 Feb. 2013.

Grausam, Daniel. "Games People Play: Metafiction, Defense Strategy, and the Cultures of Simulation." *English Literary History* 78, no. 3 (Fall 2011). Web. *Project Muse*, 9 September 2013.

_____. "'It Is Only a Statement of the Power of What Comes After': Atomic Nostalgia and the Ends of Postmodernism." *American Literary History* 24, no. 2: 308–336. Web. 9 September 2013.

_____. *On Endings: American Postmodern Fiction and the Cold War*. Charlottesville: University of Virginia Press, 2011.

Gray, John. *Black Mass: Apocalyptic Religion and the Death of Utopia*. London: Penguin, 2007.

_____. *Straw Dogs: Thoughts on Humans and Other Animals*. New York: Farrar, Straus and Giroux, 2003.

Griswold, Charles L., Jr. *Adam Smith and the Virtues of Enlightenment*. Cambridge, U.K.; New York: Cambridge University Press, 1999.

Gunn, James, ed. *The Road to Science Fiction, Volume 3: From Heinlein to Here*. Clarkston, CA: White Wolf, 1979.

Habermas, Jurgen. *Communication and the Evolution of Society*. Oxford: Polity, 1991.

_____. *Toward a Rational Society: Student*

Protest, Science, and Politics. London: Heinemann, 1971.

Hanson, Christopher. "Some Last Words on The Wire." *Film Quarterly* 62, no. 2 (Winter 2008): 66–67. JSTOR 11 August 2012.

Haraway, Donna. *Simians, Cyborgs and Women: The Reinvention of Nature.* London: Free Association, 1991.

Hargreaves Heap, Shaun P., and Yanis Varoufakis. *Game Theory: A Critical Introduction.* London: Routledge, 1995.

Harvey, David. *A Brief History of Neoliberalism.* New York: Oxford University Press, 2005.

———. "Neoliberalism Is a Political Project." *Jacobin Neoliberalism Is a Political Project Comments.* N.P., n.d. Web. 31 Aug. 2016.

Heims, Steve Joshua. *John Von Neumann and Norbert Wiener: From Mathematics to the Technologies of Life and Death.* Cambridge: MIT Press, 1982.

Herr, Michael. *Dispatches.* New York: Picador, 1977.

Herring, George C., ed. *The Secret Diplomacy of the Vietnam War: The Negotiating Volumes of the Pentagon Papers.* Austin: University of Texas Press, 1985.

Hill, Michael. *The Public Policy Process*, 4th ed. Essex: Pearson Education, 2005.

Hodgson, Godfrey. *America in Our Time: From World War II to Nixon—What Happened and Why.* Princeton: Princeton University Press, 1976.

Hofstadter, Douglas R. *Godel, Escher, Bach: An Eternal Golden Braid.* Sussex: Harvester, 1979.

Horkheimer, Max. *Eclipse of Reason.* New York: Oxford University Press, 1974.

Horkheimer, Max, and Theodor Adorno. "Dialectic of Enlightenment: Philosophical Fragments." Stanford: Stanford University Press, 2002. Web. 16 April 2013.

Inskeep, Steve. "*Glory, Wild Bunch* Among David Simon's DVD Picks." *National Public Radio: Morning Edition.* 19 Dec. 2008. Web. 7 February 2013.

Jacques, Martin. "Neoliberalism Has Had Its Day. So What Happens Next?" *The Guardian.* The Guardian News and Media, 2016. Web. 31 Aug. 2016.

Jameson, Fredric. *Archaeologies of the Future: The Desire Called Utopia and Other Science Fictions.* New York: Verso, 2005.

———. *Postmodernism, or: The Cultural Logic of Late Capitalism.* London: Verso, 1991.

———. "Realism and Utopia in *The Wire*." *Criticism* 52, no. 3–4 (Summer/Fall 2010): 359–372. Web. 22 May. 2013.

John, Andrew A., Rowena A. Pecchenino, and Stacey L. Schreft. "The Macroeconomics of Dr. Strangelove." *American Economic Review* 83, no. 1 (March 1993): 43–62.

Johnson, David K. *The Lavender Scare: Cold War Persecution of Gays and Lesbians in the Federal Government.* Chicago: Chicago University Press, 2004.

Kaplan, Fred. "Truth Stranger Than 'Strangelove.'" *New York Times,* Oct. 10, 2004. NY Times. Web. 23 March. 2012.

———. *The Wizards of Armageddon.* Stanford: Stanford University Press, 1983.

Kasinitz, Philip. Ed. *Metropolis: Centre and Symbol of Our Times.* New York: New York University Press, 1995.

Kauffman, Linda S. *Bad Girls and Sick Boys: Fantasies in Contemporary Art and Culture.* Berkeley: University of California Press, 1998.

Kermode, Frank. *The Sense of an Ending: Studies in the Theory of Fiction.* New York: Oxford University Press, 2000.

Kim, Younghoon. "Rogue Cops' Politics of Equality in *The Wire*." *Journal of American Studies* 47, no. 1 (February 2013): 189–211.

Kinder, Marsha. "Re-Wiring Baltimore: The Emotive Power of Systemics, Seriality, and the City." *Film Quarterly* 62, no. 2 (Winter 2008): 50–57. JSTOR. 11 August 2012.

Klein, Naomi. *The Shock Doctrine: The Rise of Disaster Capitalism.* London: Penguin, 2007.

Kubrick, Stanley. Dir. *Barry Lyndon.* Warner Bros., 1975.

———. *A Clockwork Orange.* (1969). DVD. MGM, 1998.

———. *Dr. Strangelove: Or How I Learned to Stop Worrying and Love the Bomb.* (1964). DVD. Columbia Tristar Home Video, 2001.

———. *2001: A Space Odyssey.* MGM, 1968.

Lentricchia, Frank, ed. *Introducing Don DeLillo.* Durham, NC: Duke University Press, 1999.

Bibliography

Leonard, Robert J. "From Parlor Games to Social Science: Von Neumann, Morgenstern, and the Creation of Game Theory 1928-1944." *Journal of Economic Literature* 33, no. 2: 730-761.

Lewis, Jeremy, and J.G. Ballard. "An Interview with J.G. Ballard." *Mississippi Review* 20, no. 1/2 (1991): 27-40. JSTOR. 13 July 2012.

Lifton, Robert Jay. "'In the Lord's Hands': America's Apocalyptic Mindset." *World Policy Journal* 20, no. 3 (Fall 2003): 59-69. JSTOR. 24 July 2012.

Linden, George W. "Dr. Strangelove' and Erotic Displacement." *Journal of Aesthetic Education* 11, no. 1 (1977): 63-83. JSTOR. 16 August 2011.

Lindley, Dan. "What I Learned Since I Stopped Worrying and Studied the Movie: A Teaching Guide to Stanley Kubrick's *Dr. Strangelove*." *Cambridge Journals* 34: 663-667. Journals.cambridge.org. 16 May 2002.

Love, Chris. "Greek Gods in Baltimore: Greek Tragedy in *The Wire*." Readperiodicals. 1 July 2010. Web. 7 February 2013.

Lyotard, Jean Francois. *The Postmodern Condition: A Report on Knowledge*. Manchester: Manchester University Press, 1983.

Maland, Charles. "Dr. Strangelove (1964): Nightmare Comedy and the Ideology of Liberal Consensus." *American Quarterly* 31, no. 5, Special Issue: Film and American Studies (Winter 1979): 697-717.

Marcuse, Herbert. *One Dimensional Man*. London: Sphere, 1968.

Martins Rosa, Jorge. "A Misreading Gone Too Far? Baudrillard Meets Philip K. Dick." *Science Fiction Studies* 35, no. 1 (March 2008): 60-71.

Martins, Susana S. "White Noise and Everyday Technologies." *American Studies* 46, no. 1 (Spring 2005): 87-113. JSTOR. Web. 24 July 2012.

Marx, John. "Pleasures of Sex and Tech." Rev. of *Literature, Technology, and Modernity, 1860-2000* by Nicholas Daly. *Novel: A Forum on Fiction* 39, no. 2, Postcolonial Disjunctions (Spring 2006): 291-294.

Marx, Leo. *The Machine in the Garden: Technology and the Pastoral Ideal in America*. London: Oxford, 1964.

Mather, Philippe. Review: Jerold J. Abrams, ed. *The Philosophy of Stanley Kubrick. Film Philosophy* 11, no. 3 (2007): 224-230. http://www.film-philosophy.com/2007v11n3/mather.pdf.

McGregor, Craig. "Nice Boy from the Bronx." *New York Times*, 30 January 1972. Web. 23 March 2012.

McHale, Brian. "Telling Postmodernist Stories." *Poetics Today* 9, no. 3, Aspects of Literary Theory (1988): 545-571.

Mennell, Stephen. *The American Civilizing Process*. Cambridge: Polity, 2007.

Méró, László. *Moral Calculations: Game Theory, Logic, and Human Frailty*. Trans: Anna C. Gosi-Greguss. Ed. David Kramer. New York: Springer-Verlag, 1998.

Metropolis. Dir. Fritz Lang. Universal Film AG, 1927.

Mills, C. Wright. *The Power Elite*. London: Oxford University Press, 1956.

Mills, David. "Q&A: David Simon." *Undercover Black Man* (blog). 22 January 2007. Web. 7 February 2013.

Mittell, Jason. "All in the Game: The Wire, Serial Storytelling, and Procedural Logic." *Electronic Book Review*. 18 March 2011. Web. 4 February 2013.

———. "The Wire in the Context of American Television." *Media Commons: A Digital Scholarly Network*. 9 Feb 2010. Web. 11 August 2012.

Monbiot, George. "The Age of Loneliness Is Killing Us." *The Guardian*. The Guardian News and Media, 2014. Web. 31 Aug. 2016.

———. "Neoliberalism: The Ideology at the Root of All Our Problems." *The Guardian*. Guardian News and Media, 2016. Web. 31 Aug. 2016.

Moraru, Christian. "Consuming Narratives: Don DeLillo and the 'Lethal' Reading." *The Journal of Narrative Technique* 27, no. 2 (Spring 1997): 190-206. JSTOR. 24 July 2012.

Naremore, James. *On Kubrick*. London: British Film Institute, 2008.

Nasar, Sylvia. *A Beautiful Mind*. Faber and Faber: London, 1998.

Nash, John F., Jr. *Essays on Game Theory*. Cheltenham, UK: Edward Elgar, 1996.

Nash Smith, Henry. *The Virgin Land*. New York: Faber, 1989.

Bibliography

Nirenberg, David. *Communities of Violence: Persecution of Minorities in the Middle Ages*. Princeton: Princeton University Press, 1996.

O'Brien, Tim. *In the Lake of the Woods*. London: Flamingo, 1995.

———. *The Nuclear Age*. London: Penguin, 1996.

O'Rourke, Meghan. "Behind *The Wire*: David Simon on Where the Show Goes Next." *Slate Magazine*. 1 Dec. 2006. Web 7 February 2013.

Osteen, Mark. *American Magic and Dread: Don DeLillo's Dialogue with Culture*. Philadelphia: University of Philadelphia Press, 2000.

Outwaite, William. *Habermas: A Critical Introduction*. London: Polity, 1994.

Packard, Vince. *The Hidden Persuaders*. Harmondsworth: Penguin, 1961.

Paret, Peter, ed. *Makers of Modern Strategy: From Machievelli to the Modern Age*. Oxford: Clarendon, 1986.

"Reich, Willhelm." *Encyclopedia Britannica Online*. Web. 26 September 2012.

Rodley, Chris, ed. *Cronenberg on Cronenberg*. London: Faber and Faber, 1992.

Rollins, Peter C., and John E. O'Conner. *Hollywood's West: The American Frontier in Film, Television and History*. Lexington: University of Kentucky Press, 2005.

Rothman, William. *The "I" of the Camera: Essays in Film Criticism, History, and Aesthetics*. New York: Cambridge, 1988.

Ruddick, Nicholas. "Ballard/Crash/Baudrillard." *Science Fiction Studies* 19, no. 3: 354–360.

Saull, Richard. *Rethinking Theory and History in the Cold War: The State, Military Power and Social Revolution*. London: Frank Cass, 2001.

Schlosser, Eric. *Fast Food Nation: What the All-American Meal Is Doing to the World*. London: Penguin, 2002.

———. *Reefer Madness: And Other Tales from the American Underground*. London: Penguin, 2003.

Schneck, Peter. "'To See Things Before Other People See Them': Don DeLillo's Visual Poetics." *Amerikastudien/American Studies* 25, no. 1, Transatlantic Perspectives on American Visual Culture (2007): 103–120. JSTOR. 24 July 2012.

Scott, Peter, Dale. *Deep Politics and the Death of JFK*. Los Angeles: University of California Press, 1993.

Seed, David. *American Science Fiction and the Cold War: Literature and Film*. Edinburgh: Edinburgh University Press, 1999.

———, ed. *Imagining Apocalypse: Studies in Cultural Crisis*. Basingstoke: Macmillan, 2000.

Sennett, Richard. *The Culture of the New Capitalism*. New Haven: Yale University Press, 2006.

Sheehan, Helena, and Sheamus Sweeney. "*The Wire* and the World: Narrative and Metanarrative. *Jump Cut* 51 (Spring 2009). Web. 11 October 2012. http://www.ejumpcut.org/currentissue/index.html.

Simmel, Georg. *The Conflict in Modern Culture and Other Essays*. New York: Teachers College, 1968.

———. *The Philosophy of Money*. David Frisby, ed. London: Routledge, 1978.

———. *Simmel on Culture: Selected Writings*. David Frisby and Mike Featherstone Eds. London: Sage, 1997.

Sinclair, Iain. *Crash: David Cronenberg's Post-Mortem on J.G. Ballard's "Trajectory of Fate."* London: British Film Institute, 1999.

Slotkin, Richard. *Gunfighter Nation: The Myth of the American Frontier in Twentieth-Century America*. New York: Maxwell Macmillan, 1992.

———. *Regeneration Through Violence: The Mythology of the American Frontier, 1600–1860*. Middletown: Wesleyan University Press, 1973.

Smith, Marq. "Wound Envy: Touching Cronenberg's Crash." *Screen* 40, no. 2 (1999): 193–202. Web. 27 August 2013.

Sorlin, Pierre. "The Cinema: American Weapon for the Cold War." *Film History* 10, no. 3, The Cold War and the Movies (1998): 375–381. JSTOR. 31 July 2013.

Southern, Terry. "Notes from the War Room." The Kubrick Site. Web. 6 March 2012. http://www.visual-memory.co.uk/amk/doc/0081.html.

Stanley Kubrick: A Life in Pictures. Dir. Jan Harlan. DVD. Warner Bros., 2001.

Bibliography

Strategic Air Command. Dir. Anthony Mann. Paramount Pictures, 1955.

Stillman, Grant B. "Two of the MADest Scientists: Where Strangelove Meets Dr. No; or Unexpected Roots for Kubrick's Cold War Classic." *Film History* 20, no. 4, Politics and Film (2008): 487–500. *JSTOR*. 31 July 2013.

Storr, Anthony. *Human Destructiveness: The Roots of Genocide and Human Cruelty*, 2d ed. London: Heinemann and Chatto & Windus, 1991.

Strathern, Paul. *Dr. Strangelove's Game: A Brief History of Economic Genius*. London: Penguin, 2002.

Talbot, Margaret. "Stealing Life: The Crusader Behind *The Wire*." *The New Yorker*, 22 Oct. 2007. Web. 7 February 2013.

Taleb, Nassim Nicholas. *The Black Swan: The Impact of the Highly Improbable*. London: Penguin, 2007.

Terminator 2: Judgment Day. Dir. James Cameron. Tristar Pictures, 1991.

There Will Be Blood. Dir. Paul Thomas Anderson. DVD. Miramax, 2007.

Thoreau, Henry David. *Walden*. Boston: Beacon, 1997.

Threads. Dir. Mick Jackson. BBC, 1984.

TonyMacklin.net: Film, Fiction, and More. "Sex and Dr. Strangelove." (*Film Comment*, June 1, 1965). 16 August 2011.

Tunander, Ola. "The Logic of Deterrence." *Journal of Peace Research* 26, no. 4: 353–365.

Tyree, J.M. "The Wire: The Complete Fourth Season." *Film Quarterly* 61, no. 3 (Spring 2008): 32–38. *JSTOR*. 11 October 2012.

"Venturing Into 'The Capitalist Labyrinth' (Video)." *Truthdig Main News*. N.p., 2016. Web. 31 Aug. 2016.

Wagar, W. Warren. "J.G. Ballard and the Transvaluation of Utopia." *Science Fiction Studies* 18, no. 1 (March 1991): 53–70.

Wall Street. Dir. Oliver Stone. 1987. DVD. 20th Century Fox, 2009.

The War Game. Dir. Peter Watkins. BBC, 1965.

Weber, Eugen. *Apocalypses: Prophecies, Cults and Millennial Beliefs through the Ages*. London: Hutchinson, 1999.

White, Mark D., and Robert Arp, eds. *Batman and Philosophy: The Dark Knight of the Soul*. Hoboken, NJ: Wiley, 2008.

Wiggershaus, Rolf. *The Frankfurt School: Its History, Theories and Political Significance*. Trans. Michael Robertson. Oxford: Polity, 1994.

Wilcox, Leonard. "Baudrillard, DeLillo's *White Noise*, and the End of Heroic Narrative." *Contemporary Literature* 32, no. 3 (Autumn 1991): 346–365. *JSTOR*. 3 August 2012.

Williams, Linda. "Ethnographic Imaginary: The Genesis and Genius of the Wire." *Critical Inquiry* 38, no. 1 (Autumn 2011): 208–226. *JSTOR* 11 October 2012.

Woodard, David J. *The America that Reagan Built*. Westport, CT: Praeger, 2006.

Zizek, Slavoj. *Living in the End Times*. London: Verso, 2010.

Index

Above and Beyond 51, 189
The Accursed Share see Bataille, Georges
Adam, Ken 42
agonistic apraxia 54
Akinnagbe, Gbenga 142
Al Qaeda 173
Alas Babylon 98
Allyson, June 51
altruism 4, 10, 13, 26, 27
Alvarez, Ralael 130, 131, 134, 135, 140, 144, 146, 151, 153, 154, 162, 164, 189
American Dream 58, 114, 134, 143, 171
American exceptionalism 10
American Football 73, 83, 93, 94, 95
American Psycho 121
Anatole Bloomberg 83, 94
anti-fluoridation 50
apocalypse, cleansing 24, 57
Apocalypse Now 139
apocalypticism 55, 69, 124, 148, 175
Armageddon 57, 71, 93, 99
Arms Race 165
ascetic journey 70, 74, 90, 93, 98
Atlas Shrugged see Rand, Ayn
The Atrocity Exhibition 104, 120, 189
Atwood, Margaret 2, 117
austerity 29, 40, 142, 176, 187
autogeddon 24, 72, 99, 116
Avon Barksdale 129

Baker, Tyrell 167
Ball, Philip 7
Baltimore 1, 122, 125, 126, 129, 130, 132, 135, 137, 138, 139, 140, 141, 142, 143, 144, 145, 146, 148, 149, 151, 152, 154, 157, 161, 162, 163, 164, 167, 168, 169, 172, 179, 187, 188, 192, 193
Baltimore Sun 109, 125, 141, 142, 144, 145, 146, 147, 148, 149, 169
banality of evil 170
Barksdale 128, 129, 139, 140, 141, 142, 150, 151, 152, 153, 154, 155, 156, 157, 158, 159, 160, 161, 162, 165, 167, 188
Bat Guano 59, 62
Bataille, Georges 5, 110, 120, 187, 189
Baudrillard, Jean 5, 36, 56, 66, 69, 76, 78, 86, 87, 91, 93, 96, 97, 114, 127, 148, 173, 185, 187, 189, 193, 195
Bauer, Chris 135
"The Beaubourg Effect" 78, 148
A Beautiful Mind 16
Beckman, Karen 108, 117, 189
Benjamin, Marina 66
Bercovitch, Sacvan 35, 91, 183, 189
Berlin Wall 119
Bill Rawls 135, 143
binding narratives 10, 24, 27, 39, 129, 132, 150, 157, 160, 163, 178, 179, 180, 181
Binmore, Ken 16
Black Mass 14, 71, 175, 176, 178, 183, 185, 191
Bodie 157, 165, 166, 167, 169
body count 21, 22, 126, 179, 185, 187
Boltzmann, Ludwig 181
"The Boys of Summer" 142
Brian Tweego 83
Broken Arrow 56
Bubbles 172
Buchanan, James 21, 126, 128, 131, 183, 187
Buck Turgidson 43
Bunk 143, 157, 172
Burns, Ed 125, 140, 187
Burrell 129, 137, 139, 155, 159, 165, 167, 168
Burroughs, William 100
Bush, George W. 125, 140, 173, 188

Candy 50
Cantor, Georg 181
capitalism and apocalypse 10
capitalist technocracy 6, 24
Carcetti 141, 142, 143, 147, 165
Carver 171
Caserio, Robert L. 79, 105, 109, 184, 190
Chernus, Ira 72
Chew, Robert F. 151
Chicago School 8, 119, 187
Chris Partlow 142
Christian teleology 6
Civilization and Its Discontents 106
Clarence Royce 137
Clay Davis 154
cleansing, apocalyptic 14, 31, 33

197

Index

A Clockwork Orange 40, 41, 111, 169, 170, 179, 188, 190, 192
Cohen, Sam 42
Cold War 16, 17, 25, 45
Coleman, Chad 160
Colin Seagrave 100
Collins, Phil 122
Colvin 138, 139, 143, 147, 155, 156, 167, 168, 171
common good 6, 18, 19, 20, 131
Communication and the Evolution of Society 19
COMSTAT 167
"The Concept of Enlightenment" 164
Consumer Society 114
The Corner: A Year in the Life of an Inner City Neighborhood 125
Cosmopolis 81, 103
Costabile, David 147
Cowart, David 94, 190
Crawford, Jermaine 141
Cronenberg, David 118, 186, 194
Cuban Missile Crisis 69, 71, 185
The Culture of Cities 123
Culture of the New Capitalism 133
Curtis, Adam 22, 42, 44, 51, 57, 125, 126, 186, 187, 190
Cutty 160

D'Angelo 152, 157, 165, 167
Dangerous Knowledge 180
Daniels 141, 143
Davis, Nick 105, 120, 154, 155
The Day After 55
"Dead Soldiers" 167
Dean Moriarty 100
Dean, James 115
de Chardin, Teilhard 100
dehumanization 7, 21, 35, 57, 66, 69, 70, 73, 87, 112, 114, 116, 117, 124, 169, 170, 172
de-libidinization 54, 57, 154
De Sadesky 2, 63, 65
deterrence: logic 68; strategies 78, 89, 126, 185
Devil's Doorway 56
Dick, Philip K. 117
Dickens, Charles 169
Discipline and Punish 170
Dr. Strangelove 2, 11, 35, 36, 37, 39, 41, 43, 44, 45, 46, 47, 48, 49, 50, 51, 53, 54, 55, 57, 59, 61, 63, 64, 65, 67, 88, 92, 133, 177, 191, 192, 193, 195
Doman, John 135
doomsday machine 2, 32, 37, 38, 39, 47, 62, 63, 64, 65
Ducker, Eric 124, 191
Dukie 141

Eclipse of Reason 123
"The Economic Problem of Masochism" 105

economic theocracy 15
Eden 89, 91, 149, 175
Edward Teller 44
efficiency, institutional 126, 177
Elba, Idris 129
Eleanor Parker 51
Ellis, Brett Easton 121
Emmet Creed 75, 81, 83
empathy 2, 3, 4, 10, 21, 22, 25, 32, 38, 42, 49, 59, 62, 64, 65, 110, 113, 114, 128, 129, 158, 159, 160, 161, 163, 171, 177, 178, 179, 180, 188; and altruism 2; for your enemy 25, 179
The End of History and the Last Man 119
The Enlightenment 7, 35, 78, 92, 100, 116, 164, 168, 170, 185, 191, 192
Enola Gay 51
Enthoven, Alain 21, 89, 126, 128, 131, 187
Eric Packer 81
Eros and Thanatos 35, 73, 77
Evergreen Review 50

The Fable of the Bees 121
Fail-Safe 50, 51
Faison, Frankie 137
The Fate of the Earth see Schell, Jonathan
The Fog of War 21, 38, 171, 179, 185, 187, 189, 191
Fonda, Henry 53
Foster, Dennis 105
Foucault, Michel 170, 188, 191
Frank Sobotka 135
Frank, Pat *see Alas Babylon*
Franklin Towers 150
Freamon 142, 143, 144, 146, 147, 149, 151, 162
free-market capitalism 124, 176
Freed, Sam 147
Freud, Sigmund 43, 104, 105, 106, 191
Friedman, Milton 48, 119, 131, 183
frontier 55, 56, 89
Fukuyama, Francis 119, 175

Gabrielle 101, 107, 108, 111
Game paradigm 124, 127, 132, 133, 135, 147, 149, 150, 153, 157, 162, 163, 164, 165, 167, 168, 171, 176, 177, 179
Game Theory 9, 13, 16, 42, 44, 45, 48, 64, 94, 95, 123, 125, 127, 129, 131, 133, 135, 137, 139, 141, 143, 145, 147, 149, 151, 153, 155, 157, 159, 161, 163, 165, 167, 169, 171, 173, 183, 184, 187, 189, 192, 193
Gannon, Charles 35, 54
Gary Harkness 70, 72, 73
A Gathering of Eagles 51, 52, 191
Gekko, Gordon 121
General Ripper 43
George, Peter 41
Ghamari-Tabrizi, Sharon 45
Gillen, Aidan 141

198

Index

Gilliam, Seth 171
Gilliard, Larry, Jr. 152
Glover, Anwen 140
Godel, Kurt 181
Grausam, Daniel 90, 191
Gray, John 71, 128, 175, 176, 178, 183, 185, 191
The Greek 135
Greek Tragedy 130, 168, 193
Greggs 143, 159
Groeteschele 53
Group Captain Lionel Mandrake 58
"The Gulf War Did Not Take Place" 148
Gunfighter Nation 56, 91, 93, 183, 194
Gutierrez 144

HAL 9000, 40
Hamsterdam 138, 147
Harrell, Maestro 141
Harris, Wood 129
Harvey, David 9
Hayden, Sterling 43
Hayek, Friedrich von 8, 183, 187
Haynes 145, 148
HBO 125, 134
Hector, Jamie 129
Helen Remington 101, 106, 111
Hiroshima 51
Homicide: A Year on the Killing Streets 125
Homicide: Life on the Street 125
homo economicus 9, 24, 75
Horkheimer, Max 5, 9, 77, 123, 128, 164, 170, 192
Hornby, Nick 140
Hudson, Rock 52
The Hudson Institute 48
human trafficking 125
Hume, David 18
Huxley, Aldous 100

Imagining Apocalypse 57
incentivization 126
industrialization 127, 169
Inskeep, Steve 170
instrumentalism 19, 46, 49, 69, 83, 99, 102, 110, 114, 127, 131, 170, 174

Jack Gladney 81
James Ballard 70, 72, 111
Jameson, Frederic 96, 186, 192
Johnson, Clark 145
Jordan, Michael B. 165

Kafka, Franz 169
Kahn, Herman 41, 42, 44, 45, 46, 47, 48, 49, 50, 53, 55, 73, 77, 84, 89, 97, 178
Kaplan, Fred 46, 125
Kennedy, John F. 63, 84, 110, 115
Kermode, Frank 66, 71, 72, 192

Kinder, Marsha 144
Kissinger, Henry 44
Kissoff 22, 38, 64, 65
Klebenow 148
Kostroff, Michael 146

Landsman 142
Lang, Fritz 54
Laplanche, Jean 105
Laurence, William L. 57
Lehane, Dennis 162
LeMay, Curtis 44
Leviathan 7
Levy 146, 154, 162
Lewis, C.S. 100
libidinal 45, 57, 70, 73, 103, 104, 110, 117
Libra 81
Lippy Margolis 75, 76
Little Kevin 167
Logos 70, 73, 74, 75, 76, 81, 88, 95, 180
Lovejoy, Frank 52

machine rationality 2, 36
MAD (Mutually Assured Destruction) 12, 46, 84
Maddaddam 3
The Magic Christian 50
Major "King" Kong 43
Major Staley 81, 83, 93, 154
Maland, Charles 45
Malone, David 180
Mandeville, Bernard 121
Mandrake 37, 59, 60, 61, 62, 63
Mann, Anthony 51
Mansfield, Jayne 115
Marlo Stanfield 128, 129, 140, 142, 143, 144, 146, 152, 158, 159, 160, 161, 162, 167, 179, 180, 187
Matthau, Walter 53
McCarthy, Senator Joseph 59
McCarthy, Thomas 144
McCullum, Julito 141
McNamara, Robert 21, 22, 25, 38, 65, 78, 84, 171, 179, 185, 188, 189, 191
McNulty 1, 128, 135, 141, 143, 144, 146, 147, 151, 152, 157, 158, 159, 162, 167
Mencken, H.L. 169
Metropolis 54
Middle Ground 152
millenarian 24, 57, 58, 59, 71, 89, 92
miscegenation 37, 58, 59, 61, 66
Monbiot, George 12
Morgenstern, Oskar 16
Morris, Errol 21
Mouzone 140, 150, 151, 155
Muffley 2, 22, 38, 44, 47, 58, 59, 61, 62, 63, 64, 65, 172, 177, 179, 184
Mumford, Lewis 123

Index

Mutual Assured Destruction *see* MAD
Myna 92, 93, 98
The Myth of the Frontier in Twentieth Century America 91, 183
mythology: apocalyptic 70, 98, 116; exceptionalist 28, 92, 115, 133, 175

Nagasaki 57, 84, 88
Namond 141
Naremore, James 46
narratives of shared purpose 6
Nash Equilibrium 16, 158
Nash, John 16, 23, 183, 184
neoliberal capitalism 8, 10, 11, 14, 15, 24, 26, 36, 80, 89, 93, 95, 96, 150, 183
neoliberalism 1, 2, 3, 8, 9, 11, 14, 16, 26, 27, 43, 48, 114, 158
Neumann, John von 16, 44, 61, 183
Neumann, Kohn von 44, 45, 48, 50, 192, 193
NHS 126
Nicky 136, 137
No Child Left Behind 125
"No Corner Left Behind" 140
NORAD 97
Nuclear Madness: Religion and the Psychology of the Nuclear Age 72

Oedipal 106, 107, 108, 109, 118, 120, 178
O'Herlihy, Dan 53
Omar 140, 150, 151, 155, 159, 172
On the Road 105
On Thermonuclear War 41, 46, 47, 73, 77
Oppenheimer, Robert 44
Osteen, Mark 79, 80, 185, 194
Oswald, Lee 81

Pandora's Box 42
panopticon 170
Paress, Michelle 144
Paths of Glory 32, 169
Patrick Bateman 121
Paul Krassner 50
Paul Tibbets *see Enola Gay*
Peach, Mary 52
Pearson, Felicia 142
performance target 14, 21, 22, 25, 126, 179, 187
Peters, Clarke 142
Pickens, Slim 43
Pierce, Wendell 143
Pimp My Ride 105
Political Arithmetick 7
postindustrialism 6, 7, 70, 72, 103, 134, 135, 136, 137, 164, 168, 169, 170, 172, 175, 180, 187
Potlatch 118, 120, 121
Potts, Michael 140
Powers, Richard 90
"The Precession of Simulacra" 85
The Prisoners' Dilemma 17

Proposition Joe 151
psychopathology 110
Public Choice Theory *see* Buchanan, James
Pulitzer Prize 145
The Puritan Origins of the American Self 58, 91, 183, 189
Puritans and Pilgrims 33, 58, 61, 175

RAND 16, 17, 21, 42, 44, 45, 46, 48, 49, 53, 55, 65, 77, 78, 89, 95, 126, 177, 184
Rand, Ayn 113
Randy 141
Raoul Duke 115
Rawls 139, 143, 155, 159, 165, 167
Raymond, Bill 135
"Re-Wiring Baltimore" 144
Reagan administration 119, 136; Star Wars program 119
Realist see Krassner, Paul
Reddick, Lance 141
Reed, Tracey 46
Reformation 171
refugees 161
reset-to-zero 25, 77, 92, 95, 97, 102, 186
Ride of the Valkyries 139
Ripper 37, 45, 50, 58, 59, 60, 61, 62, 184
The Rites of Ascent 35, 183, 189
Robert Vaughan 100
Robert's Rules of Order 151
Rodley, Chris 118
Royo, Andre 172

SAC movies 56, 57, 59, 82, 154
Schell, Jonathan 79
Schelling, Thomas 46, 89
Schreiber, Pablo 136
Scientism 5, 6, 181
scientism 8, 27, 71, 99, 103, 104, 114, 163, 174
Scott, George C. 43
secular theology 134, 174
Seed, David 44, 57, 184, 194
self-advancement 2, 19, 27, 126, 131, 159
Sellers, Peter 37, 44
Sennett, Richard 133, 136, 187, 194
The Sense of an Ending 66, 71, 192
sex and paranoia 68, 113
Shakespeare 169
Sheehan, Helena 132
Simmel, Georg 5
Simon, David 123, 124, 125, 128, 130, 131, 134, 135, 140, 141, 144, 145, 146, 153, 154, 159, 164, 169, 173, 187, 188, 192, 193, 194
Simulacra and Simulation 69
The Sioux 83
Slotkin, Richard 8, 56, 89, 91, 92, 93, 115, 134, 183, 186, 194
Smith, Adam 9, 14, 18, 191
Snoop 142

Index

The Soft Machine 119
Sohn, Sonja 143
Southern, Terry 42, 50
Soviet Union 44, 119, 175, 184
spectator, exemplary 95, 96, 98, 99
Spiros Vondas 135
stevedore union 125
Stevenson, Adlai 44
Stewart, James 51
Stillman, Grant 46
Stone, Oliver 121
"Straight and True" 156
Strategic Air Command (SAC) 44, 50, 51, 195
Stringer Bell 129, 132, 150, 153
Sweeney, Sheamus 132
Symbolic Exchange and Death 87, 189

Taft Robinson 98
"The Target" 154
Taylor, Elizabeth 101, 102, 106, 110, 115
Taylor, Rod 52
technological *liebestod* 110
technology and technocracy 15, 32, 175
teleologic 7, 76, 87, 92, 99, 104
Templeton 144, 145, 146, 147, 148
Terminator 2: Judgment Day 55
Thatcher, Margaret 20, 28, 121, 126, 131, 186
theology of the bomb 83, 88, 96, 175
theory of communicative action 19
Theory of Games and Economic Behavior 16
Thinking the Unthinkable 77
Threads 55
Tommy Carcetti 141
transcendence 38, 55, 58, 73, 101, 102, 103, 104, 105, 106, 108, 110, 114, 115, 116, 117, 171
"The Transvaluation of Utopia" 100
The Trap 20, 22, 125, 126, 183, 187, 190
Treatise on Human Nature see Hume, David
tribal-sexual breeding 37
Turing, Alan 181
Turman, Glynn 137
Twin Towers 139
Two Hours to Doom 41

The Ugly American 52
uncertainty theory 181
"Unconfirmed Reports" 143, 149
"'An Unrehearsed Theatre of Technology': Oedipalization and Vision in Ballard's Crash" *see* Davis, Nick

utopian 6, 39, 71, 87, 100, 103, 104, 106, 109, 111, 112, 113, 117, 119, 164, 179, 185, 186

Victor, Paul Ben 135
Vietnam 38, 65, 126, 139, 148, 171, 179, 185, 187, 190, 192
Vietnam War 21, 22, 23
violence: regenerative 89, 91, 92, 93, 106, 115, 134, 139, 183; sublimated 37, 54, 116
von Braun, Wernher 44

Wagar, Warren 100, 105, 111, 112, 184, 195
Wall Street 121
Wallace 165, 191
The War Game 55
War on Drugs 21, 22, 25, 30, 32, 38, 125, 127, 134, 139, 141, 147, 148, 149, 155, 163, 164, 170, 171, 172, 177, 179
War on Terror 22, 30, 31, 140, 141, 148, 150, 164, 171, 172, 173, 179
War Room 38, 46, 47, 58, 61, 63, 84, 88, 184, 194
Warhol, Andy 118
"We'll Meet Again" 38
The Wealth of Nations 121
Weber, Eugen 7
White Noise 81, 94, 98, 185, 188, 190, 193, 195
Whiting 147, 148, 169
Whitlock, Isiah, Jr. 154
"Why I Want to Fuck Ronald Reagan" 121
Wilcox, Leonard 86, 87, 195
Wilds, Tristan 141
Williams, Delaney 142
Williams, J.D. 157
Williams, Linda 124, 140, 142, 144, 145, 187, 195
Williams, Michael Kenneth 140
The Wire: Truth Be Told 123
Wisdom, Robert 138
Wizards of Armageddon 46, 125, 186, 192
Wohlstetter, Albert 42, 89

"Xerox and Infinity" 76

The Year of the Flood 3

Ziggy 137

www.ingramcontent.com/pod-product-compliance
Ingram Content Group UK Ltd.
Pitfield, Milton Keynes, MK11 3LW, UK
UKHW041938210426
5322IPUK00016B/243